Me and You and Memento and Fargo

ME AND YOU AND MEMENTO AND FARGO

How Independent Screenplays Work

By J.J. Murphy

continuum

NEW YORK • LONDON

2007

The Continuum International Publishing Group Inc
80 Maiden Lane, New York, NY 10038

The Continuum International Publishing Group Ltd
The Tower Building, 11 York Road, London SE1 7NX

www.continuumbooks.com

Copyright © 2007 by J.J. Murphy

Printed in the United States of America

Library of Congress Cataloging-in-Publication Data

Murphy, J. J., 1947-
  Me and you and Memento and Fargo : how independent screenplays work / J.J. Murphy.
    p. cm.
  Includes bibliographical references.
  ISBN-13: 978-0-8264-2804-2 (hardcover : alk. paper)
  ISBN-10: 0-8264-2804-5 (hardcover : alk. paper)
  ISBN-13: 978-0-8264-2805-9 (pbk. : alk. paper)
  ISBN-10: 0-8264-2805-3 (pbk. : alk. paper)
1. Motion picture authorship. 2. Motion pictures--United States. 3. Independent filmmakers--United States. I. Title.
  PN1996.M84 2006
  791.43'75--dc22

                                                          2006034121

Contents

Acknowledgments

In choosing the films for this book, I tried to pick examples that represent a broad spectrum of contemporary American independent films. In terms of criteria, the twelve films had to receive major distribution and exert substantial critical impact upon the field. My approach is an inductive one, and the resulting schematization grew out of certain issues of story structure, which only became apparent through the process of writing about the films. I've tried to base what I have to say on a close analysis of specific films. There are now a number of excellent books that deal with the subject of American independent cinema, but my focus here is on the screenplays. A subtext of this book suggests that if someone were to follow the prescriptions found in the standard manuals, it would be virtually impossible to write a truly independent film. Thus, I hope this study might help to open up the creative process of screenwriting from what I consider to be a rather narrow conception of cinema.

In writing this book, I need to acknowledge a number of people who have been a source of inspiration, assistance, and advice. First of all, several lectures by Kristin Thompson really challenged my own ideas about screenwriting and made me to want to write about an alternative practice. Although we take very different positions, my debt to her work should be obvious. I'm sure I would never have written this book without the encouragement of David Bordwell. He has been a close friend and colleague for thirty-five years. I've pestered him with questions throughout this process. Only David would have the patience to answer each query with boundless enthusiasm. In addition, David generously offered invaluable criticism of early drafts of the manuscript. Thanks also to Mary Francis for her perceptive suggestions, and to Erik Gunneson for providing technical support.

I'm also indebted to my colleagues Vance Kepley, Lea Jacobs, Kelley Conway, Ben Singer, Julie D'Acci, Michele Hilmes, Michael Curtin, and Mary Beltrán, and to Richard Neupert and Cathy Jones for their professional advice. While writing the book, my production colleague and close friend Nietzchka Keene, a gifted independent filmmaker, passed away unexpectedly. Two years later, I still can't write her name without feeling an immeasurable sense of sadness and loss. I really miss her and the benefit of her feedback. My heartfelt gratitude goes to my partner of twenty-five years, Nancy Mladenoff, who has been an ardent supporter of this project from its inception. Marie Karczewski and Madeleine Gekiere are two people whose belief in me has made a considerable difference in my life.

Several former graduate students provided research assistance on this project: Jim Kreul, Jonathan Walley, and Jane Greene. Eric Crosby, my current graduate advisee, assisted me in preparing the manuscript for publication, and his knowledge, dedication, and efforts are greatly appreciated. A version of my chapter on *Gummo*, entitled "Harmony Korine's *Gummo*: The Compliment of Getting Stuck with a Fork," first appeared in *Film Studies: An International Review*, 5 (Winter 2004), and benefited from the editorial advice of Murray Smith. Thanks to Manchester University Press for permission to reproduce it here. A research grant from the University of Wisconsin-Madison Graduate School provided much-needed support for the book in its early stages.

Special thanks go to the various screenwriters and filmmakers whose works I discuss in the book. Finally, I consider myself lucky to have David Barker as my editor at Continuum. It has been a total pleasure working with him on this project.

Introduction

There is no doubt that most of the dullness of our movies is con-
cocted in advance, in the so-called heads of the so-called scriptwriters. Not only the dullness: They also perpetuate the standard film
constructions, dialogues, plots. They follow closely their textbooks
of "good" screenwriting. Shoot all scriptwriters, and we may yet have
a rebirth of American cinema.

—Jonas Mekas, *Village Voice* (Nov. 25, 1959)

I intend to follow all the "rules" of screenwriting (3-act structure,
etc.). There's no point in writing if nobody will ever see it.

—David Boring in Daniel Clowes's *Eightball*

I do believe that in order to break rules, you have to know what they
are.

—Jim Jarmusch, *Jim Jarmusch: Interviews*

Within the last twenty-five years, an enormous burst of innovative features has emerged from American independent
filmmakers. From *Stranger Than Paradise* (1984) and
Slacker (1991) to *Elephant* (2003) and *Me and You and Everyone We
Know* (2005), indie cinema has become an important part of mainstream American culture. Independent cinema now has its own Web
site (indieWIRE), cable television channels (Sundance and the Independent Film Channel), theaters (Landmark theater chain, Film
Forum, Angelika Film Centers, IFC Center), film festivals (Sundance,
Slamdance), film publications (*Filmmaker, The Independent*), special-
ized distributors (Miramax, Focus Features, Sony Pictures Classics,
Fox Searchlight, and so forth), and a separate category on Netflix.

Indeed it is impossible to imagine American cinema today without such important indie writer/directors as Jim Jarmusch, Hal Hartley, Charles Burnett, Allison Anders, Todd Haynes, Todd Solondz, David Lynch, John Sayles, Julie Dash, Gregg Araki, Nancy Savoca, Quentin Tarantino, Victor Nunez, Harmony Korine, Kimberly Peirce, Gus Van Sant, Richard Linklater, the Coen brothers, or Miranda July. Through their practice, they have revitalized American cinema by creating sophisticated and challenging narratives that have provided a much-needed alternative to an industry that at times has become less concerned with producing quality films than in orchestrating the next megablockbuster.

But what makes these films and their scripts independent? Is it simply a matter of budget and production values? Or are there aesthetic qualities which set them off from ordinary Hollywood entertainment? The term "independent film" has always been rather hard to define. First of all, it suggests that a work has been created outside the dominant Hollywood studio system. This is exactly how Harvey Weinstein defines it: "On a business level, it's a movie that isn't being released by one of the seven major studios. It's independently released, independently distributed, independently marketed."[1] Such a definition, however, attempts to disguise the economic relation that all commercial films, even independent ones, bear to Hollywood. In her book *Shooting to Kill*, Christine Vachon (producer of films by Todd Haynes, Todd Solondz, and Kimberly Peirce) explains:

> While it's true that, in the best of all possible worlds, independent films are genuinely alternative visions, there's no such thing as an absolutely independent film. There's still an economy at work: The movie has to go into the marketplace, and people have to want to see it. Much of the money I get comes from Hollywood sources, and not because they want to underwrite my brilliant career. To do what I do, I have to believe that the films I produce will be so vital that they find an audience—or else will create one of their own.[2]

Issues of film financing and distribution today have become even more complicated by the fact that all the major Hollywood studios now have smaller classics or art divisions, such as Fox Searchlight, Sony Pictures Classics, Fine Line, Paramount Classics, and Focus Features, to handle independents, or they simply own smaller distribution companies, as was the case for many years with Disney and Miramax.

In 2002, Vivendi Universal acquired Good Machine for $10 million and created an entirely new entity, Focus Features, out of USA Films, Universal Focus, and Good Machine, to be run by former Good Machine partners James Schamus and David Linde.

Studios' interest in smaller-budget niche products arises from their need not only to reduce production costs, but to create prestige films worthy of Oscar nominations. In addition, studios view the specialty arms as a way to keep a lock on talent. As *Variety* reported at the time of Vivendi Universal's creation of Focus Features: "Focus is also meant to serve, in part, as a magnet for talent, keeping filmmakers like Ang Lee, Steven Soderbergh, Spike Jonze, Neil LaBute, Mira Nair and Todd Haynes—all have made pics for Good Machine or USA Films—in the Universal fold, and creating an incubator for emerging filmmakers and stars."[3] In terms of the symbiotic relationship between independents and the Hollywood industry, it should also not be forgotten that the Sundance Film Festival, the single most powerful independent showcase and an event that has almost become synonymous with independent film, depends on the financial backing of Robert Redford, a Hollywood star. The label "independent" becomes even trickier when it starts to be used as a marketing concept, in much the same way that the larger multinational record labels push the "indie" sound.

The codependence between the Hollywood industry and independent cinema has caused some to lament the impossibility of a truly independent cinema at all, and others, including filmmaker Jon Jost and producer Ted Hope, to declare its death knell. As early as 1989, Jon Jost wrote a scathing critique entitled "End of the Indies: Death of the Sayles Men," in *Film Comment*. Jost acknowledged "a small body of works built on both American experimentalism and the European 'art film,'" citing kindred 16mm works by a number of '70s and early '80s filmmakers—Yvonne Rainer, James Benning, Mark Rappaport, Bette Gordon, Charles Burnett, Lizzie Borden, and Jim Jarmusch—as creating a genuine alternative to Hollywood.[4] Jost contended, however, that the independent tradition, as represented by indie directors such as Spike Lee, Susan Seidelman, Wayne Wang, and the Coen brothers became coopted by the studios in the 1980s. He writes: "Except in the most venal of senses, little of the American Indie wave staked out anything that could legitimately claim any kind of independence from the Hollywood aesthetic model, its motives, or the preponderance of lawyers, dealmakers, and money talk, which fills those seminars dotting the filmworld landscape."[5] Ted Hope, the producer of Hal Hartley's films, also declared independent film to be dead in a 1995 issue of *Film-maker*: "Although we celebrate our independent 'spirit,' the logic of the studio film— its range of political and social concerns, its marketing dictates, and even its narrative aesthetic— is slowly colonizing our consciousness."[6] Not so surprisingly, Hope's diatribe elicited a spirited response from his then Good Machine business partner, James Schamus, who thanked him in closing for "alienating every distributor with whom we attempt to do business here in the States."[7]

The complicated economic relationship between independent film and the studios also causes problems of definition. For some, independent film represents a sort of minor leagues for the Hollywood majors, a place for debut directors to show their stuff before graduating to lucrative studio deals and big bucks. For others, such as Jim Jarmusch, it remains primarily an issue of creative artistic control. He contends: "Anyone who makes a film that is the film they want to make, and it is not defined by marketing analysis or a commercial enterprise, is independent."[8] Neither financing nor budget alone seem enough to justify the term, for there is also a political aspect to the notion of independence. It implies a more open, more democratic and oppositional stance toward Hollywood's monopolistic control of production and distribution in this country. Independent films are closer in spirit to the international art film in the sense that they are products of a personal vision either ignored or at odds with the studio system.

Yet it seems clear that there are certain films, often classified as independent, that are clearly no different from mainstream Hollywood films. As a means of clarifying how blurry the lines have become, it might be instructive to discuss an example of what I consider to be a pseudo-independent film, namely, *My Big Fat Greek Wedding* (2002), which grossed over $241 million domestically and nearly $354 million worldwide, making it the second-highest grossing "independent" film of all time. Adapted from Nia Vardalos's one-woman theatrical monologue about the problems of growing up as a Greek-American female, the film was produced on a $5 million budget by Tom Hanks and his Greece-born wife, Rita Wilson, along with Gary Goetzman, executive producer on the Oscar-winning film *The Silence of the Lambs* (1991), in association with Home Box Office.

In naming *My Big Fat Greek Wedding* one of the worst films of the year, *Entertainment Weekly*'s Owen Gleiberman writes: "You can't fool all of the people all of the time, but Nia Vardalos comes close. What looks like a genial romantic comedy is actually the most shrill and teeth-grating ethnic sitcom of the year. . . . *MBFGW* may have to triumph at the Oscars before people realize that there's something wrong with this picture."[9] There are many things wrong with this picture. For openers, Vardalos's screenplay is riddled with ethnic clichés. The Greeks are portrayed as loud meat eaters who love to dance, hug, slug ouzo, and practice weird customs, such as spitting on people for good luck. Everyone in Toula's family is wacky—from the chauvinistic Gus, who believes Windex to be a medicinal cure for everything and imagines all words to be derived from Greek, to the puerile brother, Nick, who delights in feeding sexually loaded Greek phrases to the naive Ian, to the senile grandmother who imagines countless threats from the Turks. For Ian Miller, the North Shore Chicago WASP, Toula and her family represent the exotic. Like a hunter on an urban safari, Ian seeks excitement and retreat from the boring and homogenous upper-class world in which he was raised, which is presumably why he is so willing to assume someone else's ethnic identity.

In the short middle act, Vardalos seems unable to create any real obstacles to Toula and Ian getting together. Toula accepts both the date and wedding proposal without the slightest hesitation. Toula's family is more of a nuisance than any real obstacle. In Vardalos's improbable fairy tale, religion, class, and ethnic differences are merely occasions for farce. Rather than providing insight into real difference, we are fed the same bromides again and again. For Ian, we are all members of the same species; for Gus, we're the same fruit; both are weak arguments for a melting-pot thesis that represents pure Hollywood hokum. By glossing over serious dramatic conflicts with pious platitudes, *My Big Fat Greek Wedding* blocks any type of interethnic understanding. In its use of clichéd dialogue, vulgar caricatures, broad humor, and overemphasis on a Greek wedding as spectacle, Vardalos's film turns out to be much closer to an extended television sitcom than a Hollywood romantic comedy, never mind a bona fide independent film. It came as little surprise when *My Big Fat Greek Wedding* was developed into a television sitcom (that quickly failed).

This book argues that the American independent feature film over the last twenty-five years has developed a distinct approach to filmmaking, centering on new conceptions of cinematic storytelling. The film script is the heart of the creative originality to be found in the independent movement. Even directors noted for idiosyncratic visual style or for the off-beat handling of performers typically originate their material and write their own scripts. By studying the principles underlying the independent screenplay (or treatment or outline), we gain a direct sense of the originality of this new trend in American cinema. Beyond that, my central concern is the nature of the independent film screenplay itself. As the blueprint for production and the "selling point" of getting a project into production, the script is often the cornerstone of the filmmaking process. This takes on particular importance in the independent sector, where budgets must be very carefully planned in advance and where prospective investors need to be assured that the project is both original and well-conceived. From an aesthetic standpoint, the script is also the beginning of the creative process, and the first place where the filmmaker can start to express his or her individuality.

There are many screenwriting manuals and guidebooks on the market, but they pose problems for the aspiring independent filmmaker. First, they rely on formulas believed to generate salable Hollywood projects. For instance, most writers, including Syd Field (*Screenplay*), Richard Walter (*Screenwriting*), and Linda Seger (*Making a Good Script Great*), present a "three-act paradigm" as gospel and proceed to lay down very stringent rules for characterization, plotting, the timing of climaxes, and so on. Some writers, notably Field and Seger, go so far as to demand that the screenwriter present a dramatic turning point within specific pages. Even advice books that appear to be open about such rules (e.g., Robert McKee's *Story*) turn out to be just as inflexible. Unfortunately, the most popular screenwriting manuals tend to ignore the fact that Hollywood companies do not want only formula; they also want novelty, which is hard to teach as a set of rules. The independent filmmaker is usually aware of the rules but treats them as flexible guidelines, to be used as necessary but also to be rejected or reworked if it will yield a creative benefit. As Julie Dash, who made *Daughters of the Dust* (1991), puts it, classical story structure is "a good thing to learn when you don't know what you're doing. Then abandon it," particularly if you're an independent who wants "to explore and expand upon narrative forms, like I'm trying to do."[10]

What are these rules? The screenplay manuals spell them out very explicitly. Syd Field's *Screenplay: The Foundations of Screenwriting* has been the highest-selling manual since its first publication in 1979. Field's ideas have had an enormous influence not only on novice screenwriters, but on later screenwriting books, as well as the profession itself. According to Field, one page equals one minute of screen time. Except for comedies, which tend to be shorter (approximately 90 minutes), the average screenplay should be 120 pages long, and Field advises screenwriters never to exceed this limit. Dramatic films follow a basic paradigm—the three-act structure—corresponding to beginning, middle, and end. This is *"the foundation of dramatic structure."*[11] According to Field, all good screenplays fit this paradigm.

The first act, or beginning, is the "setup," where you establish both the goal of your main character as well as the basic dramatic premise for the story. The first ten minutes are crucial because, as he explains: "You've got to hook your reader immediately."[12] This is the amount of time it takes for viewers or readers to decide whether they like or dislike the movie. The second act, or middle, involves the "confrontation." This is the event in which your goal-driven protagonist confronts the hurdles or obstacles he or she must get through. The third act, or resolution, resolves the dramatic conflict. Field contends that the third act, the ending, presents the greatest challenge for the writer and argues that a writer must know the ending before starting to write the script.

Field's three acts follow a neat division in terms of their length: the first and third acts are thirty pages long, while the middle act consists of sixty pages. Field's structure hinges on what he terms "plot points." The function of the plot points is to keep the story dramatically interesting. The plot points turn the story in a different direction and usually occur at precise moments between each act. The first plot point can usually be found between pages 25–27, while the second one happens between pages 85–90.

Field has elaborated on his structural concepts in other books since *Screenplay*, especially *The Screenwriter's Workbook* (1984) and his more recent effort, *The Screenwriter's Problem Solver* (1998). In *The Screenwriter's Workbook*, which functions as an exercise guide, Field offers a refinement of the basic three-act paradigm. Field has changed his mind in terms of which act presents the greatest difficulty. He now claims that the second act is the most difficult to write because it is the longest. Field suggests that it is actually divided by what he terms a "Mid-Point." This can be an "incident or episode or event" that serves as a structuring aid in organizing the long second act. According to Field, the midpoint occurs at page 60, or exactly at the midway point between the first and second plot points. The midpoint thus breaks the script into four thirty-page segments of equal length. Field suggests a further division of the first and second parts of the second act. He labels these "pinches" and the function of each pinch is to tie the story line together and "*keep your story on track.*"[13] According to Field, the first pinch occurs on page 45 of the 120-minute script, while the second would be found on page 75. The inclusion of the midpoint and pinches results in Field's "new paradigm." This remains virtually unchanged in his *The Screenwriter's Problem Solver*, a book basically concerned with the rewriting process. In this later book, Field reduces all script problems to issues of plot, character, or structure.

Richard Walter's *Screenwriting: The Art, Craft and Business of Film and Television Writing* (1988) presents a paradigm nearly identical to Field's, but without his authoritarian tone. Walter cites Aristotle as the basis of the three-act dramatic structure—beginning, middle, end—and also insists that structure is the most important component of a screenplay. "The three most important facets of story craft," writes Walter, "are: (1) structure; (2) structure; (3) structure."[14] While Field links three-act structure to such processes as the life cycle of humans and stars, the replenishment of cells within our bodies, and even the experience of having a job, Walter compares the structure of a story to the floors, walls, and roof of a house. Walter, in obvious reference to Field, cautions the novice screenwriter against turning the basic shape of a story into formulas. "Although script structure most assuredly adheres to certain immutable laws," he writes, "the miracle is that screenplays are at the same time as individual as the writers who write them."[15] According to Walter, beginnings and endings may vary in size, but "are invariably shorter than middles."[16] Even character is treated as related to story structure. Walter advises against having more than one protagonist because, as he puts it: "the wider the sharing, the softer the focus of the entire film."[17]

Walter agrees with Field's revised position that the middle is the most difficult section of a film, not only because it is the longest, but because this is where "the complications are played out." Walter never uses the term "plot point," but it is clear he means the same thing, at least as far as the first one is concerned. "If at the end of the Beginning a complication arises that launches the tale's fundamental conflict," he writes, "throughout the Middle the plot thickens." The elements that thicken the plot he lumps together as "wrinkles and reversals, obstacles and complications."[18] Walter explains: "Wrinkles, obstacles, impediments, complications are all clearly related to one another. Each interferes with the protagonist's forward motion, each requires him to take a step sideways, up, over, or even momentarily backward in order to arrive at that place where it is determined at the beginning of the tale he should go."[19] The function of the wrinkles and reversals, obstacles and complications is to keep the script from moving in a boring, straight-line direction. Walter, however, is vague about whether there is such a thing as a second plot point that falls between the second and third acts. The function of the ending is "to resolve and balance beginnings and middles." Whereas Field rigidly opposes ambiguous endings, Walter believes that ambiguity has its place, even in endings, provided that it "is integrated into the fabric of the entire film."[20]

Walter's second book on screenwriting, *The Whole Picture: Strategies for Screenwriting Success in the New Hollywood* (1997), does not go much beyond the basic ideas found in *Screenwriting*. Nor does it discuss how the new Hollywood differs from the old. Rather *The Whole Picture* presents a rambling, highly anecdotal account of twenty-five screenwriting principles that Walter believes to be useful in the rewriting process. While still affirming the preeminence of story and the enduring importance of the three-act paradigm, Walter makes a striking admission about the overemphasis on structure he helped to create. He writes:

> Thanks in part to the plethora of new books and seminars on screenwriting, a new phenomenon is taking over Hollywood: major scripts are skillfully, seductively shaped, yet they are soulless. They tend to be shiny but superficial. They proffer pat prescriptions for chrome-plated stories, with all the right parts in all the right places, but in the end they have no heft.[21]

Walter argues for a more personal screenplay as an antidote to what he considers the well-made but essentially inert script. He also proposes looking at "the whole picture" rather than viewing scripts as the sum of their parts, an idea that can also be found in Field's *The Screenwriter's*

Workbook. Walter calls this approach "the integrated screenplay." He explains: "The integrated screenplay is one whose every aspect—each bit of action, every line of dialogue—accomplishes simultaneously the twin tasks of (1) advancing plot and (2) expanding character. Perhaps this is just another way of saying that each piece of information needs to tell the audience something new."[22] According to Walter, the integrated script opens up the screenwriting process by negating all rules and prohibitions. In this revisionist book, Walter also acknowledges that most films are too long and that the ideal length of a screenplay ought to be 100 pages or less.

Linda Seger's *Making a Good Script Great* has been another highly influential manual. The 1987 first edition concentrated on the more advanced aspect of screenwriting, the rewriting process, but Seger has gone back and included the basics in her revised 1994 version. Seger, a Hollywood script consultant, also adheres to the three-act structure. She uses the same terms as Field for her first and third acts, but calls her middle act "development" rather than "confrontation." Seger lays out the basic structure of a feature film, but in a slightly different form than Field. She writes:

> These acts for a feature film usually include a ten- to fifteen-page setup of the story, about twenty pages of development in Act One, a long second act that might run forty-five to sixty pages, and a fairly fast-paced third act of twenty to thirty-five pages. Each act has a different focus. The movement out of one act and into the next is usually accomplished by an action or an event called a turning point.[23]

Seger's turning points are identical to Field's plot points and they serve the same function, but she is more flexible in terms of their placement. In a two-hour film, she locates the placement of the first turning point as occurring between pages 25 and 35, while the second falls between pages 75 and 90.

Seger's three acts also resemble Field's. Act one contains the setup, the function of which is to introduce the main character and "to give us a clue about the spine or direction of the story."[24] As part of the setup she also discusses an event she calls the catalyst, which "begins the action of the story."[25] The setup lasts about ten or fifteen minutes of screen time. The setup is followed by what she terms "Act One Development," which fleshes out both character and situation. In act two, Seger uses a concept that she borrows from Syd Field's *The Screenwriter's Workbook*. This is the midpoint scene, which divides act two in half. Seger admits that in her extensive consulting experience, midpoint scenes do not occur in every film. But she argues that "they are excellent structural tools to help structure the difficult second act."[26] Seger elaborates: "Besides dividing the entire script in half, the midpoint scene divides the second act in half, creating a direction for the first half of Act Two, and giving a change in direction for the second half of the act, while keeping the overall focus of Act Two which has been determined by the first turning point."[27] Seger's second-act midpoint at least suggests the possibility that some films could be broken down into four acts, but she never goes this far, other than to say that mysteries and thrillers are the genres most apt to have midpoints. Seger adds two useful concepts to act three: the climax and the resolution. "The climax usually happens about one to five pages from the end of the script, followed by a short resolution that ties up all loose ends."[28]

Seger's *Making a Good Script Great* provides a great deal more analysis of the basic elements of screenwriting than the basic paradigm, especially in comparison to the slender first manuals of both Field and Walter. Seger also discusses actual films in depth, but her examples all come from mainstream Hollywood: *The African Queen, Back to the Future, Cocoon, The Fugitive, Ghost Busters, Gone with the Wind, Jaws, Out of Africa, Places in the Heart, Tootsie, Unforgiven,* and *Witness*. Except for a passing reference to *The Trip to Bountiful*, the only time Seger mentions independent films is by way of criticism. She discusses them in terms of character or expositional scenes in which "there is little momentum or dramatic build within the individual scene."[29] This results in problematical static scenes. Seger writes:

> To understand this concept, you may want to look at two small films that received a great deal of interest in 1993: *Ruby in Paradise* and *The Bad Lieutenant* [*sic*]. These new filmmakers clearly have talent and potential; nevertheless, many scenes are static, merely descriptive, and repetitive. You can see some of these same issues in films by Robert Altman and John Cassavetes. Although they are brilliant filmmakers on many levels, they generally lack strong story beats to pull their stories forward. If you love their characters and style (and, many times, I do), you can be patient with the episodic nature of the scenes. But remember that it is possible for a scene to

function on many levels—strong character scenes and strong story scenes—while also exploring a theme and building an image.[30]

Seger clearly prefers films that adhere to classical Hollywood conventions.

Seger's bias becomes obvious from the very title of her latest book, *Advanced Screenwriting: Raising Your Script to the Academy Award Level*. In the introduction, she indicates that she is in favor of "more innovation in the art of storytelling." Seger states: "I'd like to see new subject matter and new forms to express new types of stories."[31] In line with this seemingly progressive position, she begins *Advanced Screenwriting* by discussing the structural innovations of a number of contemporary films. But her analyses of two independent films treated in depth in this book—*Memento* and *Mulholland Dr.*—end up criticizing their narrational strategies, which borrow heavily from those of art cinema, from a strictly classical Hollywood position that insists on clarity and comprehensibility. She ultimately dismisses two of the more boldly innovative films of the past several years as simply being too difficult and confusing for the average viewer to follow.

Besides their books, Syd Field, Richard Walter, and Linda Seger have also disseminated their ideas about screenwriting through short, intensive workshops around the country. But perhaps no one has achieved more notoriety and success on the workshop circuit than Robert McKee, who even appears as a character in Charlie Kaufman's clever comedy *Adaptation* (2002), a film about Kaufman's own tribulations as a screenwriter. As Kaufman labors to find a dramatic spine for a book about orchids that he is adapting to the screen, his bother Donald enrolls in McKee's screenwriting seminar, which leads to the following humorous exchange:

KAUFMAN: Anybody who says he's got "the answer" is going to attract desperate people, be it in the world of religion—

DONALD: I just need to lie down while you explain this to me. Sorry. I apologize. Okay, go ahead.

KAUFMAN: So—

DONALD: (*adjusting himself*) Sorry. Okay. Go.

KAUFMAN: There are no rules, Donald, and anybody who says there are, is just—

DONALD: Oh wait. Not rules. Principles. McKee writes that a
          rule says you must do it this way. A principle says
          this works and has through all remembered time.[32]

Although it reads very much like a parody, Donald's distinction
between rules and principles is actually a direct quote from the first
two lines of McKee's highly influential manual *Story: Substance, Structure, Style, and the Principles of Screenwriting* (1997).[33]

At least initially, McKee's *Story* promises to be a much more open-ended approach than that of the three previously discussed authors.
McKee readily admits to the decline of the Hollywood screenplay over
the past twenty-five years. He likewise laments the erosion of the European art film during this same time period, and finds Asian cinema to
be the only bright light on the international landscape. McKee, who
seems to have the utmost faith in the workings of capitalism and the
free enterprise system, refuses to place any of the blame on the Hollywood studios or on the distributors. Rather he believes it is the writers
who are at fault. Not only have writers not bothered to learn their
craft, but it is simply not being taught anymore. American universities
teach literary theory but not the principles of story, while the European universities do not believe it is possible to teach screenwriting.

McKee has a building-block approach to structure. He discusses
the smallest unit, a beat, which contains an "action/reaction." A number of beats combine to form a scene, which together create a
sequence, which leads to acts. As McKee explains: "Scenes turn in
minor but significant ways; a series of scenes builds a sequence that
turns in a *moderate*, more impactful way; a series of sequences builds
the next largest structure, the *Act*, a movement that turns on a *major*
reversal in the value-charged condition of the character's life."[34] Taken
together, the acts comprise the basic structure of the story.

McKee actually provides a chart for his basic story design. At the
top, he places what he terms the "Archplot," or classical design. These
principles, which he refers to as timeless and universal, turn out to be
the classical conventions of Hollywood storytelling: "CLASSICAL
DESIGN means a story built around an active protagonist who struggles against primarily external forces of antagonism to pursue his or her
desire, through continuous time, within a consistent and causally connected fictional reality, to a closed ending of absolute, irreversible
change."[35] McKee also includes other structuring designs on the bottom

corners of his triangle. He dubs these "Miniplot" and "Antiplot." The miniplot reduces or minimizes the archplot. The characteristics of miniplot include: either a passive protagonist or multiple protagonists, internal conflict, and an open ending. Based on his list of examples, European art films tend to have miniplots. McKee also describes his other antiplot category whose characteristics include the use of coincidence, nonlinear time, and inconsistent realities. According to McKee, the antiplot film "doesn't reduce the Classical but reverses it, contradicting traditional forms to exploit, perhaps ridicule the very idea of formal principles."[36] These films also tend to be European films from the post-World War II era, but also include such American independent films as Jim Jarmusch's *Stranger than Paradise* and David Lynch's *Lost Highway* (1997).

Although McKee refers to filmmakers such as Horton Foote, Robert Altman, John Cassavetes, Preston Sturges, and François Truffaut as "masters," and even talks about the unique visions of independents such as Spike Lee and Quentin Tarantino, as the book goes on, this seems more a rhetorical strategy than an honest critical opinion. McKee makes a strong argument on behalf of classical design. His most compelling reasons are strictly commercial ones, but McKee goes even further by stating emphatically, without offering any evidence, "Classical design is a mirror of the human mind."[37] Novice writers must first master classical form because audiences have classical expectations. In the final analysis, McKee clearly sees miniplot and antiplot as lesser structures that are subserviently dependent on the archplot.

McKee goes on to elaborate his five steps of dramatic structure. These involve the inciting incident, progressive complications, crisis, climax, and resolution. McKee writes:

> In our effort to satisfy the audience's need, to tell stories that touch the innermost and outermost sources of life, two major reversals are never enough. No matter the setting or scope of the telling, no matter how international and epic or intimate and interior, *three* major reversals are the necessary minimum for a full-length work of narrative art to reach the end of the line.[38]

His most basic structure involves an inciting incident and three acts. But McKee also states that there can be extreme variations since this is merely a formulation and not a formula. He claims that *Four Weddings and a Funeral* has five acts, *Raiders of the Lost Ark* has seven acts, and the *Cook, the Thief, His Wife & Her Lover* has eight. "These films," he observes, "turn a major reversal every fifteen or twenty minutes."[39] More typically, in a 120-minute feature, the first act equals thirty minutes, while the last act should be shorter, perhaps twenty minutes in length. This leaves a middle act of seventy minutes. McKee discusses the use of a "Mid-Act Climax" (midpoint) in the second act as well as the use of subplots.

Despite McKee's complicated and nuanced discussion of the classical Hollywood screenplay in *Story*, his discussion of miniplot and antiplot largely ignores the recent achievements of American independent cinema. For all his examples, McKee has very little to say about the work of American independents. McKee lists Jarmusch's *Stranger Than Paradise* under the antiplot category but, except for "coincidence," the other characteristics—inconsistent realities and nonlinear—do not really seem to be an appropriate fit.

McKee's discussion reveals a second major fault of the popular screenwriting manuals. On the rare occasions when they deal with independent films, they tend not to appreciate the genuine innovations that the films introduce. This is partly due to the fact that the manuals' authors are not well-versed in the historical tradition of independent cinema. Thus McKee's treatment of *Stranger Than Paradise* as an antiplot film cannot adequately analyze what the film does positively; it does not lack a plot, it has a different kind of plot. Ironically, it has a three-act structure, but the structure becomes geographical rather than plotted as a dramatic arc. Moreover, *Stranger Than Paradise* derives its approach to storytelling from an amalgam of 1970s minimalist cinema, punk subculture, and the Beat tradition of *Pull My Daisy* (1959) and *Shadows* (1957–59).

American independent cinema represents an alternative approach to the classical Hollywood film, and the screenplays differ in significant ways from the formulaic rules promulgated by the manuals. It is not that independent filmmakers are unfamiliar with the rules that govern the classical Hollywood screenplay. After all, many of the screenwriters of the films featured in the following chapters have attended film schools where such concepts are routinely taught.[40] The academic backgrounds of these screenwriter/directors, as well as remarks they've made in interviews, suggest that they are quite familiar with such concepts as the three-act paradigm and character arcs. Nevertheless, they choose to take a more innovative approach to their scripts rather than mimic the tried-and-true formulas. Rather than creating a naive cinema, independent filmmakers use their understanding of narrative conventions to challenge them.

My analysis of the screenplays in this book suggests that although independent cinema represents a rather broad category of many different types of films and genres, its narrational strategy lies somewhere between classical Hollywood cinema and art cinema. David Bordwell has provided a detailed account of art cinema narration by arguing that "the art cinema defines itself explicitly against the classical narrative mode, and especially against the cause-effect linkage of events."[41] According to Bordwell, characters in art cinema, while often displaying complex psychology, "lack clear-cut traits, motives, and goals" of classical narration.[42] Character subjectivity plays an increasingly greater role in art cinema and, as a result, the ensuing narratives tend to be much more ambiguous and open-ended. Whereas classical narration attempts to create and maintain a seamless illusion in the telling of the story, art cinema creates inexplicable gaps and problems, which often make us more keenly aware of the mediating presence of the author. Art cinema also shows a propensity to disrupt classical notions of space and time.

American independent film does not constitute a unique and separate category, but instead represents a hybrid form that bridges the divide between classical Hollywood and art cinema by freely incorporating elements from both of them. While independent cinema has created definitional problems that make it hard to pin down exactly what constitutes an independent film, my analysis of twelve American independent films—*Stranger Than Paradise, Safe, Fargo, Gas Food Lodging, Trust, Me and You and Everyone We Know, Reservoir Dogs, Memento, Elephant, Mulholland Dr., Gummo,* and *Slacker*—suggests that independent films always manage to distinguish themselves from classical mainstream films in terms of story concept, structure, character, dialogue, visual storytelling, representation, and overall narrational strategy in some very significant way.

Nothing is more central to the manuals than their structural approach to screenplays, in particular, the importance of the three-act paradigm. Rooted in the theories of Aristotle, this audience-oriented model tries to keep the viewer continually engaged in the narrative by making the story varied and interesting through the incorporation of major turning points that spin the story in a new or different direction. In *Alternative Screenwriting: Writing Beyond the Rules*, one of the few non-Hollywood manuals, Ken Dancyger and Jeff Rush use Spike Lee's *She's Gotta Have It* and Jim Jarmusch's *Stranger Than Paradise* as examples of "counter-structures."[43] They argue that *She's Gotta Have It* has "an ironic two-act structure" and that *Stranger Than Paradise* has a one-act structure. My own analysis, on the contrary, indicates that most independent films, including *She's Gotta Have It* and *Stranger Than Paradise,* actually do have three-act structures, which should not be surprising given the commercial considerations all feature films face. There are, in fact, only a small number of independent films that defy act breakdown. I discuss two such examples—*Gummo* and *Slacker*—in the final section.

In *Storytelling in the New Hollywood,* Kristin Thompson proposes that feature-length Hollywood films tend to have four acts rather three acts. More precisely, she argues that most films break down into four large-scale parts of roughly twenty to thirty minutes. David Lynch's *Mulholland Dr.* is the only one of the twelve films analyzed here that seems to break into four acts. In the other nine films that have three-act structures, there turns out to be a wide variation where the turning points occur and very few fall where the manual writers would place them.

For one thing, many independent films are a good deal shorter than Field's conventional 120-minute length. Only *Mulholland Dr.* has a running time over 120 minutes. One obvious reason for this in terms of independent films has to do with the fact that shorter scripts are a sure way to reduce production costs. Thompson acknowledges the fact that features "less than 100 minutes may break into three parts."[44] That certainly seems to be the case here, but it also seems to be true of independent films longer than 100 minutes as well, with the notable exception of *Mulholland Dr.* Three films—*Stranger Than Paradise, Gas Food Lodging*, and *Reservoir Dogs*—have short middle acts that result in a 1/3–1/3–1/3 pattern, while *Trust, Fargo, Elephant*, and *Memento* follow the conventional 1/4–1/2–1/4 division. The other two films—*Safe* and *Me and You and Everyone We Know*—have more flexible, asymmetrical patterns in terms of their act structures. None of the films turns out to have what might be considered a clear midpoint.

The structural approach of the manuals tends to emphasize the three-act paradigm, but generally ignores alternative storytelling patterns. In the section on temporal structures, I discuss three examples—*Reservoir Dogs, Memento,* and *Elephant*—that demonstrate a range of storytelling possibilities other than straightforward linear progression. Quentin Tarantino's *Reservoir Dogs*, for instance, undercuts audience expectations through a flashback structure that scrambles the time frame of the events and by withholding and delaying crucial exposition. Christopher Nolan's *Memento* has the most unusual overall shape. Rather than being a reverse structure, as it is often described, *Memento* is a puzzle film in which two stories go in opposite directions, then overlap at the tattoo parlor, and connect again as part of a small loop. In *Elephant*, Gus Van Sant moves back and forth in time, while creating a sense of real-time duration and simultaneity in exploring the Columbine shootings.

Temporality and causality are, of course, intricately linked concepts. David Lynch creates what Evan Smith dubs "thread structure" by developing multiple story threads that confuse the time sequence of the narrative by incorporating abrupt identity changes and the kind of logic usually found in dreams.[45] In *Mulholland Dr.*, only after the film is over can a viewer even begin to piece together and understand the implications of its initially repressed romantic plotline. Along with the dream structure of *Mulholland Dr.*, I discuss two other noncausally based films in the final section, namely, Harmony Korine's *Gummo* and Richard Linklater's *Slacker*. Noncausal structures depend heavily on the viewer to make the connections between scenes. *Gummo* relies on a type of poetic free association, while the structure of *Slacker* depends on the interactions of its various characters. As Richard Linklater suggests: "The relationship between various scenes can be connected later (or before—cause can follow effect)."[46]

Many commentators have a tendency to equate independent films with character-driven stories. An article in *scr(i)pt*, by Bob Verini, is somewhat typical in the way it uses the character/plot dichotomy to differentiate independent films from mainstream studio fare:

> Allowing for the odd exception, there's no getting away from the vast gulf between today's "studio pictures"—action- and plot-driven, technologically complex, and often "dumbed down" to attract a mass-audience—and the character-driven, psychologically complex "indies" that increasingly represent the most interesting work in contemporary film. There's work to be had for writers in each broad movie type, but one needs to know and follow the informal but inescapable rules that govern each.[47]

Verini never spells out these inescapable rules, but he does argue that
independent film offers several advantages for writers interested in
creating rich and complex characters. These include being able to
write characters based on real people rather than bankable stars, and
not being forced to create likeable characters who are redeemed at the
picture's end. For Verini, "surprise 'everyday' behavior, [and] an
absence of cliché" can be useful counterpoints to the predictability
found in mainstream movies.[48] Although most independent films can
be described as fundamentally character-driven, the character/plot
distinction between independent films and Hollywood films represents something of an oversimplification. It does not explain, for
instance, the stylistic and structural workings of many of the independent films discussed in the following chapters.

Only two of the films in this study—*Safe* and *Memento*—have
clearly defined, single protagonists. In fact, the tendency in recent
years has been for many films to have multiple protagonists and multiple plotlines. I discuss this phenomenon in my analysis of multiple-
plot structures such as *Trust, Gas Food Lodging*, and the ensemble film
Me and You and Everyone We Know. Many of the independent films
contain dual protagonists, multiple protagonists, or they problematize
the issue. Moreover, Robert McKee considers the passive protagonist to
be "a regrettably common mistake." He writes: "A story cannot be told
about a protagonist who doesn't want anything, who cannot make
decisions, whose actions effect no change at any level."[49] Yet *Safe* and
Stranger Than Paradise have passive or ambivalent protagonists who
can hardly be thought to be goal-directed. Because the protagonist of a
film serves as the main agent for the narrative, I discuss the implications of passive or ambivalent protagonists, namely, Willie in *Stranger
Than Paradise* and Carol White in *Safe*, in my discussion of problematic protagonists in the opening section of the book. I also discuss the
Coen brothers' attempt to shift protagonists midstream in *Fargo*.

Manual writers all suggest that protagonists undergo a transformation, often referred to as "character arc," in the course of the film.
McKee, for instance, writes: "Taking this principle further yet: The
finest writing not only reveals true character, but arcs or changes that
inner nature, for better or worse, over the course of the telling."[50]
Although less emphatic in the need for screenwriters to employ a character arc, Linda Seger suggests that the best films have them: "Not
every film needs a transformational arc, although many of the best

films will show at least one of the characters becoming transformed in the process of living out the story. Usually the character transformed is the protagonist."[51] Richard Walter's similar requirement that characters must "grow and develop throughout the tale" is violated in quite a number of independent films.[52] Willie does not really change in *Stranger Than Paradise*. Neither do Jerry and Marge in *Fargo*, nor Carol in *Safe*, nor Leonard Shelby in *Memento*, nor any of the characters in *Elephant*, *Gummo*, or *Slacker*.

Only seven independent films described here have what could be construed as traditional romance characters. Not many of the actual romances in the films that do have them, however, end very happily. Syd Field writes: "If you're ever in doubt about how to end your story, think in terms of an 'up' ending."[53] Yet very few independent filmmakers do. In fact, of the twelve films analyzed in the following pages, only *Me and You and Everyone We Know* and *Fargo* have what could be termed an upbeat ending, and *Fargo*'s ending easily could be interpreted as a parody of that very notion.

Romance usually serves as one of two plotlines—the main one having to do with the protagonist's goals—in classical Hollywood films, and, as Kristin Thompson points out, the two plotlines are "causally linked."[54] Independent films, however, often deviate from this. Because Willie does not have any real goals in *Stranger Than Paradise*, his repressed feelings for Eva have no causal connection to another plotline. Shade's romances with Darius and then Javier in *Gas Food Lodging* have no connection with her desire to have a normal family. As a matter of fact, her own goals play a secondary role to those of her sister, Trudi, and her own romantic interests turn out to be less important than those of both her sister and mother. In *Mulholland Dr.*, the romantic plotline doesn't actually surface until the fourth act. In *Safe*, Carol meets Chris at Wrenwood, which holds out the possibility that this new relationship will cure her health problems. This proves to be a red herring, however, and Carol ends up isolated and alone.

While romance characters are not considered absolutely essential in narrative films, antagonists are usually considered to be an indispensable element because they create the dramatic conflict and tension within the story. Teddy in *Memento*; Mr. Slaughter and Jean Coughlin in *Trust*; Carl Showalter, Gaear Grimsrud, and Wade Gustafson in *Fargo*; Mr. Blonde in *Reservoir Dogs*; and the Castigliane brothers, Mr. Roque, the Cowboy, and Adam in *Mulholland Dr.* would be considered strong, colorful antagonists. But some of the other films, notably, *Stranger Than Paradise, Safe, Gas Food Lodging,* and *Me and You and Everyone We Know,* lack the strong external antagonist insisted upon by the manual writers. *Stranger Than Paradise* does not have an antagonist because Willie's conflict remains an internal one. *Gas Food Lodging* is short on dramatic conflict precisely because it lacks a clear antagonist, unless this turns out to be something so broad as "fate." Anders substitutes lots of romance—each of the three women has at least two lovers—in order to compensate for the lack of dramatic conflict. *Safe* diffuses the notion of an external antagonist into either the environment or Carol's own body, depending on your point of view. *Me and You and Everyone We Know* lacks an antagonist in virtually every plotline, except for Christine's desire to show her video at the art museum. Nancy, the curator, might be seen as Christine's nemesis when she refuses to accept the work in person, but the two characters only meet once. On the other hand, there are no obstacles preventing Christine from having a romantic relationship with Richard because he's already been dumped by his wife. In *Mulholland Dr.,* Diane Selwyn creates a number of antagonists, but the film leaves open the question of whether any of them actually deserve to be, or whether they are merely projections of her own disturbed mind.

The fact that so many of the films here do not have external antagonists suggests that these films lack the strong dramatic conflict of the classical Hollywood style. In fact, a number of them are dramatically flat. *Stranger Than Paradise* is a road movie that moves from New York to Cleveland to Florida, where the characters actually do very little other than mundane activities in the course of the film. They eat, watch television, go to the racetrack, play cards, go to the movies, drive around, and sit around. Nothing much happens to them, which is precisely the point of the film. Coincidence plays a major role in the final act when Eva stumbles into a drug deal and obtains money through a case of mistaken identity. This provides her with the means to fly back to Budapest. Her last-minute decision not to return home is as arbitrary as any of the other events in the film. Lacking a goal-driven protagonist, dramatic conflict, and a consistent plotline, *Stranger Than Paradise* turns out to be much closer to art cinema in terms of its narration.

In *Safe,* which is as dramatically flat as *Stranger Than Paradise,* Carol wanders aimlessly around an incredibly sterile landscape that becomes more menacing as the film progresses. Since she lacks any real goals other than a concern for her own health, *Safe*, like *Stranger Than Paradise*, has an episodic rather than dramatic structure. *Gas Food Lodging* takes on an episodic quality as well because Shade gets sidetracked from her own goals by the problems of her mother and sister. Her initial goals to find her dad and a man for Nora are easily achieved. Her desire to make it with Darius dissolves when he turns out to be gay and incapable of responding. But Shade has the mentality of a survivor, and she manages to shift her goals according to the situation. An ensemble film such as *Me and You and Everyone We Know* is also more episodic than dramatic.

In classical films, the behavior of characters is expected to be motivated, but that's not true of art cinema. The same could be said of the characters in several of these independent films. Willie's behavior in *Stranger Than Paradise* is not motivated, nor is that of the other characters, Eva and Eddie. Todd Haynes deliberately creates gaps in our understanding of Carol White in *Safe*. He does not provide a rational explanation for her illness, but leaves it up to the viewer to conjecture what is wrong with her. We know little backstory about Mr. White in *Reservoir Dogs*, especially why he becomes so sentimental about Mr. Orange. Gus Van Sant doesn't attempt to provide viewers with an easy explanation for what prompted the Columbine shootings, but instead offers an observational meditation on the events. Nor does Richard Linklater provide motivation for any of the myriad characters we meet in *Slacker*. We also don't know what causes Christine's obsession with Richard in *Me and You and Everyone We Know*, while the totally subjective point of view of Leonard Shelby in *Memento* makes it nearly impossible to gauge any of the information provided about him. In independent films, character motivation is often buried, which reflects a desire to create characters that are less heroic figures than people we find in real life.

Traditionally, the dialogue in a film not only helps to reveal character, but also serves to advance the story. The manuals do not privilege dialogue as much as we might expect. Because they emphasize plot more than character, three-act structure turns out to be the far more important element for them. As a result, Field devotes only two pages to dialogue, Seger and McKee several pages, while Richard Walter, who seems to consider it much more important, has a short chapter devoted to it. When they deal with the subject, the manual writers, more or less, all offer the same set of prescribed rules. Dialogue should be concise and economical as well as naturalistic. It should avoid repetition, long monologues, chitchat, clichés, dialect, and exposition. Yet, as Sarah Kozloff points out in *Overhearing Film Dialogue*: "Perhaps these 'rules' have been proclaimed so often out of desperation. For my researches have consistently indicated that no matter how loudly they have been shouted, *in actuality they have never been followed by American cinema.*"[55] Nor have the rules been followed by independent cinema, where a great deal of experimentation has taken place in the realm of dialogue, which contradicts the advice found in the manuals.

Instead of being concise, much of the dialogue found in independent films is written to mimic the rhythms of everyday conversation. As a consequence, indie dialogue often meanders. The characters in *Reservoir Dogs* and *Slacker*, for instance, consistently engage in extremely long-winded monologues and are interested in talk for its own sake. The genre-based dialogue in *Reservoir Dogs* is hardly economical, nor does it always advance the plot of the film. It is also full of the kind of chitchat frowned on by the manuals. Rather than maintaining a consistent focus, Tarantino's dialogue creates numerous digressions, as does the dialogue in *Slacker* and *Gummo*. Both *Slacker*, which employs scripted improvisation, and *Gummo* contain numerous non sequiturs. Korine's dialogue also includes bits of pure nonsense, as well as disguised quotation from other sources.

The manual writers discourage the use of dialect, but the Coen brothers poke fun at their native Minnesota in *Fargo* by incorporating the regional dialect of the upper Midwest. The Coens also create a humorous contrast between the talkative Carl and his taciturn sidekick, Grimsrud. Both Jerry and Carl attempt to control the inarticulate locals by the sheer volume and velocity of their dialogue. Facility with language is shown to be a form of power in *Fargo*, but it proves no match for sheer physical violence. In *Stranger Than Paradise*, what characters cannot say to each other becomes just as important as what they are able to say. In many ways, the extended silences between them become even more meaningful than any verbal dialogue.

Hal Hartley's stylized dialogue is perhaps more idiosyncratic than that of any other independent screenwriter, and it certainly does not conform to the naturalistic conventions advocated by the manual writers. Hartley's dialogue employs obvious clichés, as well as aphorisms. It is full of repetitions of certain words and phrases, which gives it a distinct poetic and musical quality. In *Trust*, Maria and Rachel speak right past each other as they sit on the bench in front of the deli,

turning their dialogue into a pair of separate, almost interior monologues. Sarah Kozloff refers to this technique, which places the specta-
tor in a privileged position to the characters, as "dialogues of the
deaf."[56] Hartley's dialogue displays the push and pull typically found in
dramatic films and is full of unexpected surprises, but his scenes do
not necessarily build toward traditional dramatic climaxes. Hartley is
also capable of eliminating the need for dialogue in a scene. The clarity
of what Hartley articulates through the images and sound makes the
need for dialogue seem redundant and unnecessary.

Kristin Thompson points out: "Virtually all Hollywood films achieve
closure in all plotlines and subplots. The open, ambiguous endings that
often characterize art films like *Bicycle Thieves* (1947) or *The 400 Blows*
(1959) are typically avoided."[57] Not surprisingly, manual writers, such as
Syd Field, strongly advocate closed rather than open endings. As Field
puts it: "When you see a well-made film, you'll find a strong and directly
stated ending, a definite resolution. The days of ambiguous endings are
over."[58] But quite a number of independent films have open-ended reso-
lutions, notably *Stranger Than Paradise*, *Safe*, *Memento*, and *Gas Food
Lodging*. In addition, *Elephant* and *Mulholland Dr.* resist Field's "No
loose ends" dictum by introducing an element of ambiguity.[59]

As hybrid forms, independent films borrow freely from classical
Hollywood and art cinema, which is what often makes the results such
an interesting amalgam. Some independent films—*Mulholland Dr.*,
Memento, *Stranger Than Paradise*, *Safe*, *Trust*, *Gummo*, *Slacker*, and
Elephant—seem much closer to art cinema in terms of their narrational procedures, while others, such as *Fargo*, lean closer toward classical Hollywood, and *Reservoir Dogs*, *Gas Food Lodging*, and *Me and
You and Everyone We Know* are probably somewhere in the middle. In
order to gain either financing or commercial distribution, independent films must walk a fine line between novelty and convention, which
is why the successful ones contain elements of both. For all of the
emphasis placed on mainstream conventions by the manuals, there
can be no denying that some of the best writing over the past twenty-
five years has shifted to the independent sector, which has become the
laboratory for more innovative storytelling. As I hope to show in the
following chapters, today's independent screenwriters have moved
beyond the hardened rules and formulas advocated by the manuals to
embrace a much broader and flexible conception of cinema than one
governed solely by the principles of classical Hollywood.

Part One

Problematic Protagonists

Chapter 1

The Ambivalent Protagonist in
Stranger Than Paradise

As the main agent of the narrative, the goal-driven protagonist is fundamental to classical storytelling. It is his or her aspirations and desires that will create the impetus for subsequent narrative actions. Without Leonard Shelby's obsession to find and avenge his wife's murderer, there would be no *Memento*. Without Mr. White's dogged belief that Mr. Orange can't possibly be the infiltrator of the criminal gang's botched diamond heist, *Reservoir Dogs* would grind to an abrupt halt in the first act. Without Diane Selwyn's buoyant desire to succeed as a Hollywood star, she would never fall down the rabbit hole of her own tormented mind in *Mulholland Dr.* Without Christine's surreal attraction for a sad-sack shoe salesman and persistence to be recognized as a performance artist, *Me and You and Everyone We Know* would never get going. Goal-driven protagonists certainly exist in independent films, as the above examples indicate, but indie screenwriters also employ alternative strategies. "What I want to do is make films that are narrative films, that tell stories," Jim Jarmusch said at the time he made *Stranger Than Paradise* (1984), "but somehow in a new way, not in predictable form, not in the usual manipulative way that films seem to work on their audiences."[1] Jarmusch's elliptical approach to narrative is one more often found in art cinema than in mainstream commercial films. The plot of his second feature consists of a series of loosely connected incidents, filmed as continuous extended takes and separated by black leader. The action of the film is minimal. The major accomplishment of *Stranger Than Paradise* rests on its ability to employ an ambivalent protagonist, while still managing to create an entertaining and engaging story.

Jarmusch has linked the more unconventional aspects of *Stranger Than Paradise* to his own idiosyncratic method of constructing a narrative: "That comes from the way I write, which is backwards: Rather than finding a story that I want to tell and then adding the details, I collect the details and then try to construct a puzzle or story. I have a theme and a kind of mood and the characters but not a plotline that runs straight through. I think that's partly why the narrative takes the form that it does."[2] Such an approach to story construction runs directly counter to the structured pre-plotting advocated by the manuals. As is often the case with independent films, Jarmusch privileges character as his main story element. He uses only the most basic semblance of a traditional plot, in this case, a romantic triangle that takes the form of a road movie.

At the heart of this love triangle stands the film's protagonist, Willie, a kind of anti-hero, whose lack of ambition and internal confusion sends the story in a number of amusing and unpredictable directions. Despite the fact that his main conflict remains internal throughout the course of the film, Willie makes several pivotal decisions that appear to be arbitrary rather than motivated by established traits in his character. To say that Willie is impulsive or operates solely on whims implies that he lacks that consistency classical film characters are expected to display.[3] Willie's decision to leave New York for Cleveland has the effect of turning *Stranger Than Paradise* into a road movie, which allows Willie and his pal, Eddie, to reconnect with Eva. Willie later decides to detour to Florida and to backtrack and rescue Eva from her dreary life in Cleveland. Even though Willie has been affected as a result of his interactions with Eva, his character does not undergo the kind of transformational arc usually associated with traditional protagonists. Jarmusch also makes no attempt to create audience identification with Willie nor to tell the story from his point of view.

If the protagonist's pursuit of clearly delineated goals provides the direction in a classical film, Willie's lack of ambition and bohemian lifestyle prevent him from having any such master plan. Jarmusch explains this aspect of Willie's character as a conscious and deliberate strategy on his part: "I'm interested in people who are outside normal structures. I'm not interested in ambitions. I'll never make a film about ambitions, about characters who have some kind of dream and fight to achieve it. I'd rather make films about the way people actually exist, from day to day."[4] Because Willie lacks drive and ambition, *Stranger Than Paradise* focuses on the more mundane aspects of his life.

As we learn early on, Willie's real name is Bela Molnar, and he is an immigrant like the rest of his family. Willie refuses to speak Hungarian to either Aunt Lotte or Eva, and he acts rude to both of them initially because they remind him of his past. Even though *Stranger Than Paradise* succeeds largely as an affectionate portrait of these young bohemians, the film does not provide much backstory about Willie or any of the other characters. We know little about their current lives other than what we see in the film. There is no evidence, for example, that Willie and Eddie work at any sort of regular jobs. They are presented as marginal figures, small-time hustlers who cheat at cards and gamble at the racetrack. Willie and Eddie do not seem to have any friends other than each other, and the relationship between the two men is a codependent one. Willie is clearly the dominant figure, while Eddie seems content to be a follower. When the two leave Cleveland together, Eddie complains that Willie is always telling him what to do. Willie defines the dynamic of their relationship by replying, "It seems like if I don't tell you what to do, you don't do anything at all." But neither really knows very much about the other, as becomes evident when Eddie seems surprised to learn, through Eva's visit, about Willie's real name and Hungarian background.

The three main characters are all, for the most part, inarticulate and unable to verbalize their feelings, but Willie, in particular, seems to have the most difficult time because his own feelings remain a mystery even to him. What does he really feel about Eva? Why does he feel such melancholy when she leaves? Why does he get so jealous about Eva's friend, Billy, in Cleveland? Why does Willie revert to his old self in Florida? Since the characters are not able to express their thoughts and feelings, what they say—the actual dialogue of the film—does not propel the story forward or reveal character in the conventional sense suggested by the manual authors.[5] Rather the dialogue (or the lack of it) becomes a kind of stylistic mannerism of each character. Flo Leibowitz, who sees *Stranger Than Paradise* as what she terms a "New Character" film, offers some insightful observations on this issue:

In *Stranger*, however, talk is a *behavior*, and something that acts as the basis for one's inferences about the fictional characters who do the talking. We learn a lot about characters in this film from their conventional habits: when do they talk? when do they not? When they converse, what do they talk about? How do they say what they say? what tones of voice do they use? when do they speed up? and when do they slow down? One watches *Stranger* as one watches the behavioral repertoire of zoo animals or newly acquired pets, in order to make inferences concerning the temperament of the behavers.[6]

For this reason, despite the ambiguity of their responses, the characters in *Stranger Than Paradise* are not opaque to us.

They, in fact, remind us of the characters in John Cassavetes' early independent classic *Shadows*, a film that played a crucial role in the development of the tradition of American independent cinema I am concerned with here. *Shadows* grew out of a series of improvisations with aspiring, but nonprofessional, actors. The ambivalence of its characters, especially Ben and Lelia, adds an element of unpredictability to the narrative. In terms of motivation, they remain open to the possibility of the moment instead of being constrained by defined character traits. As a result, their personal identities remain very much in flux. As Ray Carney suggests, individual scenes do not build dramatically, but involve a series of abrupt tonal shifts:

> The scenes are less documentary records of what conversations really sound like than they are efforts to present as many shifting feelings, moods and alliances as possible. No mood lasts for more than a few seconds. Every relationship keeps changing. It's all tonal jumps and jitterbug jukes. Experience does not progress in a straight line like a plot, but zigzags through a series of changing emotional positions and counterpositions, thrusts and parries, approaches and withdrawals, bits and pieces of this and that.[7]

Cassavetes conceived of narrative not in terms of the contrivances of plot, but as a character-centered process that more closely resembles real life. This is what connects *Shadows* to *Stranger Than Paradise*, and later American independent films, such as *Elephant*, *Gummo*, and *Slacker*.

Stranger Than Paradise has what might be considered a three-act structure—Jarmusch himself describes its structure as "three acts and a coda"—but the act-breaks stem as much from geography as from traditional turning points.[8] There are three parts to the film; each takes place in a different location. We start in New York with the arrival of Eva, move to Cleveland when Willie and Eddie go there to visit Eva at Aunt Lotte's, and end up eventually in Florida. Jarmusch reinforces this three-part geographical structure by providing chapter titles before each section: "The New World" (New York); "One Year Later" (Cleveland); and "Paradise" (Florida). The geographical dichotomy, however, is actually not as clear-cut as I have just suggested, because the second section includes the card game as well as a couple of other scenes in New York. The "Paradise" section also includes scenes on the road both before and after Willie and Eddie come back for Eva.

From a screenwriting perspective, *Stranger Than Paradise* deviates from manual conventions in a number of significant ways. One page of script usually equals one minute of screen time, but Jarmusch's original script runs only about fifty-five pages (and many of these are not even complete pages), which is extremely short for the film's length. Jarmusch, in fact, calls his 1982 script a "film proposal," which suggests that he himself thought of it only as a blueprint. In actuality, it reads more like an extended treatment for a film rather than a full-blown screenplay. A number of scenes contain no dialogue and are simply short descriptions of actions. It would be difficult to make a financing decision based on Jarmusch's script because *Stranger Than Paradise* is not the kind of literary film that exists on the page, but a film that operates on a more purely visual and stylistic level.[9] Christine Vachon, the noted independent producer, refers to this type of film as "execution dependent." As she explains, "But the bottom line is that when you're making a film which is what they call 'execution dependent'—meaning that there's no way for the average Joe to be able to tell what's going to happen between the script and screen—the financiers have to take a leap of faith."[10] Interestingly, Jarmusch and John Lurie, who plays Willie, collaborated on the script for the first section of the film, which ends with the scene of Willie and Eddie drinking beers after Eva has left New York, while Jarmusch wrote the remainder of the screenplay by himself. Recognizing the fact that *Stranger Than Paradise* was execution dependent, Jarmusch actually shot and exhibited the first section as a short at two European film festivals, on the basis of which he was then able to raise additional financing to complete the feature.

On a stylistic level, *Stranger than Paradise* is comprised of sixty-seven single-take shots interspersed with black leader. Jarmusch claims that the opaque transitions allow him to make ambiguous temporal shifts, but they also have the effect of fracturing the narrative by bracketing each scene as an isolated event rather than reinforcing its connection to the next.[11] The camera remains fixed in a slight majority of the shots in the film; otherwise it moves to follow the actions of the characters by framing and reframing them into various configurations within the shot. There seems to be no discernible structure or pattern to the scenes involving camera movement, except that they increase in frequency as the film progresses. The camera only moves in six of twenty shots in the first section, while it increases to ten of twenty-two shots in the middle section, and finally to fourteen of twenty-five shots in the third section. Throughout *Stranger Than Paradise,* Jarmusch relies on wide-angle shots and extended takes rather than traditional shot/reverse shot setups. He never once cuts into an action, and often stages actions by having characters walk into and out of the frame. Jarmusch favors objectively neutral rather than subjective shots. He also more or less avoids point-of-view shots or poetic flourishes, except for the one instance where the camera moves from a shot of Eddie driving to one of Eva asleep in the back seat, as her hair blows in the breeze.

Stranger Than Paradise begins with sounds of an airplane over opening credits. A young woman, Eva, stands with a suitcase and shopping bag at the vast wasteland of an airport. She looks around and then exits the frame, as a plane glides slowly down the runway in the background. After more credits over black, a phone rings in the foreground of a room. Willie, wearing a black leather jacket and stingy brim, learns from Aunt Lotte that she has to go into the hospital for ten days and that Eva, his teenage Hungarian cousin, needs to stay at his place in the meantime. Willie makes it clear to her that he considers this to be a major imposition.

The words "The New World" appear as an intertitle over black, as we hear the sound of footsteps. Eva walks forward in the frame, stops, and hits the button on a cassette recorder. Screamin' Jay Hawkins's song "I Put a Spell on You," which will become emblematic of her character, plays over an extended tracking shot of Eva as she walks through the litter-strewn streets of lower Manhattan. Willie doesn't hide his resentment by refusing to greet Eva or invite her inside. When she introduces herself as "Eva Molnar," he responds harshly, "Yeah, no kidding." Willie's ethnic denial is once again manifest when he insists, as he did with Aunt Lotte, that Eva only speak English and not Hungarian. Willie begrudgingly tells her, "You can stay here tonight, and I don't know what you're gonna do after that."

Conflict develops between Willie and Eva, but the beginnings of a romantic triangle surface when Willie's friend, Eddie, drops by on the way to the racetrack. The love triangle is reinforced on a stylistic level by Jarmusch's careful staging and framing of the action. The camera isolates Eva as she reads a comic book, moves toward the door as Eddie enters, and into a two-shot of Eddie and Willie, who shaves in front of a tiny mirror. After Willie indicates that Eva is his cousin, Eddie, eyeing her several times, comments, "Yeah. She's cute." Willie tells him to shut up. The camera then follows Eddie over to Eva, creating another two-shot as he introduces himself and sits down next to her on the couch. Willie interrupts their conversation by asking Eddie about the horses in the second race. As Eddie reads off the entries, which include references to Ozu films, Willie reenters the frame and lights a cigarette. After looking at the horses scheduled for the third race, Eddie asks Willie whether Eva can come along, but Willie refuses to include her and exits the frame, leaving Eva and Eddie in a two-shot. Eddie gets up and again asks about taking Eva, as the camera now

Eva's arrival in New York

frames Eddie and Willie together. As Eddie follows Willie out the door, he continues to glance over at Eva, but Willie remains adamant about not taking her with them. The camera tracks back over to Eva and again isolates her in the frame, as she tosses the comic book in frustration and reclines on the bed.

The next three scenes—in which Eva and Willie watch a football game and a late-night science-fiction film, and Eva watches morning cartoons while Willie sleeps—delineate the boredom and inertia of Eva and Willie's life in New York City. The first thaw in their chilly relationship occurs when Eva attempts to clean Willie's filthy apartment and he plays a joke on her by telling her that the slang expression for using the vacuum cleaner is "choking the alligator." She plays along with Willie's juvenile sense of humor and, as she vacuums, tells him, "I'm choking the alligator right now." It is, however, only after Eva steals cans of food, a carton of Chesterfields, and a frozen TV dinner from the grocery store that Willie is willing to concede, "You're all right, kid."

Willie's growing acceptance of Eva gets confirmed when he gives her a dress as a present. After she protests that the dress is ugly and clearly not her style, Willie, who repeatedly espouses assimilation, responds, "You know, you come here and you should dress like people dress here." As Eva later packs for her trip to Cleveland, she wears the dress Willie has given her. At the door, Willie asks, "So you're sure you don't want me to go with you to the station?" Eva, however, insists on going there alone. She gives Willie a goodbye peck on the cheek, but he doesn't respond. Head lowered, he opens the door for her. As they stand there, an awkward tension exists between them. Willie seems on the verge of saying something to Eva:

> WILLIE: So, Eva?
> EVA: Yeah?
> WILLIE: Uh, maybe I'll see you again sometime.
> EVA: Yeah, maybe.

In reverting back to his usual indifference, this parting exchange represents a missed opportunity for Willie. After Eva leaves, he stands pensively by the closed door. Once on the street, Eva's reason for wanting to go to the station alone becomes obvious when she changes out of the dress and throws it in a trash can. As Eddie happens to pass by, she tells him, "This dress bugs me."

Jarmusch uses gesture and silence rather than dialogue to suggest the impact Eva's departure has on Willie, a point which is also underscored by somber violin music as he mopes around his apartment. When Eddie shows up and mentions that he saw Eva, Willie inquires about the dress. Even though Eddie knows that Eva has thrown away Willie's gift, he is unable to reveal this to his friend. For over a minute after they get beers, no more words are spoken. Instead, we experience an awkward silence between the two men. Deprived of language, we are forced to concentrate on their various gestures: Eddie tapping nervously on the beer can before opening it, his sudden and abrupt body shifts, his periodic glances over to Willie, their occasional slugs of beer, Willie's vacant stare, the sight of Eddie looking down. Willie cannot admit his sense of loss; Eddie cannot reveal the truth. The poignant scene is about things that cannot be verbally communicated by these characters, yet we know and understand precisely what is transpiring through the nonverbal, gestural cues, which are heightened by the extended silence and our own sense of the inexorable passage of time. The entire scene, which takes up only three-quarters of a page in the script, lasts two minutes and twelve seconds.

By the end of this last scene, the traits of the three main characters have been established. In Willie, who is rude, arrogant, controlling,

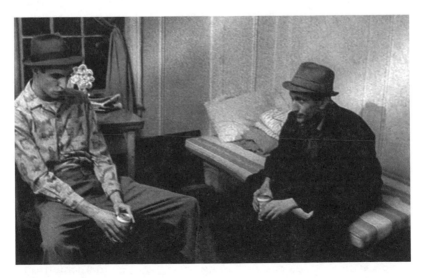

Willie and Eddie after Eva's departure

and sexist, Jarmusch goes against the convention of having a likeable protagonist, despite the fact that Willie's initial hostility toward Eva gradually softens. On some level, he seems to be smitten by her, but this can only be inferred from the subtext of the last several scenes. Eddie, on the other hand, finds Eva cute and wants to take her to the racetrack, but he nevertheless goes along with Willie's desire to exclude her. While Eddie lacks the ability to think on his own, Eva has a stubborn independent streak that clashes with Willie's attempts to dominate her. Her outsider perspective enables Eva to critique aspects of American culture that Willie embraces wholeheartedly—she finds football to be stupid and TV dinners to be anything but wholesome. After Willie puts down her favorite music, Eva responds, "It's Screamin' Jay Hawkins and he's a wild man, so bug off!" Her use of American slang seems especially appropriate given the fact that she has picked up this phrase from Willie. In Willie and Eva, Jarmusch creates strongly contrasting characters, and the underlying tensions between them serve as the basic conflict of the film.

The first section of *Stranger Than Paradise* establishes the traits of the three main characters, but little else. Jarmusch's scenes, in fact, consist of much that would be left out of most films: watching television, eating dinner, vacuuming, packing, and drinking beer. The introduction of Eddie at thirteen minutes creates the third element of the romantic triangle, but as yet there has been no catalyst or inciting incident to give us a clear sense of direction to the story. As Jarmusch explains:

> The form of this film as a narrative is so minimal it almost tricks you. It has elements like a traditional plot and it has three sections, but those sections don't do . . . what you would expect: introduce the characters, then some kind of conflict, and then a resolution. Instead the narrative is very minimal. If you stop the film at any point and ask the audience what was going to happen next, they would have no idea. They wouldn't really be thinking about it, but would be more concerned with the characters and what's happening to them.[12]

As Jarmusch suggests, *Stranger Than Paradise* works primarily on the level of character. Although character has been defined by manual writers such as Linda Seger as a tight nexus of goal, motivation, and action, Jarmusch's characters actually represent the antithesis of this.

Yet their distinctive personalities still manage to hold our interest, even when we are not always clear about the spine or direction of the story. Once the triangle has been set up and Eva departs, the logic of the narrative would demand that she needs to come back into the story, but we are not sure exactly how this will happen.

The middle section begins with a title which indicates that it is now "One Year Later." After Willie and Eddie get caught cheating at cards, Willie expresses a desire to get out of town. In a more classical dramatic plot, this event might serve to provide motivation for the road trip, but the card players never end up posing an actual threat to either Willie or Eddie, nor do they appear again. Willie even downplays their significance by referring to them as a "bunch of lightweights." Nevertheless, the money the two have just obtained through cheating at cards turns out to have an important function—it provides them with the actual means to take a trip. Eddie asks Willie where they would go, but their destination is left as one of the few dangling causes in the film.

Willie's desire for a change of scenery at thirty-three minutes functions as the first turning point. As Willie and Eddie head out of town in a borrowed car, we glimpse the sense of male camaraderie and affection that exists between these two characters. But the nastier side of Willie surfaces, as he and Eddie drive through the cold, wintry streets of New York City on their way out of town. When he spies a man shivering on the street, Willie tells Eddie to pull over. After summoning the guy to the car, Willie asks, "Can you tell me which way is Cleveland?" Willie's question provides important exposition by indicating their ultimate destination. Even though the scene does nothing to advance the plot, it reveals a good deal about Willie's character. When the guy turns out to be a factory worker on his way to work, Eddie comments, "Can you imagine working in a factory?" Willie, of course, cannot. Eddie, who would probably never do something like this on his own, becomes culpable through his silence during the interaction. When Eddie does say something to Willie afterward, Willie seems regretful momentarily, but Eddie quickly exonerates him. Nevertheless Willie's cynical and aggressive attitude, reminiscent of punk, remains partially hidden by the film's deadpan comic humor.

Music critic John Piccarella picks up on the disguised subcultural aspect of *Stranger Than Paradise*, which he sees as a means of avoiding stereotyping. He writes:

Its characters show no redeeming motivation, no real ability to relate. But they have no criminal vices, no malice, no sociopathy. They're not part of a subculture, just old-style bohemians with a nostalgia for hipsterism and a barely perceptible affection for each other. They have undeniable charm. Because they're not sensationalized punk misfits, they're worth believing in.[13]

This actually seems to be a deliberate strategy on the part of Jarmusch, who, at the time of its release, talked about not wanting the film to be associated with "New Wave" music or "with some kind of fashion or some kind of trend."[14] Elsewhere, he elaborated on this issue: "I wasn't trying to make a statement about a certain generation. This is a group that's always there, throughout history. There are always people who exist on the margin, and they happen to make good stories."[15] Jarmusch was after all a part of the East Village scene that spawned punk and "No Wave" music. He was a member of the rock band the Del-Byzanteens, and both his two male leads, John Lurie and Richard Edson, also played in bands. Jarmusch was also familiar with the work of punk filmmakers, such as Beth and Scott B, Amos Poe, and Eric Mitchell, for whom Jarmusch did sound on *Underground USA*.[16] *Stranger Than Paradise* has the punk attitude but not the obsession with the iconography of violence emblematic of these other films. The punk attitude is embodied in the character of Willie, but it is so downplayed that the film comes across as less punk than neo-Beat and was never really characterized as part of the movement.

While Willie's reference to Cleveland in the last scene indicates their destination, the motivation behind it becomes clarified once the two are on the highway when Eddie (who does all the driving while Willie relaxes in the front seat) asks, "When we get to Cleveland, where are we gonna stay? With your aunt, and Eva?" Eddie also wonders aloud whether Eva will remember him, but Willie responds, "I doubt it, Eddie," and changes the subject by asking him how much money they have from their card winnings. It turns out to be almost $600, causing Eddie to boast that they're rich. On the outskirts of Cleveland later on, Eddie confesses to Willie that prior to Eva's visit, he never even knew that Willie was "from Hungary, or Budapest, or any of those places." Eddie tells him, "I thought you were an American." This causes Willie to respond defensively, "Hey, I'm as American as you are." We see their large American car pass the Greyhound bus station, Nite Life

Lounge, a power plant with large smokestacks, and other postindustrial structures before they pull up at a small working-class house.

The middle section, or second act, is notable for introducing two additional characters—Billy and Aunt Lotte—but neither presents much of an obstacle for Willie. Billy, who makes demands on Eva, has the potential to become a formidable rival, and, in a classical narrative, no doubt he would serve this function. At the very least, Eva would be conflicted enough by her relationship with him that she would not allow herself to be whisked off to Florida, but Billy, despite his assertiveness, never provides enough of a challenge to Willie. Aunt Lotte, in fact, proves to be a much more colorful character, who manages to beat the young hustlers at cards, to force Eva to be chaperoned on a date, and to slip in humorous slang expressions whenever the situation calls for it.

Since she hasn't seen him in ten years, Aunt Lotte does not recognize Willie when he first appears at her door. Willie learns from her that Eva's working at a hot dog place and he and Eddie later slip into the seedy joint and surprise her when she walks up to wait on them. Eva seems genuinely happy to see them and Eddie is especially glad that Eva remembers his name. The two decide to wait in the car for her to get off work and she arrives shortly, accompanied by a friend named Billy who pesters her to go to the movies with him.

Life in Cleveland turns out to be no more exciting than it is in New York, as Willie, Eddie, and Aunt Lotte watch television and play cards. "Yeah, we're not doing anything," Eddie complains. Tension arises once Eva announces she's going to the movies and Aunt Lotte wants Willie and Eddie to be her chaperones. The subsequent scene threatens to turn the romantic triangle into a foursome. We see Billy, Eddie, Eva, and Willie lined up together in a row of a nearly empty movie theater, as they watch a kung fu movie and shadows flicker over their faces. Eva sits between Willie and Eddie, thus isolating Billy, who furtively glances in Eva's direction. Afterward, Eddie thanks Billy for paying for them and Billy asks Eva to walk him to his door. Willie, who seems jealous, mimics Billy's line, which disgusts him enough that he follows it by asking Eddie, "What are we doing here?" Eddie responds, "I don't know." The next day, as they hang out together on the railroad tracks, Eddie indicates that he wants to leave. After Willie throws a snowball, Eddie comments, "You know, it's funny. You come to someplace new and everything looks just the same." Willie retorts, "No kidding, Eddie!"

Willie finally gets a chance to spend time alone with Eva, who indicates that she'd like to get out of Cleveland. Willie asks her about Billy—a further indication of his jealousy—but Eva avoids the issue by calling him "a nice friend." Their conversation, like the one before Eva left New York, becomes punctuated once again by long pauses. Willie even tries telling Eva a joke, but despite several feeble attempts, he can't remember it. The sound of a passing train outside only heightens the awkward tension between them.

Jarmusch's staging of the next scene suggests Eva's romantic conflict involving Willie and Billy. As Willie and Eddie play cards with Aunt Lotte, who manages to win every hand, the phone rings. Eva walks into the frame, picks it up, and moves away, so that the composition becomes divided in half. Willie's head remains prominently visible in the mirror that occupies the upper quadrant of the left side of the frame. The depth of the right-hand side becomes evident, as Eva paces backward and forward as she talks with Billy, who pressures her to get together. Eva offers the excuse that her cousin and his friend are planning to leave the following day. After their conversation ends, Eva returns to the living room and asks them whether they want to see the big lake. Eddie is a bit taken back when Aunt Lotte smacks him on the thigh and tells him in her heavy accent, "Go jump in the lake."

As the wind howls and light snow falls, Willie, Eddie, and Eva exit the car into the blistery cold. The three stand at a railing overlooking Lake Erie, which appears to be a huge white void. Eddie, of course, gives his standard response that "it's beautiful." The awkwardness once again returns in the form of long, extended gaps in the dialogue, with Eva once again reiterating, "It's kind of a drag here, really." The next morning Eva gives Eddie a peck on the cheek and kisses Willie goodbye, but this time he returns the kiss. She tells them, "So, if you guys win a lot of money at the racetrack, you should come and try to kidnap me." Willie answers, "We'll take you someplace warm. This place is awful." The car exits the frame, leaving Eva standing there. For the second time now, Eva and Willie have become separated, causing us to wonder whether their last dialogue is intended as a dangling cause, a foreshadowing of subsequent events that will bring them back together. In the last several scenes, Eva has clearly telegraphed her dissatisfaction with Cleveland, as well as hinted at her desire to hit the road with Willie and Eddie.

It doesn't take long before our questions about Eva get answered. After a title that indicates the start of the third section, "Paradise," Willie demands to know how much money they have left on their way out of town. When he finds out that they have only spent fifty dollars, Willie asks Eddie whether he's ever been to Florida. Eddie responds that Florida is beautiful, but after detailing its many wonders (white beaches, girls in bikinis, Cape Canaveral, Miami Beach, pelicans, and flamingos) he admits that he's never been there. Willie proposes going to Florida, and adds that they can even take Eva along, a plan that Eddie prefers to heading back to New York. When they return to get Eva, Aunt Lotte protests loudly in Hungarian and calls them "good for nothings." As Aunt Lotte waddles back toward her house, she mutters, "You son of a bitch."

Willie's decision to rescue Eva and take her with them to Florida represents the film's second turning point, which occurs at fifty-eight minutes. Since the overall film is approximately eighty-six minutes excluding final credits, such a structure would divide the film into three acts (thirty-three minutes, twenty-five minutes, and twenty-six minutes). If such a breakdown is indeed accurate, then each act turns out to be approximately the same size. According to the manuals, the middle act is usually the longest, often twice the size of the first and third acts, but here it turns out to be the shortest.

The third act begins on a buoyant note, as the three start the long drive to Florida in the front seat. Eddie even teases Eva about bringing her bikini along—the only overt sexual reference in an otherwise chaste movie. Willie chooses to ignore the comment, but he seems to be in a foul mood in the next scene. In Jack Kerouac's classic Beat novel *On the Road*, the open road causes the characters to feel a sense of wild exuberance, but in *Stranger Than Paradise* the long car drive results in monotony and tedium. As they drive at night, Eva has been relegated to the backseat. The awkward tension has once again returned and it is reinforced by the extreme duration of the shot. Nearly thirty seconds of silence pass before Eva puts on "I'll Put a Spell on You." Willie growls, "Not that." When Eva tells him it's Screamin' Jay, Willie responds, "Oh, that's awful." Eva, however, defends Screamin' Jay as her "main man" and ends up converting Eddie into a fan as well. "It's horrible," Willie tells them, and shows his disdain by covering his face with his hat. As Eddie drives along the highway, he

Eddie, Eva, and Willie in Florida

looks to his right and then over his shoulder at Eva, whose hair blows
in the night breeze, as lights flicker over and behind her.

At a sleazy motel in Florida, Willie tries to pawn off the portable cot
on the exhausted Eva, but she lies down on one of the two beds. Willie
grabs the other, leaving Eddie to struggle with trying to open the
portable cot. The three of them sleep with their clothes on. The old
issues in their relationship return the next morning when Eva awakens
and discovers that Willie and Eddie's belongings are still there, but
they have both left. She paces angrily around the room, then slumps on
the day bed. When Willie and Eddie return, Eva complains about their
utter lack of consideration—the first time we see her anger. She tells
them, "I'm here alone in the middle of nowhere. I don't know anybody,
and you can't even do that much . . . leave me a note when you leave."
Willie tells her to shut up, and continues to argue with Eddie about his
poor intuition about the dog track. After Eddie tells Eva they lost nearly
all of their money, her outward disgust causes Willie to knock over a
vase holding a tropical plant. Willie storms out after this violent outburst, but the contradictions of his ambivalent behavior become obvious when he comes back in and apologizes. Eva asks, "What are we
going to do now?" This serves as another rare instance of a dialogue
hook, as the three of them stare at the ground. They go for a walk along

the beach, but relations between them are so strained that they don't speak to each other. At one point Eddie and Eva wait for Willie to catch up with them, but he simply walks right past them and out of the frame. Back inside their hotel room, the tension persists. As Willie and Eddie start to head out to the horse track, Eva gets up to go with them. Willie, however, refuses to allow her to come along. This causes a vigorous argument between Willie and Eddie, but Willie refuses to relent. As he did with Aunt Lotte, Eddie attempts to placate Eva, but she responds, "You're the same . . . just go." Eddie apologizes, but he follows Willie out the door, leaving Eva in the motel.

The next scene comes as a kind of deus ex machina in terms of the plot, even for a film whose narrational strategy lies closer to art cinema. We watch Eva, wearing a dark straw hat with two white bands, walk slowly out of a gift shop. As she passes a beach entrance, an African-American man approaches her and complains about her being forty minutes late. After telling her that he's fed up, he hands her an envelope and leaves. Dumbfounded, Eva slips it into her coat. Moments later, another woman in a similar outfit—raincoat and identical dark straw hat with two light bands—appears and looks around, indicating that the earlier incident has been a case of mistaken identity. Back at the hotel, Eva closes the curtains and is amazed when she discovers the envelope contains a stash of money. She places part of it on the table along with a note, and splits. Rather than being set up previously and motivated by events in the plot, the last scene relies solely on coincidence. Even the dialogue resorts to overt exposition in attempting to justify the case of mistaken identity, as the guy tells Eva, "You got the hat on . . . Man, I see the dome piece on your top." That the envelope would also contain the means for Eva to escape strains credibility even further.

Willie and Eddie return from the horse track, slightly drunk and in high spirits, but they soon realize that Eva has left behind the note, money, and her straw hat. At the airline counter, Eva learns that the only flight to Europe goes to Budapest (another coincidence) and leaves in forty-five minutes. After talking to the same ticket person, Willie buys a ticket in order to dissuade her from leaving. He also tells a confused Eddie that he will meet him back at the car in ten minutes. In the next scene, Eddie watches as a plane takes off and flies overhead. "Oh Willie," he says aloud, "I had a bad feeling." Eddie then gets in the car, wonders what they're going to do in Budapest, and drives away. Meanwhile, Eva returns to the empty motel room to find that Willie and

Willie's estrangement from Eddie and Eva on the beach

Eddie have already vacated it. She sits down in a chair and holds the straw hat in her lap. Eva closes her weary eyes, as the screen goes black and Screamin' Jay's "I Put a Spell on You" plays over the final credits.

The sense of melancholy that *Stranger Than Paradise* evokes has largely to do with its downbeat ending and the ultimate plight of Eva, who is clearly the film's most sympathetic character. The love triangle—slight as it is—creates certain expectations in the viewer, but actually turns out to be a red herring because it does not lead anywhere. Like the road trip itself, it merely becomes a pretext for the interaction of the three main characters. Willie and Eddie never really discuss Eva between themselves. We know that Eddie likes Eva—he thinks she's cute and wants to include her—but it is Willie who will not let her accompany them to the racetrack. *Stranger Than Paradise* is, after all, a buddy road movie, which almost by definition would demand that Eva be excluded. There is certainly a sexist side to Willie. He has trouble accepting Eva's self-assertiveness in matters of music and style in the New York section, and he is equally critical of her choice in men, namely, Billy, either out of jealousy or because Willie does not deem him cool enough, a factor which seems to matter a great deal to him.

Willie can accept Eddie, who dresses in a similar manner, because he provides a mirror image of himself. Toward the end of the film, when Eddie tries to apologize to Eva for leaving her, she lumps him together with Willie. Of course, Eva is right. Although Eddie comes across as charming, polite, and funny, he is also naive and a bit slow, which is the reason Willie can take advantage of him. At various times in the film, we also witness the sense of male camaraderie that exists between Willie and Eddie, but, for whatever reason, it cannot be extended to women, especially independently minded ones such as Eva. There is a sense of poetic justice in the fact that Willie winds up on a plane back to Budapest, the place he has most tried to forget, while Eva gets stuck in the false paradise of a Florida motel room. Despite its absurdist sense of humor, the vision of *Stranger Than Paradise* is a rather dark one, presenting a world of deadbeat losers, missed connections, and unrealized possibilities.

As an American independent film, *Stranger Than Paradise* turns out to be much closer to art cinema than a classical Hollywood film. Willie's passivity flattens the potential drama, but his ambivalence regarding Eva creates underlying tension and adds elements of both unpredictability and surprise. The film shifts the narrative emphasis from the written page to the performances as well as the mise-en-scène. On a stylistic level, Jarmusch's use of wide-angle shots and continuous single takes separated by black leader continually draws our attention to the compositional frame, which determines the actors' movements and actions within it, such as the scene where Eddie and Eva walk toward us on the beach and stop, while Willie proceeds to walk out of the shot, indicating his estrangement. Episodic incident replaces drama, and the film substitutes bohemian hanging out for the goal-oriented determinism of conventional plot. There is a conflict at the heart of *Stranger Than Paradise*—the repressed love triangle between the main characters—but, largely as a result of Willie's ambivalence, the romantic plotline is not acted upon and does not lead anywhere, which is precisely the point of the film. The real brilliance of *Stranger Than Paradise* has to do with its young and disaffected characters who, through their erratic behavior, nevertheless manage to engage us with their idiosyncratic sense of style, deadpan humor, and unexpected charm.

Chapter 2

The Passive Protagonist in *Safe*

An ambivalent protagonist, as we have seen with Jarmusch's film, can have positive attributes. For one thing, such a protagonist creates an instability that keeps the narrative unpredictable and full of surprises, because we're not always sure where the story is heading. An ambivalent protagonist has a tendency to shift the focus from the plot, which gets de-emphasized, back toward character. In *Stranger Than Paradise*, Willie's ambivalence contributes to a sense of drift rather than forward direction, which very much reflects his marginal lifestyle. For Willie to change as a result of his encounter with Eva would seem somehow too contrived and phony. After all, most people don't really change in real life, an important referent for many independent screenwriters. They often repeat certain patterns of behavior. They are not necessarily heroes, a term that Michael Hauge uses interchangeably with "protagonist" in his manual.[1] In fact, Jarmusch's decision to put someone like Willie at the center of his story represents a deliberate affront to this notion.

A character can be active, ambivalent, or passive. In short, there are broader options when it comes to conceiving of agency in a screenplay. An active protagonist, an obsessive type almost by nature or inclination, will create greater drama. The sheer force of her or his behavior will provoke a reaction of some kind. Such passion and energy will be held in check or countered by an equally determined antagonist who represents either dark forces, nearly insurmountable obstacles, or, at the very least, cold reality. Ambivalence, as we have already seen, can cause erratic, tonal shifts that often mitigate some opposition. But what happens in a narrative where the protagonist is the opposite of goal-driven? How does a passive protagonist affect both story structure and storytelling? Todd Haynes's *Safe* (1995) provides just such a case study.

Haynes's second feature, *Safe*, managed to confound audiences by its seemingly odd mixture of art-film stylistics with unseen horror. Todd McCarthy's Sundance review in *Variety* set the tone for the film's initial reception when he wrote that *Safe* "delves into the ominous condition of 'environmental illness' in an arid, pretentious way that will try the patience even of viewers who come to it sympathetically."[2] Waiting for unexpected twists in the plot to develop or for the film to become a satire, McCarthy found *Safe* to be a disappointment. Not all critics panned *Safe*. In fact, the film received generally favorable reviews, but some, like McCarthy, obviously did not know what to make of its utterly passive protagonist, Carol White, its dramatic flatness, and its unflinching ambiguity, especially concerning Wrenwood, the New Age oasis where Carol spends the last portion of the film. Whereas Willie, the protagonist of *Stranger Than Paradise*, turned out to be incapable of knowing exactly what he wanted, Carol White challenges the classical Hollywood notion of the energetic, goal-driven protagonist by being so completely passive that the story's main action unfolds in a slow, downward trajectory, as Carol withdraws and then fully retreats from the pervasive chemical threats in her environment.

Despite the fact that *Safe* managed to puzzle some viewers, the film nevertheless has become an independent classic in the subsequent period since its release. It wound up being ranked number eleven in *Filmmaker*'s poll of the most important American independent films.[3] And, even more surprisingly, *Safe* was named the top film of the 1990s in the *Village Voice*'s First Annual Film Critics' Poll, consisting of forty-six national film critics. In earning this distinction, *Safe* placed ahead of such international art-house favorites as Lars von Trier's *Breaking the Waves* (1996), Hou Hsiao-hsien's *Flowers of Shanghai* (1998), Abbas Kiarostami's *Taste of Cherry* (1997), and Scorsese's more mainstream *GoodFellas* (1990).[4]

By the time he made his first feature, *Poison* (1990), Todd Haynes was already a familiar figure within the New York independent-film community. Shortly after graduating from the semiotics program at Brown, Haynes had teamed with Christine Vachon and Barry Ellsworth to start Apparatus, an incubator-type funding agency for stylistically innovative shorts by emerging filmmakers. Apparatus was an attempt to bridge the gap between the more rigidly experimental tradition of independent film and more commercial notions of entertainment. As Vachon explains in her independent producer's guide *Shooting to Kill*:

> Actually, there were two camps in the New York independent scene. People were making either super-experimental films, which were often like watching paint dry for two hours, or slick calling-card movies that were essentially mini-Hollywood pictures. There was little in between. We wanted to make films that were both avant-garde and entertaining—such as *Blue Velvet*, which had just come out and seemed to signal a new direction. One of the strong mandates of the company was to change people's perception that "experimental" was synonymous with "excruciating."[5]

One of Apparatus's early efforts was Haynes's own forty-three minute short *Superstar: The Karen Carpenter Story* (1987), which used Barbie dolls to portray the anorexic singer's downward descent. The film created a strong buzz at Sundance, but it also led to threats of a lawsuit from a Carpenter family member, which prevented the film from being shown more widely. *Superstar* nevertheless managed to achieve a certain underground cult status as a result of the ban.

Haynes followed *Superstar* with *Poison*, a first feature that employed an associative structure and a medley of three separate stories, each one shot in a different style, to explore issues of gay desire in the context of AIDS. Made for the sum of $250,000, the Genet-inspired film won the Grand Jury prize at the 1991 Sundance Film Festival. Expected to appeal to a small niche market, *Poison*'s commercial appeal increased considerably when it found itself the target of a virulent right-wing campaign against the National Endowment for the Arts, which had provided a small portion of the film's funding.[6] After *Poison*'s unexpected success, one might have guessed that it would have been relatively easy for Haynes to raise financing for his next feature, but this proved not to be the case. Although distributors and financial backers were anxious to produce a New Queer Cinema follow-up to *Poison*, Haynes chose to chart a new direction by writing a script that dealt with gay issues only obliquely. Despite Haynes's reputation as one of the more innovative American independent filmmakers, it took several years for Haynes and his producer, Christine Vachon, to raise the $1 million needed to produce *Safe*. Vachon reported receiving widely varying reactions to the script among financiers:

> I think they just didn't know what to make of it. A lot of people would recognize the power of the script. Whatever you thought of it, you couldn't deny that the script was beautifully written. Every single word was like a knife. But they reacted to the script much the same way people are reacting to the film. . . . Unfortunately, the financiers who thought it was brilliant didn't have fat cheque books, and a whole other lot of people simply said, 'I don't know what he's trying to do.' And Todd would explain what he was trying to do until he was blue in the face, but they just didn't get it.[7]

Eventually funded from a variety of different sources, including England's Channel Four and American Playhouse, *Safe* is a boldly formal study of a wealthy woman suffering from chemical sensitivity, an allegory about certain aspects of the AIDS epidemic, and a subtle exploration of the loss of personal identity. Like *Stranger Than Paradise*, *Safe* shares a great deal more affinity with art cinema than with classical Hollywood, especially in flattening out the potential dramatic elements of the story. It lacks the strongly inflected turning points found in most mainstream films. This is undoubtedly why the script proved to be such a hard sell for Vachon, even with a hot young director and a rising star, Julianne Moore, cast in the lead role.

Safe begins with an extended, moving car shot through a wealthy, suburban neighborhood in the San Fernando Valley, which makes the night landscape appear otherworldly. When Carol White and her husband, Greg, arrive home, they make love, but it's obvious that Carol remains detached. Once Carol discovers that the wrong-colored couch has been delivered the next day, she becomes visibly upset, especially when she can't get through to anyone at the store. When Carol comes downstairs in the morning, her kitchen is a swirl of activity—housekeepers and painters busily at work. She cannot find the telephone book, but her housekeeper, Fulvia, shows her where she has moved it. Carol reaches for the phone directory, but she becomes dizzy and tries to stabilize herself by drinking a glass of milk. As Carol stares straight ahead, we hear the faint sounds of a helicopter and other eerie noises on the soundtrack. This scene, which occurs at thirteen minutes, serves as the film's inciting incident.

Carol drinks a glass of milk in her house

While driving home from the furniture store, the fumes from a truck in front of her cause Carol to have a severe coughing attack. Forced to pull into an underground parking ramp, she ends up doubled over, gasping for air. Carol later experiences difficulty sleeping. At lunch, her friend Linda suggests that they both go on fruit diets. After Carol dozes off during an off-color joke at an upscale restaurant, she consults her physician, Dr. Hubbard, complaining of stress. The doctor tells her to forgo the fruit diet, but he can't find anything medically wrong with her. The first turning point occurs at twenty-eight minutes when Carol gets a nosebleed at the hair salon. "Oh my God," she screams as dark blood seeps out of her nostril, which serves as a horrific marker that something must be terribly wrong, a point that is underscored by the ominous soundtrack.

There are not many major complications during the middle act other than the fact that Carol gets progressively sicker, and ends up taking on the identity of an environmentally ill person. Carol's decision to seek refuge at a New Age retreat called Wrenwood occurs at sixty-six minutes. Although Wrenwood represents a major change in Carol's life, one in which she essentially abandons her family, it does not result in any real change in her condition, which raises the question of whether the film has a two-act or a three-act structure. Assuming that Carol's move to Wrenwood represents the second turning point, which I would argue, the film has a first act of twenty-eight minutes, a second act of thirty-eight minutes, and an extremely long third act of forty-nine minutes. Instead of accelerating the pace, which is more typical of third acts, Haynes's excessively lengthy third act makes the Wrenwood section not only the longest act of the film, but nearly twice the length of the first act.

Haynes's dissection of the film's protagonist, Carol White, is a brilliant portrait of bourgeois sterility, as we watch her identity begin to dissolve right before our eyes. Carol is really the opposite of McKee's notion of a willful protagonist. After her whole world starts to tumble, Carol seems incapable of mustering much willpower or psychic resistance. Her downward spiral happens in stages. She gets dizzy while reaching for the telephone book, has a coughing fit on the freeway, falls asleep while dining with her husband's clients, suffers a nosebleed at the beauty salon, vomits in her bedroom while embracing Greg, becomes totally confused in her own home, gasps for breath at a friend's baby shower, and collapses at the dry cleaners, which lands her in the hospital. Carol consults various professionals—her medical doctor, a psychiatrist, and an allergist—throughout her ordeal, but they are unable to help her. She attends seminars about environmental

Carol's nosebleed at the hairdresser's

illness and begins to follow their strict regimen, but when this also fails, she abandons her family for Wrenwood.

Carol's passivity cedes agency and, hence, power to others—at first to the medical profession, and when that fails, to various New Age regimens and retreats. As a result, she really becomes the victim of factions all too willing to fill an empty void. This reverses the usual dynamic of a classical film. Carol not only lacks outer motivation—the will or determination to fight for herself—but she also lacks inner motivation as well. A passive protagonist turns out to be the equivalent of a weak antagonist because the effect on the narrative is largely the same. Since drama stems from conflict—from contrast and opposition—a passive protagonist reduces the potential for dramatic combustion, and consequently flattens the dramatic arc of the story. The lack of drama has the effect of turning *Safe* into a character study of this type of person.

Carol's illness is intricately bound up with issues of personal identity. She describes herself as a homemaker to the psychiatrist, but it's clear that her maid actually runs her home. Carol spends virtually all of her time on such activities as gardening, aerobic exercise classes, lunches at outdoor cafés, fad diets, minor household chores, interior decorating problems, and baby showers. From what we observe, Carol's complaints about being "stressed out" and "really busy" are patently absurd, given the fact that she doesn't work at any sort of job and appears to be doing very little. Carol remains divorced from her own body—she is unable to sweat during aerobics or stay connected during sex—as well as her feelings. Even the psychiatrist seems at a loss when Carol proves incapable of talking about herself in any meaningful way. Carol wonders why he's not asking more questions, but he responds: "We really need to be hearing from you. What's going on . . . in you." When the speaker at the environmental illness seminar calls on her, Carol defers to Greg to explain her condition. She is unable to discuss her feelings of remorse when Peter Dunning drops by, struggles at describing her childhood room in the outdoor session, and proves incapable of participating in group therapy.

As a rich, suburban housewife, Carol really has no identity. In her own bedroom, she becomes so disoriented and confused that she has to ask Greg where she is, and looks at family pictures and her husband for some sort of confirmation. "Who am I?" a videotape about environmental illness asks right after this, and Carol gradually attempts to

Greg and Carol at the environmental illness seminar

fill the void by assuming the identity of a diseased person. This becomes obvious during her lunch with Linda, as Carol explains the toxicity of various products, including her new couch. When Dr. Hubbard becomes irritated with her at the hospital for blaming her convulsive reaction on pesticides, Carol insists that she suffers from a chemical impairment, and (for the first and only time) actually raises her voice to a nurse, who sprays air freshener in the room.

Throughout all this, the viewer expects Carol to recover, a point which Roger Ebert makes in his original review of the film:

> The set-up scenes have all the hallmarks of a made-for-TV docudrama about the disease of the week. We settle in confidently, able to predict what will happen: Carol's problems will be diagnosed, the environment will be blamed, and there will be an 800 number at the end where we can call for more information about how to save the planet. But that isn't how *Safe* develops at all.[8]

Although Wrenwood appears to be a progressive retreat—run by an HIV-positive, chemical-sensitive gay man named Peter Dunning, an earth-mother figure as director, Claire, and an African-American staff member, Susan—our impression begins to shift once we are introduced to its various rules and proscriptions. These include segregation of the sexes, silence during breakfast and lunch meals, as well as prohibitions against smoking, drinking, recreational drugs, and sexual contact. Peter begins his first talk to the group by getting the other new member's name wrong and sounding like a bad standup comedian. He gives a sermon about love and personal transformation, but manages to preach against drugs and promiscuity while mixing in progressive-sounding buzz phrases like "sensitivity in the workplace and the men's movement and multiculturalism." He ends by getting everyone to repeat a religious mantra: "We are one with the power that created us. We are safe, and all is well in our world." The cultlike nature of Wrenwood becomes reinforced when we hear guitar music and a woman strolls out (followed by a guitar-strumming man) and sings a retro folk song entitled "Give Yourself to Love."

During their visit to Wrenwood, Greg and their son, Rory, join Carol at Peter's weekly communal session, which provides something of a reality check. Peter launches into an attack on the negativity of the media, announcing that he refuses to watch TV any longer because it's too risky to his immune system as well as theirs. This bit of news appears to contradict everything he has preached about earlier. Greg looks bewildered and Rory casts skeptical glances toward his father, especially when Peter ends with his usual prayer. As Carol walks with Greg afterward and Rory tags along at a distance, Greg inquires about the huge mansion on the hill. Carol indicates that it's Peter's house, which certainly makes us question the founder's motivations.

The next scene provides additional insight into Peter's character. In an outdoor therapy session, facilitated by Peter, several residents discuss their feelings of self-hatred, self-blame, and deep-seated hurt. When Peter calls upon Carol, she can only shake her head, indicating her inability to participate. Peter then moves on to Nell, who reveals that her husband thought she was crazy until he also became ill. Peter asks what she was feeling at the time, and Nell responds: "I just wanted to go get a gun and blow off the heads of everyone who got me like this." Peter chastises her: "Nell, nobody out there made you sick. You know that. The only person who can make you sick is you. Right? If our immune systems have been damaged, it's because we allowed them to be." Peter once again reveals himself to be a maze of contradictions, as he now rails against all the hatred and frailty he sees around him and ends with self-aggrandizing statements about how lucky and blessed he feels.

Whereas Peter Dunning continually blames the victims for their illness and encourages them to submerge their personal identities to the group, Claire emphasizes Wrenwood's focus on the individual in the infomercial Carol happened to see while in the hospital. Claire is also the one who provides solace to Carol, when she bursts into tears upon returning to her cabin one night. As Claire moves toward her, Carol steps back instinctively. Claire insists that what Carol's feeling is "natural" and commends her for her brave actions. Claire shares some of her own personal history, including the fact that she was unable even to walk when she first arrived there. She tells Carol: "I would look myself in the mirror every single day and I would say to myself, 'Claire, I *love* you, I really love you.'"

A romance character gets introduced late in the third act in the form of Chris, a male resident who volunteers to share meal duties. Our expectations that Chris might turn out to be Carol's salvation, as happens so often in Hollywood romances, become raised when the two of them flirt briefly like two shy teenagers. Nevertheless, Carol becomes more agitated during an outdoor therapy session. Claire expresses concern that Carol's increased sensitivity to car fumes might indicate that she's "spiraling down" and suggests, now that Nell's husband has passed away, that Carol might consider taking his

Peter and Susan in a therapy session at Wrenwood

more isolated "safe" house. After Greg and Rory have helped her move into the new quarters, Carol and Greg walk together, but Carol wobbles on her feet and backs away from her husband. Experiencing a shortness of breath, she blames his cologne, then something in his shirt. Greg approaches her cautiously and the two embrace awkwardly. A scene of Carol waving goodbye at Greg and Rory's departure cuts to one of Carol and Chris flirting as they prepare dinner in the kitchen. After the meal, music comes on and the residents and staff (including Peter and Claire and Carol and Chris) dance in the dining hall. Chris then surprises Carol by announcing that it's her birthday tomorrow. After Susan brings out a cake and Carol manages to blow out the candles, the other residents urge her to make a speech. Carol begins by thanking Chris and the others. She continues:

> CAROL: I don't know what I'm saying, just . . . it's true how much I . . . (*she stumbles, her eyes filling unexpectedly*) hated myself before I—came here, so I'm . . . trying to be more—aware . . . seeing myself more as I hopefully am.

> *Carol smiles as tears are replaced by a slight shortness of breath. She continues.*

> CAROL: More positive, like seeing the pluses—like, I think it's slowly opening up now, people's minds, it's like educating and AIDS and other types of disease— And this *is* a disease . . . 'Cause it's out there. It's just making people aware of it and even our own selves. I mean, we have to be aware of it . . . reading labels . . . going into buildings . . .

> *Carol stops, suddenly forgetting what she was saying. She looks at the people listening to her.*

> *Everyone looks at her in anticipation.*

> *For an interminable instant, Carol is lost. She shudders.*[9]

Peter puts an end to Carol's incoherent rambling by toasting her, but Carol's fractured speech—containing jumbled bits of clichéd jargon she's heard at the environmental illness seminars and at Wrenwood—indicates not progress, but the total erasure of her identity. Her speech represents one of the most terrifying moments in the film.

Chris walks Carol back to her cabin. As they say goodnight, we expect them to kiss, but they only smile at each other instead, and Chris gives her a slight wave as he leaves. Alone in her igloolike dwelling—the inside of which Haynes likens to an "antiseptic space capsule" in the script—Carol breathes oxygen and then looks into the mirror at her emaciated face, now covered with red blotches and lesions. She tries to mimic Claire by peering at herself and saying, "I love you." The film ends on this terribly bleak note by holding on Carol's blank expression.

Like Jarmusch in *Stranger Than Paradise*, Haynes also does not attempt to create the kind of character identification found in most narratives. In the introduction to the three published screenplays for *Far from Heaven*, *Safe*, and *Superstar: The Karen Carpenter Story*, Haynes discusses the implications of his deliberate subversion of this expectation. Although *Safe* adheres to certain elements of genre, Haynes writes: "So while *Safe* pays allegiance to these kinds of issues, there's no question that the tone of the film, the coolness of its style and the inaccessibility of its central character, unsteadies the 'disease movie' genre (at times it feels more like a domestic horror flick). And this puts everything the film might be 'saying' into question."[10] Instead of identifying with Carol, we watch her with almost clinical detachment, which has the effect of making her situation and condition appear all the more frightening. Even at the moments she is most vulnerable—when she gasps for breath in the parking lot or breaks down and cries in her cabin at Wrenwood—what's striking about the film is how distant and remote she remains from us. Haynes uses other framing devices, such as compartmentalizing the spaces she inhabits, to emphasize Carol's separation. After Rory's paper about gang violence, Carol goes into the kitchen to get Greg some coffee. As she discusses her visit to the doctor, Carol, dressed in a pink outfit, becomes squeezed by the vertical lines of the narrow entrance to the pink kitchen, while Greg and Rory remain within the larger vertical lines of the recessed dining area. A similar example can be found later in the film when Carol calls Greg from a pay phone shortly after arriving at Wrenwood. During the conversation, Carol becomes enclosed by the strong vertical lines of the phone booth on the left side of the frame, while Greg appears within the confines of the doorway in the foreground of his shot, and Rory occupies a similar space in the background, which is bathed in cool blue light. Haynes's framing emphasizes the architectural elements of the spaces to reinforce the sense of isolation of each family member.

We know surprisingly little about Carol in terms of backstory, other than the letter she composes about herself to the environmental illness group. The sex we watch her have with her husband is completely detached from feelings of intimacy. The conversation she has with her mother at the film's beginning also suggests avoidance. Her friends are more or less strangers. Her conversations with them are sprinkled with tidbits of information about diets, gurus, and other fads. Both sides seem to share a steadfast determination not to discuss their feelings. This is evident, for example, from the following exchange between Carol and her friend, Linda:

> LINDA: *Hi.*
> CAROL: Hi. Did you forget?
> LINDA: No, it's inside. I just—Something happened.
> CAROL: What?
> LINDA: Come in.

CUT TO: INT. LINDA'S HOUSE—DAY

Carol and Linda sit in silence over a milk and a Diet Pepsi in Linda's kitchen. Although reasonably good friends, their manner with each other is somewhat formal.

> LINDA: (*Breaking the silence*) It's just—was so sudden.
> CAROL: How old was he?
> LINDA: Five years older. He was the oldest of my mom's kids.
> CAROL: It wasn't—umm . . .
> LINDA: *No*—that's what everyone keeps—not at all.

They are frozen for a moment.

> LINDA: 'Cause he wasn't married.
> CAROL: Right.
> LINDA: It's just . . . so unreal.

Silence.

> LINDA: Did you see the den?
> CAROL: At your party. It's gorgeous.

LINDA: You know I'm suing the contractor? Did I tell you?
CAROL: No.
LINDA: You don't even want to know.[11]

Carol's awkwardness in social situations is painfully evident from the above conversation. The death of Linda's brother has affected Linda enough for her to bring up the subject, but Carol proves incapable of responding in any emotional way. In fact, the two women are only able to talk to each other about his death through circumlocution. Both of them speak in fractured sentences with huge gaps. When Carol tries to ask the cause of death, she cannot even manage to get the thought out. The word "AIDS" is only hinted at by what neither woman is capable of saying. The only comment Linda can muster is: "It's just . . . so unreal." Refusing to allow death to penetrate her world too deeply, she changes the subject to more "safe" suburban topics, such as interior decorating and lawsuits with contractors.

Even around her own husband, Carol remains uncomfortable. Haynes's extensive use of wide shots allows us to watch their awkward body language when she and Greg appear in the same frame. Sex is obviously a problem for them. As Greg pumps away on top of her at the film's beginning, we see Carol's head and flattened long hair, which makes her appear like a Barbie doll beneath him—her distracted expression and mechanical hand gestures indicate she's only going through the motions. When Carol begins to become sick, Greg interprets her illness as an excuse for denying him in bed. He tries to be sympathetic and supportive, but he also exhibits flashes of irritation and frustration, as well as skepticism about her actual condition. Unnatural pauses punctuate their conversations, which take on a tentative quality. Carol and Greg don't talk to each other so much like a married couple, but like two people who don't know each other. In an interview, Haynes discusses this aspect of the dialogue, arguing that he is attempting to capture a quality of actual conversation: "*Safe* is the first film I've made where I was interested in the awkwardness of real speech. I was trying to incorporate people's inability to really talk to each other—that's what real speech has in it more than 'movie speech.'"[12] When Carol comes back from the environmental illness center, she and Greg struggle to connect with each other. Both actors exaggerate the strained awkwardness between them by adding pauses, which gives a stammering quality to the lines:

GREG: Carol?

Carol turns, gasping, startled.

Greg stands at the other end of the living room.

CAROL: You scared me.
GREG: Sorry.
CAROL: No—I was just—I'm sorry—
GREG: I just took Fulvia down. You just get home?
CAROL: Yeah.
GREG: So how'd it go?
CAROL: What?
GREG: Your thing, this morning—What was it on?
CAROL: Oh, it was just this thing on getting sick on fumes
          and bug sprays and stuff.

He stares at her a moment.

GREG: You mean on—like, pollution?
CAROL: Well, more just about people who get sick from
          chemicals and what it does to you.
GREG: Who told you to go to this?
CAROL: No, I just—at the health center I saw a flyer.
GREG: So you think this is what you've been—I mean—
          why you've been sick? Because of bug spray?
CAROL: No, I just—

Silence. They look at each other.

CAROL: I don't know why.[13]

Haynes shoots the scene in a wide-angle shot/reverse shot so that we see the couple full-frame, thus magnifying the distance between them.

Carol's estrangement from people also extends to her stepson, Rory. There are only a few actual exchanges between them, involving only a handful of lines. When Rory reminds his mother not to forget to pick him up from soccer practice, Carol seems sensitive to the implied accusation. She claims not to have forgotten the last time, but attributes the oversight to a mix-up. Later on, Rory reads his school essay about drug and gang wars in Los Angeles to his parents over dinner. Greg responds positively, but Carol asks: "Why does it have to be so gory?" Rory responds: "Gory! That's how it really is." As Carol gets sicker, she and Rory do not really interact, and he retreats into being more of a background character in the film, primarily because Carol's self-absorption with her illness leaves no place for him. When the psychiatrist asks her about having one child, Carol tries to separate herself from him even more by responding: "Yes, my husband's little boy, Rory. He's ten." Near the end of the film, Rory walks at a distance from Carol, and the strain in their relationship becomes obvious from the tone of their brief exchange.

Carol's isolation is an essential part of her character. Haynes's description of her in the script indicates this: "She is most comfortable when the world goes about its business, accepting (by ignoring) her as one of its own. The thin weakness of her speaking voice combined with a kind of emotional laxity make her seem removed at times, distant from herself. As a result, Carol always seems somewhat stumped by life."[14] Haynes doesn't attempt to explain Carol to us. It is certainly ambiguous whether her problems stem solely from environmental causes, but Haynes is careful to motivate every major allergic reaction Carol experiences. When she has her first bout of dizziness while reaching for the telephone book, not only are there painters in the kitchen, but we have just watched her housekeeper demonstrate to a trainee how to clean the silverware with some type of spray. We see the fumes belching from the truck on the freeway, the liquid being applied to the curlers during her hair permanent, the little girl coloring in her book with Magic Markers at the baby shower, and the exterminator spraying pesticides at the dry cleaners. Although Carol never notices the large truck behind her when she eats lunch with Linda, her difficulty speaking coincides with its passing, which at least provides some evidence that her problems are not entirely psychosomatic. Even so, Haynes refuses to provide pat psychological explanations:

> It was very much a strategic plan on my part to try to exclude a lot of information that we usually think we require to know about character in a film. What that meant was basically excluding the sense of psychological access to a character. When you look at the way we are made to feel secure about knowing a character in a movie, it's so facile and silly—it's such a short-hand way. If *Safe* mentioned that Carol's father had hit her when she was a child—if that was just planted early on in the film—people would say, "Oh,

OK, now I know why." It explains everything in the entire film and you don't need anything more. It makes it all very easy. I wanted to exclude those kinds of pieces of information, in combination with the distance and the stylistic treatment of her. That way, there would be an anxiety about her that would be akin to the suspense of her finding out who she is and what is wrong with her life as it starts to fall apart. It also encourages people to begin to make conjectures about why she's sick.[15]

By not providing the normal kinds of character clues we come to expect, Haynes hopes to create gaps in our understanding of Carol White, gaps that viewers would fill in. This strategy of eliminating cause-and-effect, psychological explanations of character is also one more typically found in art cinema.

Our sense of Carol's character is conveyed more through visual means. The rigorously formal *Safe* abounds in striking visual details. The opening tour of the neighborhood hurtles us into the architecture of Carol White's world. Haynes not only describes the shot in his script, but also the texture of what we are seeing:

> A shot from the hood of a car as it passes the large, night-lit homes of a wealthy suburb of the San Fernando Valley. The shot is slightly slowed down as the car snakes uphill, each house becoming progressively larger and newer, each in a different style (Roman, Spanish, Modern, Tudor, etc.). All the houses are lit. The colors are ice greens and acid yellows.[16]

When we later see Carol outside, Haynes again provides very precise descriptive detail: "Carol's hand in a yellow rubber gardening glove snips a yellow rose from a bush."[17]

The script for *Safe* not only contains descriptions of shots—which the manuals decry as sure signs of amateurism—but also provides visual detail relevant to the story. Haynes's description of Carol's living room indicates exactly how he wants the location to look and sound, including the fact that the couches should be covered with plastic. After her coughing fit on the freeway, Carol has difficulty sleeping and goes outside. Haynes writes: "Outside, Carol stands in front of the house. She is frozen in a stare. Her pale pink robe reflects the little light there is. A slight breeze makes it move."[18] In the film, Carol stands next to the gazebo as she looks out, with her back to us. Light—perhaps reflected from the swimming pool—shimmers on her robe, creating an eerie image that seems right out of a science-fiction film (and which we will connect later to the huge power lines Carol will observe on the drive home after her doctor suggests that she see a psychiatrist). The scene ends with another image of yellow roses. Haynes describes the image in the script: "The roses look frozen, like daguerreotypes."[19] Virtually every scene is described this way. We get powerful images— Carol's shimmering robe and the frozen roses—as well as the color palette of each scene. In doing this, Haynes reduces the importance of dialogue as the most important element in a script in favor of the film's overall mise-en-scène.

Haynes has cited Stanley Kubrick's *2001: A Space Odyssey* (1968) as a major stylistic influence on *Safe*, where many of the interiors have a kind of minimal, denatured, space-age look. Haynes's mise-en-scène and framing differ from the style of someone like Jarmusch, despite the fact that they both use long static shots. Haynes's mise-en-scène is more rigorously formal and more the product of scripting and art direction, whereas Jarmusch's mise-en-scène is more casual and grounded in naturalism, which can be explained in terms of the type of protagonist the films employ. In *Stranger Than Paradise*, the frame defines an open space in which the characters have a certain freedom of movement. In *Safe*, Haynes's framing creates a geometry that restricts or confines Carol's actions.

Haynes creates a strong contrast between warm peach/orange and cool blue in many scenes. He also favors placing his protagonist in wide shots—the film unfolds mostly in master shots—while keeping close-ups to a minimum. Like Antonioni's heroines, Carol becomes defined by the architectural spaces that surround her. Haynes's compositions have the effect of reducing her in size, as well as emphasizing Carol's growing estrangement from her environment and from those around her. Besides Kubrick, Haynes acknowledges Chantal Ackerman's highly formal approach to narrative as another influence, including her attention to mundane detail. As Haynes comments in one of his many interviews: "What you see in it [an Ackerman film] in real time is what every other movie would cut out. But it creates a suspense and curiosity, and a huge role for the viewer in the telling."[20]

Haynes combines many elements from art cinema with those of genre—not only melodrama, but the horror film (which is how Sony's trailer tried to pitch *Safe*). Suspense in the film comes from the expectations Haynes creates in the viewer. For Carol, suffering from chemical sensitivity, physical danger seems to lurk everywhere. Virtually every situation contains a potential "monster"—the car exhaust on the freeway, a hair permanent at the beauty salon, a new couch, her husband's hair spray and deodorant, an exterminator spraying at the dry cleaners, or the fumes from a Magic Marker in a child's hand. One of the women at the environmental illness seminar describes this aspect of the disease:

> PATIENT 1: It's true, it's like, you go into a building, you're walking down the hall. It's like—you don't know if that monster's gonna jump out at you. You're just, like, going along the wall like any normal person—[21]

In screenwriting terms, the antagonist has become dispersed to include potentially anything or anyone. Even the hospital does not provide a safe haven, nor does Wrenwood, situated in such close proximity to the highway. No matter where Carol tries to hide, she can never be safe, because, as Haynes shows, the whole notion of "safety" amounts to an illusion.

Haynes undercuts conventional viewer expectations at crucial points in *Safe*, especially in relation to his protagonist. Carol's pathetic rather than heroic attempt to regain her health leads not to the epiphany we have come to expect in disease films of this type, but to further isolation, when both Wrenwood and the romantic tease, Chris, turn out to be red herrings. Instead of making progress, Carol continues to regress throughout the film, becoming more disoriented and confused about her own identity. A rich, suburban housewife, Carol has so little personal identity that she's willing to accept that of a diseased person, but Wrenwood, with its cultlike focus on blaming the victim, manages to strip even that away, so that what we are left with by the end is an utterly blank portrait. Given its disturbing subject matter, enervated protagonist, and lack of traditional plot, *Safe* is a highly demanding work that does not necessarily aim to be a crowd-pleaser. Yet Haynes's emphasis on visual storytelling, formal rigor, and critical perspective on classical narration are precisely the qualities that differentiate his more truly independent vision from those films that strictly adhere to the more predictable conventions of the mainstream.

Chapter 3

Shifting Protagonists in *Fargo*

Ethan and Joel Coen's debut feature, *Blood Simple* (1984), showed a unique ability to combine their particular brand of offbeat humor with a clever reworking of film noir, and their subsequent films have continued this penchant for innovative twists on classic American film genres. The Coen brothers have shifted between large-budget, studio-produced works and independent productions throughout their careers. After their $25 million *The Hudsucker Proxy* (1994) proved to be a fiasco, the Coens returned to their independent roots with the much lower-budget, regionally flavored *Fargo* (1996), which unexpectedly became their biggest critical and commercial success. *Fargo* wound up being nominated for seven Academy Awards, eventually winning in the best actress and best original screenplay categories. *Fargo* also swept the Indie Spirit Awards in six categories, including Best Feature, Best Director, and Best Screenplay. While it is difficult to think of a $6.5 million film as truly independent, *Fargo* nevertheless exhibits the sensibility of a small regional film with superb production values. By setting the film in the incongruous snowy location of the Upper Midwest, the Coens literally invert the meaning of film noir, while maintaining the crime genre's sinister overtones. The real innovation of *Fargo*, however, rests less on its play on genre than on its somewhat unorthodox script, which not only seems to lack a clear protagonist, but incorporates a dramatic structure that most screenwriting manuals do not admit is even possible.

In this first section, I've used the term "problematic protagonists," to discuss alternative strategies to the goal-driven protagonist, but I wish to clarify that I don't really consider either an ambivalent or passive protagonist to be a problem. They are bona fide options. Such protagonists, as we have seen in the previous two chapters, result in their films having less drama and different strategies of narration. They are only considered problematic in terms of the classical tradition advocated by most manuals. In fact, most manuals also make it seem as if the protagonist of a film is patently obvious, yet I don't always find this to be the case. Who's the protagonist of such films as Neil LaBute's *In the Company of Men*, *Gas Food Lodging*, or *To Sleep With Anger*? Does it matter? In terms of writing a script, Linda Aronson argues that it does. She writes, "The reason we need to identify the protagonist is because giving this job to the wrong characters can make plot and characterization fall apart."[1]

Multiple-plot films, the subject of the next section, often raise questions regarding the main protagonist. In *Fargo*, which has this type of structure, the issue turns out to be a central one. Many commentators have chosen to sidestep the issue entirely. One asserts that *Fargo* is an ensemble film with no lead character.[2] As we will see later, while Richard Linklater's *Slacker* doesn't have a main protagonist, I don't find this to be the case in *Fargo*. Yet who functions as the film's protagonist? There are four main characters: Jerry, Marge, Carl, and Grimsrud. If we decide that Carl and Grimsrud, rather than Jerry, serve as the obvious antagonists, that leaves only two real possibilities for the protagonist. It has to be either Jerry or Marge. The film begins with Jerry, and most of the film is concerned with his ransom scheme—the central element of the plot—without which there would be neither Carl and Grimsrud nor Marge. If Jerry is the protagonist, however, he is certainly not a terribly likeable one. He tries to extract ransom money from his own father-in-law, uses cars he doesn't own as collateral, sticks it to customers by insisting on adding rust-proofing to the price of a new car, and seems to care very little for his son, Scotty.

Despite Jerry's less-than-admirable behavior, he is not a truly bad person—like Carl, Grimsrud, or even Shep Proudfoot—but a bumbling loser who has managed somehow to find himself in over his head. The Coen brothers' predilection for such a character stems from a desire to go against the typical Hollywood characterization of the "super-professional who controls everything," resulting in a film they find "closer to life than the conventions of cinema and genre movies."[3] If Jerry is not the film's protagonist, then the Coens certainly spend a good deal of time establishing his character traits and motivating his behavior. Jerry is a virtual outsider within his own family unit, which is dominated by his blustering millionaire father-in-law, Wade Gustafson, who clearly has very little respect for him. Jerry has become so frustrated by his own personal situation and inability to pull off his cockeyed get-rich schemes that several times in the course of the film he explodes into childlike temper tantrums. Jerry does not really intend to hurt anyone—he simply needs to come up with a large amount of money—and he is so obtuse that he never anticipates that something might go wrong with his ransom scheme, even though his own twelve-year-old son seems to grasp this possibility. That Jerry's plan involves kidnapping his own wife, Jean, and extorting money from his father-in-law adds a sad and pathetic dimension to his character. Even the two low-life thugs, whom Jerry hires to do the dirty work, indicate that they find the whole scheme to be contemptible.

Throughout *Fargo*, we also spend a good deal of time following Marge Gunderson, the pregnant police chief of Brainerd, Minnesota, as she attempts to solve the murders. Besides her detective work, there are additional scenes of her home life with her house-husband, Norm, a wildlife painter who aspires to have his work displayed on postage stamps—that is, when he is not out ice fishing. There is also a rather curious scene involving Mike Yanagita, a former classmate, whom Marge meets at the Radisson Inn in the Twin Cities. The most obvious question is: What function does the scene with Mike Yanagita—which takes up three and a half pages in the script and four minutes of screen time in the actual film—serve in the story?

Marge first receives a late-night phone call from Mike, who has seen her on the TV news. Marge surprises even Norm by heading to the Twin Cities, ostensibly to investigate a lead involving Shep Proudfoot, but her real reason for the trip seems to be to meet Mike. As they sit in the hotel bar and Mike begins to talk about his wife, Linda Cooksey, he slides next to Marge and tries to put his arm around her. Marge, however, makes it clear that she would prefer that he continue to sit across from her. Mike apologizes to Marge and then proceeds to discuss how his wife died of leukemia. After a toast to "Better times," the scene takes a very strange turn:

> MIKE: It was so . . . I been so . . . and then I saw you on TV, and I remembered, ya know . . . I always liked you . . .
>
> MARGE: Well, I always liked you, Mike.
>
> MIKE: I always liked ya so much . . .
>
> MARGE: It's okay, Mike—Should we get together another time, ya think?
>
> MIKE: No—I'm sorry! It's just—I been so lonely—then I saw you, and . . .

He is weeping.

> . . . I'm so sorry . . . I shouldn't a done this . . . I thought we'd have a really terrific time, and now I've . . .
>
> MARGE: It's okay . . .
>
> MIKE: You were such a super lady . . . and then I . . . I been so lonely . . .
>
> MARGE: It's okay, Mike . . . [4]

Marge's motivation for meeting with Mike is never very clear. The fact that she does not tell Norm about it, however, suggests that there might have been some type of previous romantic interest. When Marge arrives at the hotel bar, it is also the only time we really see her really dressed up and trying to look attractive. After Mike tries to put the moves on Marge, she discourages his advances very politely. Marge, however, does admit to Mike that she always liked him. When Mike indicates the intensity of his feelings for her, Marge responds, "It's okay, Mike—Should we get together another time, ya think?" Right after this, Mike falls completely apart.

The scene between Marge and Mike Yanagita seems to be there to develop Marge's character. In fact, without the scene it would be more difficult to make the case for Marge as the protagonist because, by itself, the scene (like the later one involving Officer Gary Olson and a local bartender) appears to be extraneous to the plot. When Marge later finds out that Mike has made up the story about his wife dying of leukemia, it does cause her to pay a surprise visit to Jerry at the dealership. Even so, the sheer length of this particular scene suggests that the Coens do not really need to create such a long scene in order to motivate Marge's second visit to Jerry, especially since she proves to be an

Mike Yanagita at the Radisson Inn

astute detective from the moment she appears at the scene of the triple homicide. The fact that Marge finds out later that Mike has lied to her catches her off-guard, adding an element of personal disequilibrium to the banality of her small-town life.

Yet if Marge is the actual protagonist of *Fargo*, there are at least two anomalies. The first is that rather than Marge, Jerry is the one who has the dramatic conflict. The second, and even more unusual aspect, would be the fact that Marge does not appear until the second act, about thirty-three minutes into the film. The convention, of course, is for a protagonist to be established early in a narrative film, especially since the story would often be told from his or her point of view. Richard Walter, for example, insists, "Each movie needs its protagonist with clear needs, and hurdles obstructing the path to satisfying those needs. And that character, those needs, those hurdles, and that tone must be asserted in the film's beginning."[5] Syd Field espouses a similar position. In the *Screenwriter's Workbook*, he discusses the film *Absence of Malice* in considerable detail. Concerning the film's structure, Field writes:

> This screenplay is one in which the main character doesn't appear until the end of Act I. Before you get too excited about that,

though, notice that Michael Gallagher has been talked about and referred to from page 1. If you write a script like this, you still have to introduce your main character in the first ten pages.[6]

Marge is certainly not introduced or mentioned within the first ten pages or ten minutes of the film, even though it would have been easy enough to establish her as a character before the triple homicide is committed.

John Egan suggests that a new type of structure emerged in the 1990s that violates conventional dramatic structure. He deems this the "multiple plot structure" and his examples include *Secrets and Lies, The English Patient, Pulp Fiction,* and *Kansas City.* He explains, "The traditional Hollywood *formula film* focuses on the central lead throughout the film. At certain plot points something will happen to the lead, allowing the plot to develop. All other characters are subordinate, existing only to develop the lead character's relationship to the plot."[7] Egan's formula example embodying the above is *Jerry Maguire,* but many Hollywood films conform to this pattern. "In the '90s New Wave," he writes, "there are no easily recognizable leads and no clearly defined plot in relation to a lead."[8] He goes on to describe the essence of the multiple-plot alternative as "multiple plots and casts fusing in spurts of action that lead to the revelation of the 'true plot' in the final act" and suggests, in terms of relevance here, that such a structure is "perfect for stories in which the main character is objectionable and loathsome."[9] Egan's multiple-plot structure clearly differs from Robert McKee's concept of "Multiplot," which refers to the kind of structure found in Robert Altman's *Shortcuts,* in which there is no central plot, but only a series of interweaving subplots.[10]

Fargo fits Egan's version of a multiple-plot structure only partially. It does not focus on one central lead, but instead follows Jerry, Carl, and Marge at various points in the film. Since Marge doesn't even appear in the first act, the actual focus of the film seems to shift from Jerry to Marge as it progresses, especially because Jerry has very little to do with the film once Wade supplants him at the ransom meeting. By the film's end, Marge clearly appears to be more central than Jerry, which is why the film ends on her. And while Jerry is, in fact, a fairly loathsome main character, in contrast to Marge, who's extremely likeable, there is no true plot that is revealed in the third act. Norm's postage stamp art competition can only qualify as a minor subplot.

Although it is an unusual structural strategy to shift protagonists during the course of the film, it is not unprecedented, since this is exactly what happens in Alfred Hitchcock's *Psycho* (1960). McKee, in fact, acknowledges this possibility in discussing his notion of a "Plural-Protagonist":

> It's even possible, in rare instance, to switch protagonists halfway through a story. *Psycho* does this, making the shower murder both an emotional and a formal jolt. With the protagonist dead, the audience is momentarily confused; whom is this movie about? The answer is a Plural-Protagonist as the victim's sister, boyfriend, and a private detective take over the story.[11]

Despite their similarity in shifting protagonists, *Fargo* and *Psycho* differ in that *Fargo* has a multi-protagonist rather than a plural-protagonist, because Marge and Jerry have contrary rather than collective objectives.

Although *Psycho* is really a story about a deranged murderer, Norman Bates, it was the film's screenwriter, Joseph Stefano, who came up with the idea to begin the story with the victim, Marion Crane, a woman who wants to get married so desperately that she steals $40,000 from her employer and flees town.[12] The character of Norman is not introduced until twenty-six minutes into the film, when a rainstorm forces Marion to stop at the run-down Bates Motel. There, she is brutally murdered, presumably by Norman's jealous mother, as she takes a shower. Hitchcock and Stefano manage to confound viewer expectations by killing off the film's ostensible protagonist at forty-seven minutes. After Marion is killed, the film makes the viewer shift identification to Arbogast, Lila, Sam, and even briefly to Norman, who is not revealed to be the actual villain until the very end of the film. The Coen brothers, on the other hand, do not kill off Jerry in *Fargo*, but they do seem to lose interest in him. Once the ransom scheme goes awry, Jerry's role begins to diminish, especially when Marge gets introduced and Wade brushes Jerry aside in order to deliver the ransom money and confront the kidnappers. Jerry's eventual capture is decidedly anticlimactic, mainly because he has not figured directly in any of the seven murders we witness, even though his ransom ploy is responsible for unleashing the film's homicidal villains, Grimsrud and Carl.

Both *Psycho* and *Fargo* use unorthodox narrative construction to play deliberately with audience expectations. Hitchcock referred to the whole beginning of *Psycho* as a "red herring." As Hitchcock explained to the noted French director François Truffaut, "You turn the viewer in one direction and then in another; you keep him as far as possible from what's actually going to happen."[13] The lengthy introductions to both Marion and Jerry in the respective films can be seen in this light, especially in terms of the great lengths the screenwriters go to in order to motivate their behavior and to make us feel sympathy for their circumstances, which leads both of them to engage in criminal acts. It becomes clear that the Coen brothers are, in fact, referencing *Psycho* at various points in *Fargo*, not only in terms of the film's narrative construction, but also with such elements as the shower curtain and what happens to the actual ransom money.

In the introduction to the published screenplay, Ethan Coen provides the following description of *Fargo*: "It evokes the abstract landscape of our childhood—a bleak, windswept tundra, resembling Siberia except for its Ford dealerships and Hardee's restaurants. It aims to be both homey and exotic, and pretends to be true."[14] The Coens succeed admirably in turning the unending whiteness of the northern Midwest into a completely barren place. The Coen brothers also present an over-the-top rendition of the Scandinavian accent

Carl and Grimsrud at the bar

prevalent in the region, making all the locals in *Fargo*, as Thomas Goetz points out, sound like "North Country crackers."[15] The Coens's joke is, of course, at their hometown neighbors' expense. And while they are careful to wink at the telling, the film nevertheless reinforces certain Midwestern stereotypes.

Fargo begins with a tongue-in-cheek opening text announcing that this is a true story that took place in Minnesota in 1987: "At the request of survivors, the names have been changed. Out of respect for the dead, the rest has been told exactly as it occurred." The written words flare to a totally white, snowy landscape, as Jerry Lundegaard, a wimpy car salesperson in an Elmer Fudd hat, tows a new car to a bar in Fargo. Once there, Jerry meets with two young hoodlums: a loquacious, funny-looking shorter guy named Carl Showalter, and his mute sidekick, the large blond-haired, quite sinister and menacing Gaear Grimsrud. Jerry conspires to have them kidnap his rich wife for $40,000 (the same amount of money Marion stole in *Psycho*) and a brand new Ciera. The film's considerable humor becomes evident in the initial meeting between Jerry and the hired thugs. By the time Jerry arrives, Carl and Grimsrud are already angry with him for arriving an hour late, while Jerry insists there's been a simple mix-up. Almost from the second he opens his mouth, Carl manages to put Jerry in a defensive position:

> CARL: I'm not gonna sit here and debate. I will say this, though: What Shep told us didn't make a whole lot of sense.
>
> JERRY: Oh, no, it's real sound. It's all worked out.
>
> CARL: You want your own wife kidnapped?
>
> JERRY: Yah.

Carl stares. Jerry looks blankly back.

> CARL: . . . You—my point is, you pay the ransom—what, eighty thousand bucks?—I mean, you give us half the ransom, forty thousand, you keep half. It's like robbing Peter to pay Paul, it doesn't make any—
>
> JERRY: Okay, it's—see, it's not me payin' the ransom. The thing is, my wife, she's wealthy—her dad, he's real well off. Now, I'm in a bit of trouble—
>
> CARL: What kind of trouble are you in, Jerry?

> JERRY: Well, that's, that's, I'm not gonna go inta, inta—see, I just need money. Now, her dad's real wealthy—
> CARL: So why don't you ask him for the money?

Grimsrud, the dour man who has not yet spoken, now softly puts in with a Swedish-accented voice.

> GRIMSRUD: Or your fucking wife, you know.
> CARL: Or your fucking wife, Jerry.
> JERRY: Well, it's all just part of this—they don't know I need it, see. Okay, so there's that. And even if they did, I wouldn't get it. So there's that on top, then. See, these're personal matters.
> CARL: Personal matters.
> JERRY: Yah, personal matters that needn't, uh—
> CARL: Okay, Jerry. You're tasking us to perform this mission, but you, you won't, uh, you won't—aw, fuck it, let's take a look at that Ciera.[16]

The humor in the scene, of course, revolves around the reversal of roles and the way that Carl is able to turn the tables on Jerry and assume power and control of the relationship. It is also apparent that Carl and Grimsrud find it incomprehensible, even despicable, that Jerry wants to kidnap his own wife and extract ransom, which he intends to split with them. We learn important exposition, namely, that Jerry is in some kind of financial trouble and that his father-in-law is very wealthy. Carl balks at Jerry's attempt to keep his own private life separate when he presses him for information. But the two thugs raise an important question in the minds of the audience, namely, why wouldn't Jerry's father-in-law and wife help him financially, especially if he's really in trouble?

Some of our initial questions get answered when Jerry's father-in-law, Wade, stops over for dinner. Jerry asks Wade whether he's had time to consider the deal. Their conversation, however, borders on farce when it turns into a repetitious play on the word "lot," which leads to confusion rather than clarification:

> JERRY: Yah, you said you'd have a think about it. I understand it's a lot of money—
> WADE: A heck of a lot. What'd you say you were gonna put there?
> JERRY: A lot. It's a limited—

WADE: I know it's a lot.
JERRY: I mean a parking lot.
WADE: Yah, well, seven hundred and fifty thousand dollars is a lot—ha ha ha!
JERRY: Yah, well, it's a chunk, but—
WADE: I had a couple lots, late fifties. Lost a lot of money. A "lot" of money.[17]

Jerry tries to pitch the project as something that would be good for Jean and Scotty, but Wade makes it very clear that his daughter and grandson are already set financially.

Wade later calls and tells Jerry that his business associate, Stan Grossman, likes Jerry's business proposal and tells him to meet them in the afternoon. The news takes Jerry by surprise. In an effort to stave off the kidnapping, Jerry tries unsuccessfully to get in touch with Carl and Grimsrud through Shep Proudfoot, a rugged Native-American mechanic who works in the service area of the car dealership. Meanwhile tension builds between Carl and Grimsrud, as Carl tries to discuss Midwestern architecture as they approach Minneapolis. Frustrated by Grimsrud's one-word answer to a question, he finally vents:

CARL: "No." First thing you've said in the last four hours. That's a, that's a fountain of conversation, man. That's a geyser. I mean, whoa, daddy, stand back, man. Shit, I'm sittin' here driving, man, doin' all the driving, whole fucking way from Brainerd, drivin', tryin' to, you know, tryin' to chat, keep our spirits up, fight the boredom of the road, and you can't say one fucking thing just in the way of conversation.

Grimsrud smokes, gazing out the window.

... Well, fuck it, I don't have to talk either, man. See how *you* like it.

Carl looks at Grimsrud for a reaction.

... Just total fuckin' silence. Two can play at *that* game, smart guy. We'll just see how *you* like it ...

He drives.

... Total silence ...[18]

The Coens extract a great deal of humor from the juxtaposition between the talkative Carl and his near-mute partner. Carl's criticism of Grimsrud's conversational skills makes Carl sound more like the shortchanged wife in a bad marriage than a hardened criminal about to embark on a kidnapping. The monetary difficulty Jerry alluded to in the opening scene becomes clarified when Jerry receives a call from someone at the financial services company, demanding to have the serial numbers of the automobiles for which he received credit of $320,000.

Carl and Grimsrud go forward with the kidnapping as planned. After Jerry arrives home, he wanders upstairs and sees evidence of the struggle—the dislodged window screen and crowbar on the floor, open window, and scraps of the shower curtain still on the rings. As the camera continues to track from the crumpled curtain to the shattered window, we hear Jerry telling Wade about Jean in a series of variations. The shot of Jerry reveals that he is merely practicing his performance. He then picks up the phone, dials, and asks for Wade.

After the camera tracks down the huge statue of Paul Bunyan as Carl and Grimsrud drive by at night, we hear sounds of Jean whimpering in the back seat. Grimsrud threatens her, but a police car suddenly appears behind them. The first turning point occurs when Grimsrud shoots the trooper at approximately twenty-nine minutes, turning the kidnapping into murder. (The subsequent shooting of the witnesses four minutes later only seals the criminals' fate.) After the comedic setup, Grimsrud's violent rampage signals a complete shift in tone, as Jerry's ransom scheme takes the film in an unexpected direction. As we move into the middle act, we're introduced to the Brainerd police chief, Marge Gunderson, who is awakened by news of the triple homicide. At the murder scene, the seven months-pregnant Marge, after a brief bout of morning sickness, begins to piece together the clues, dazzling her affable but dim-witted colleague Lou with her shrewd detective work. She learns from the dead trooper's citation book that his last ticket was for a tan Ciera with dealer plates.

Wade wants to call in the police, but Jerry convinces Stan Grossman of the need to follow the kidnappers' ransom request. During the conversation, we learn an additional aspect of Jerry's deception, namely, that the ransom request is actually for $1 million, not the $80,000 that he had told Carl and Grimsrud earlier. Wade wants to offer the kidnappers only half of the amount, but Jerry and Stan dissuade him. When Stan mentions Scotty, it's clear from Jerry's reaction that he has completely forgotten about him. When Jerry later discusses the situation with his distraught son, Scotty worries that something could go wrong and wants to call the police.

The next several scenes shift the focus from Jerry to the kidnappers and Marge's investigation. Carl and Grimsrud take Jean to an abandoned cabin. Despite the fact that her head is covered by a black hood and her hands are tied behind her back, Jean nevertheless tries to run off. Carl chuckles as the barefoot Jean veers wildly around in the snow like a chicken without a head. After Norm brings Marge lunch at the Brainerd police station, Lou interrupts with the news that the tan Ciera has been traced to the Blue Ox, and that the two men registered there also had "company."

Marge interviews the two hookers who describe Carl as funny-looking and not circumcised and Grimsrud as the Marlboro Man. One of them also remembers that the two were on their way to Minneapolis. As Jean sits in a chair with her hands bound and Grimsrud impassively smokes a cigarette, Carl has a fit due to poor television reception. Meanwhile, after turning in for the night, Marge is awakened by a phone call from Mike Yanagita, who has seen her on the news. Jerry gets a call from Carl who tells him that circumstances have changed—"blood has been shed"—and demands more money. Each time Carl alludes to the murders in Brainerd, Jerry responds, "The heck d'ya mean?" Carl insists he's coming to town tomorrow, and now wants the entire $80,000 ransom money. Marge presses forward with the investigation by interviewing Shep and questioning Jerry, before meeting Mike Yanagita.

The second turning point occurs at seventy minutes, as Wade heads off to meet with the kidnappers on the top level of the Dayton-Radisson parking ramp. When Wade shows up instead of Jerry, Carl has had enough. He shoots the arrogant older man, but winds up taking a bullet in the face. Carl grabs the ransom money, throws it in the car, and drives off wildly down the ramp, just missing Jerry's vehicle. His face all bloody, Carl demands that the attendant open the gate. The scene cuts to the rooftop lot, where Jerry dumps Wade's body into the trunk of his car. As Jerry approaches the exit, he sees the broken gate as well as the attendant lying dead in the booth. After Jerry arrives home, Scotty tells him that Stan has called twice, but Jerry, clearly dazed, just sits in the foyer.

Since Jerry has demanded $1 million from Wade rather than the $80,000 he has promised to split with the hired kidnappers, the second turning point represents the final unraveling of Jerry's plan, not only because Wade gets killed, but because Carl ends up with the $1 million rather than Jerry. That Carl gets shot will also lead to a confrontation with Grimsrud. If I'm right in my segmentation of the structure of *Fargo*, the first act would be twenty-nine minutes in length, the second act would be forty-one minutes, and the third act would total twenty-four minutes, since the actual film is approximately ninety-four minutes long, not including the final credits.

Just as Jerry attempted to cheat the two kidnappers, Carl tries to swindle Grimsrud. He takes $80,000 of the ransom money and hides the rest of the $1 million in a snowy field. Marge learns through a friend that Mike Yanagita has fabricated the story about Linda Cooksey dying of leukemia and discovers that he had been stalking her for almost a year. This news leaves Marge dumbstruck. After a drive-through breakfast at Hardee's, she makes a surprise visit at the car dealership to question Jerry once again. While insisting the whole time that he's cooperating with her, Jerry loses patience with Marge's questions. She tells him, "Sir, you have no call to get snippy with me. I'm just doing my job here." After Marge asks to speak with Wade, Jerry

Jerry at the parking ramp

agrees to take a hand count of the vehicles, but, as Marge watches, Jerry drives off. When Carl shows up at the cabin, Jean lies dead on the floor—a victim of Grimsrud's rage. Carl gives Grimsrud his share of the money, but the two argue over the Ciera. Grimsrud wants to split it, but Carl insists that it's his reward for getting shot and starts to head off. Grimsrud rushes outside after Carl and, in Paul Bunyan–like fashion, suddenly whacks him in the neck with an axe.

The climax occurs shortly afterward, as Marge happens to see the Ciera at a cabin on Moose Lake. She proceeds to sneak up on Grimsrud, as he is disposing of Carl's body in a wood chipper. As Grimsrud pushes down on a human leg, which sticks up from the chipper, Marge orders him to surrender. Grimsrud tries to escape across the snow-covered field, but her second shot wounds him in the leg. As Grimsrud sits handcuffed in the backseat of the police car, Marge, like a disappointed parent, chides the impassive criminal: "There's more to life than a little money, you know." The anticlimactic resolution shows Jerry's arrest in a shabby motel outside of Bismarck, North Dakota. Meanwhile Norm and Marge sit in bed watching television. Norm's rendition of a mallard has been selected to be on the three-cent stamp. Although he's disappointed, Marge reassures him. The two express their love for each other as they snuggle together. Norm rests his hand on her bloated stomach. He says, "Two more months," a line which Marge repeats.

In his book *Good Scripts, Bad Scripts*, screenwriter Thomas Pope uses *Fargo* as one of twenty-five practical examples for teaching scriptwriting craft. Following the classical paradigm, Pope analyzes *Fargo* in terms of a three-act structure, but his analysis of the film's structure is quite different from mine.[19] He writes, "The structure of *Fargo* takes a number of risks, particularly in its first-act structure, its late introduction of the protagonist, and its third-act break."[20] Pope locates the first turning point as the kidnapping: "As for the act break, it comes naturally when the wife is kidnapped. Until then, nothing that happens is inevitable; after that, everything is inevitable."[21] It's not the kidnapping, however, that makes subsequent events inevitable. It is only after Grimsrud murders the trooper that everything has changed and there is no turning back; for this reason, I believe it would be more accurate to consider this to be the first turning point.

"The second act is unusual," Pope continues, "in that it introduces Marge, the protagonist, about half an hour into the movie."[22] According

Marge fires at Grimsrud

to where Pope places the turning point, this would be thirteen minutes into his second act. Also, as I have argued previously, compared to Jerry, Marge has little to do with the plot other than to follow leads rather mechanically. Pope attempts to answer this by claiming that while the first turning point occurs at a "plot juncture," the second one happens as a "thematic juncture."[23] He argues that the thematic event occurs when Marge learns from her friend that Mike Yanagita lied to her both about being married as well as about his wife dying from leukemia. Pope sees this scene as paralleling Jerry's contemplation of his eventual fate, as he sits disconsolately in the foyer after returning from the parking ramp. He writes, "Thus the dual revelations by Marge and Jerry, where each sees into the hidden workings of society and of the human soul, serve as the dividing line between the simple plot complications of the second act and the moral collisions of the third."[24] While Pope's point is certainly insightful, such thematic inflections do not seem to have enough impetus, either singularly or combined, to serve as the second turning point. Rather, what changes things for Jerry as well as for the overall plot is Wade's bravado attempt to stand up to the kidnappers, which pushes the film inexorably into its third and final act.

I bring up Pope's analysis of *Fargo* less to quibble with his interpretation than to demonstrate how unusual *Fargo* is in terms of its structure, as well as to reiterate how ambiguous the film can be in terms of determining its protagonist. Since *Fargo* clearly strays from the classical paradigm, it is precisely the kind of script that might not make it past an initial reader at one of the studios. The elements that differentiate *Fargo* as a script could easily be translated into flaws by anyone locked into the conventional paradigm.

Fargo succeeds largely as a result of its unorthodox structure, zany characters, and black humor. On a fundamental level, *Fargo* has a lot in common with David Lynch's *Blue Velvet* (1986). Beneath this placidly white surface of perpetual smiles, good-naturedness, and cheerful small talk lie vicious greed and repressed violence capable of spawning the likes of an Ed Gein (on whom Norman Bates is modeled) or a Jeffrey Dahmer, to mention just two of the more well-known Midwestern serial killers. The broad satire and comic humor mask a horrific violence. Examples include scenes in which Grimsrud splatters the blood of the trooper on Carl's face and then slays innocent bystanders, Shep interrupts Carl's romp with a hooker to assault him savagely, Carl shoots Wade in the head only to get a return bullet in the face, Jerry's wife gets her skull broken for screaming, and Carl ends up with his foot sticking out of a wood chipper.

Everyone seems to be fair game for the Coen brothers' gruesome wit. Shep, on probation for narcotics abuse, has a violent streak that parallels Grimsrud's. He not only beats Carl, but also the African-American bystander, as well as the hooker whom he chases down the hall. Even the Asian-American high school friend of Marge, who mimics the same yahoo accent as the rest of the locals, attempts to seduce Marge by making up a pathetic story about his wife dying of leukemia. And the locals, who waddle through the snowy, barren landscape like penguins, are portrayed as innocuous dimwits, incapable of distinguishing between what's important and what's not, which makes them utterly unreliable as police informants. Even the good-natured Marge has to raise an eyebrow at their obtuseness.

In terms of character, Jerry and Marge are complete opposites. While Marge is both pregnant and happily married to Norm, Jerry resents his wife and kid because their financial problems are taken care of, whereas his are not. Working at his father-in-law's car dealership, Jerry has become adept at presenting a cheery facade to the public while trying to pawn off TruCoat. He provides a striking contrast to the genuinely sincere Marge, who lets Mike Yanagita down in the gentlest possible way and politely corrects Lou's poor detective work. Marge represents a parody of the noir genre's cynical detective. She lectures Grimsrud about life's virtues in the patrol car after he's been caught. Marge later confides to Norm as they watch televison in bed, "Heck, we're doin' pretty good." Marge is largely satisfied by the simple pleasures in life, in contrast to Jerry, whose get-rich schemes mask his brooding dissatisfaction with his lowly status.

The power that comes from being able to manipulate language plays a big role in *Fargo*, adding a conceptual element to the dialogue of the film. As has already been mentioned, the good-natured verbal inarticulateness of the locals sets them up to be victims. But other characters in the film, besides Carl and Grimsrud, are defined by the ability or inability to use language. For instance, Jerry uses his verbal skills to dupe customers and stave off creditors, but he begins to stumble and stammer in the presence of the fast-talking Carl and his powerful and arrogant father-in-law, Wade. Mike Yanagita spins a tale of deceit that fools Marge completely. When she finds out that Mike has lied to her, it affects her more personally than the gruesome murders she's investigating because it introduces evil into the small talk of everyday conversation, which for the people of Brainerd, circumscribes their world. Even Shep, the Native-American outsider, will only vouch for Grimsrud and not Carl, because he remains tied to his direct experience. Shep can only say about Carl, "Never heard of him. Don't vouch for him."

Language, despite its considerable power to control and manipulate people and situations, turns out to be no match for brute violence. Grimsrud's muteness, or inability to verbalize what he feels, represents a repressed and very different sort of absolute power, which is symbolized by the oversized statue of Paul Bunyan that looms outside the city limits of Brainerd. Brute violence ends all discussions or differences of opinion for Grimsrud, as in the case of the trooper, the young witnesses who happen to drive by, or Carl, who insists on taking the Ciera as compensation for getting shot while picking up the ransom. The same is true for Shep, who does not confront Carl with words, but with unbridled force in the scene where he interrupts Carl's sexual encounter with a hooker.

Marge goes about her investigative work of this horrific criminal violence with a certain bemused acceptance, as if it is a no more unpleasant task than bringing Norm a bag of night crawlers. But her remarks to Grimsrud after his capture suggest that she has difficulty understanding why anyone would behave this way. And while Marge retreats back into the contented safety of her marriage to Norm and the prospect of their baby at the conclusion of *Fargo*, on the basis of what has already transpired in the film, there is no mistaking the bitter irony of the Coens's ending. In a classical narrative, the ending stems from the original dramatic premise, but that is not what happens here. Although *Fargo* seems to parody the kind of happy ending we might find in a Hollywood film, its focus on Marge rather than on Jerry is actually a direct result of its narrative construction, which involves the subtle shift in protagonists that has occurred during the course of the film.

Part Two

Multiple-Plot Films

Chapter 4

Multiple Plots and Subplots in *Trust*

ven though some manual writers discourage multiple protago
nists and multiple plotlines, there is no question that such
devices add greater structural complexity to narrative films and,
as a result, have become extremely common in recent years. As we saw
in *Fargo*, the shift in protagonists is a direct result of its unusual multiple-plot structure. In *Trust* (1990), Hal Hartley uses several plotlines to
explore the relationship between two family outcasts: a pregnant
teenager named Maria Coughlin, and Matthew Slaughter, a volatile
electronics whiz. Besides the main romantic plotline, in which the two
characters attempt to grapple with the meaning of true love, there are
other story lines. As a result of his bad temper and unflinching ideal-
ism, Matthew finds it impossible to hold onto a job, which causes fric-
tion between his brutally sadistic father and him. Maria has her own
share of parental problems. After she inadvertently kills her father,
Maria's mother, Jean, throws her out of the house. Hartley employs
two additional subplots in *Trust*. One involves a search for a kidnapped baby, while the other concerns Jean's unsuccessful attempt to
get Matthew to marry Maria's older sister, Peg. What's especially
unusual about *Trust* in terms of its story structure, however, is the fact
that neither one of these subplots actually affects the main plot in any
significant dramatic way.

The function of subplots, according to Linda Seger, is "to add
dimension to the script."[1] As she explains, "If a film has no subplots,

it's in danger of being too linear, without dimensionality." Just as the main plot has a structure, subplots also have structure as well. "A good subplot has turning points," Seger contends, "a clear set-up, developments, and a pay off at the end."[2] This turns out not to be the case in Hartley's *Trust* because Maria's search for the kidnapped baby actually turns out to be a red herring. By the time Maria visits Rachel and her husband at their house, she has already terminated her pregnancy and the stolen baby has already been returned, thereby undermining its original dramatic function. Although the subplot provides a parallel thematic reference in terms of Maria's decision whether or not to terminate her pregnancy, the search has really been for nothing because there is no payoff at the end. The second subplot is also established, only to be dramatically negated by Maria's seeming lack of response to finding Matthew in bed with Peg, which subverts her mother's underhandedness. But this event also has no dramatic bearing on the story in terms of cause and effect because Maria has previously indicated to Nurse Paine that she intends to proceed with the abortion.

Trust feels like a contemporary soap opera as it might be written and directed by the unlikely combination of Jean-Luc Godard and Robert Bresson. Besides Jim Jarmusch and Todd Haynes, Hal Hartley is probably the American independent screenwriter and director most heavily influenced by international art cinema, which accounts for the fact that he often undercuts the dramatic situations he manages to create through a variety of different strategies. Although his spare, pared-down mise-en-scène and spiritual concerns suggest Bresson, Hartley's films abound with other cinematic references—from indie director Mark Rappaport to the Danish master Carl Theodor Dreyer. Hartley's films are rigidly stylized, especially in the understated manner in which his actors often deliver their lines. His films dispense with establishing shots and show a penchant for fractured rather than fluid space and for tableaux-like compositions that often isolate his characters in two-shots or within the frame. Since *Trust*, his second feature, established his reputation as one of the quintessential American auteurs, Hartley has completed numerous other features, including *Simple Men* (1992), *Amateur* (1994), *Flirt* (1995), *Henry Fool* (1997), *The Book of Life* (1998), *No Such Thing* (2001), and *The Girl From Monday* (2005), all of which bear his unmistakable stamp.

The world presented in Hal Hartley's early films is a decidedly skewed and comical one. In Hartley's fictional universe, parents have a master-slave relationship with children and seem bent on thwarting their potential, often secretly conniving against them for their own selfish reasons. Parents routinely brutalize their kids, either physically or psychologically, but then turn around and demonstrate their love by making sure they have eaten. There is a strong pedophilic strain in Hartley's films, as well as hints of incest. Older men seem to get hung up on young (sometimes underage) women, who have a tendency to fall for dangerous men with questionable pasts. Nuns and priests mix easily with ex-cons and actual criminals. The criminals are the ones possessed by cosmic doubts; the cops are too preoccupied with their own problems to be effective, or their overwhelming sense of sadness can just as easily cause them to become despondent. Hartley's male protagonists are basically the pure of heart—men unable to lie or sometimes even remember their pasts. They are usually angry and violent, as well as tortured by existential doubts about such large issues as the nature of love, trust, truth, ambition, and success.

Hartley's characters discuss philosophy and theology, but also contemporary music, media, and new technologies, such as the Internet. Their conversations are riddled with clichés, aphorisms, unexpected word plays, and frequent misunderstandings rooted in language. Hartley's characters carry books and quote literature, but they are just as prone to break into guitar riffs or choreographed dance numbers. They have a tendency to slap each other in the face impulsively, or collapse to the ground from fainting. Men constantly confront each other by pushing and shoving to the point of parody. There is a tongue-in-cheek, cartoonlike quality to almost all the events, and virtually every form of human interaction entails negotiation—the working out of a deal—whether it be a marriage proposal, a new job, or the choice of a college major. In Hartley's world, people are still respected for their technical skills, their ability to fix things, and for being good at what they do. Thus factories and gas stations are privileged locations, as are such off-the-beaten-path places as the borough of Queens or Long Island, Hartley's setting for his first three feature films.

In one sense, *Trust* has dual protagonists—Maria and Matthew—who receive equal time on the screen. There are several reasons, however, to suggest that it is actually more Maria's story than Matthew's. Not only does the film begin and end with her, but she's really the one who has the major dramatic conflicts—her decisions whether or not to marry Matthew and whether or not to have an abortion. The two turning points derive from her decisions and actions. In addition, the viewer identifies more clearly with Maria's character, as she struggles to become not only more intellectually aware, but a more spiritually developed person as well. Matthew doesn't really change very much in the course of the film, in contrast to Maria, who matures significantly and manages to transform herself as a person.

The individual stories of Matthew and Maria are developed as two separate plotlines in the first act. As *Trust* begins, Maria Coughlin, a brash seventeen-year-old high school dropout, demands that her father give her five dollars. After he refuses, Maria reveals that she's pregnant. Mr. Coughlin kicks her out of the house. Maria slaps him in the face and leaves, as her stunned father collapses dead on the floor. Maria's limited ambitions include plans to marry her jock boyfriend, Anthony, whom she expects to land a job in his father's construction business after playing college football. But even Anthony considers Maria a loser, and he quickly dumps her. After the credits, we're also introduced to Matthew Slaughter, an angry, thirty-year-old computer worker, who gets into a confrontation with his superior over the company's shoddy products and winds up shoving his boss's head into a vice. When Matthew returns home, his father berates him about quitting his job, complaining: "You go through jobs like most people go through underwear."

Trust continues to shift between the two plotlines. At the women's health clinic, Maria has a revelation about the stupidity of getting knocked up by someone who only viewed her in physical terms. As she puts it: "He's seeing my legs. He's seeing my breasts. My mouth. My ass. He's seeing my cunt." She admits to Nurse Paine, "I don't know anything." Meanwhile, Matthew sits holding the hand grenade in his room, but Mr. Slaughter delivers a hard punch to his stomach for failing to clean the bathroom to his satisfaction. Upon returning home, Maria discovers that she has killed her father, causing her mother to order her out of the house.

Hartley employs a number of intriguing strategies for expanding the range of dialogue beyond the conventions. One is to have two characters talk to each other but never connect, so that "dialogue" becomes reduced to a pair of separate monologues. An example of this occurs when Maria talks to an older woman named Rachel on the bench outside a delicatessen. Only after Maria demands five dollars—a reference to the argument with her Dad—and Rachel gives it to her, does Maria open up to the other woman. Rachel's own personal problems, however, surface immediately, and neither of them seems capable of really listening and responding to what the other is saying. Hartley presents what seem to be two internal monologues that have become externalized and broken up.

MARIA: I killed my father this morning.

RACHEL: (*Not listening*) My daughter would have been just about your age.

MARIA: I didn't mean to, honest. It was an accident. We were just arguing.

RACHEL: I've spent some time in a psychiatric hospital.

MARIA: I didn't know he had a bad heart.

RACHEL: After that my husband just didn't want children.

MARIA: He always *seemed* healthy enough.

RACHEL: I wonder if deep down he blames me for her death.

MARIA: I just slapped him.[3]

The scene continues this way, until Maria, who becomes lost in her own thoughts, gets brought back to reality by Rachel mentioning that she hates Cape Holiday, the vacation resort where she and her husband go every summer. The screenplay, in fact, describes Maria's reaction: "Maria listens and realizes that Rachel is somewhere far away in her own head."[4] Rachel's sadness at the loss of a child creates a parallelism to Maria's unwanted pregnancy, but guilt is also a factor here, which connects Rachel's stream-of-consciousness rambling to both Maria and Matthew.

In a typical dramatic scene, tension usually builds through a back-and-forth exchange between the participants, often resulting in continual power shifts between the characters. What's interesting about Hartley's scenes is that they contain the same "push and pull" that provide forward energy and momentum, but they do not necessarily escalate toward a dramatic climax. The effect, in fact, is quite the opposite, because Hartley chooses to flatten rather than to exploit the inherent drama of the situation. In the above exchange between Maria and Rachel, for instance, Maria breaks down initially. But when Rachel tries to comfort her, Maria takes offense once Rachel resorts to clichés. After Maria demands five dollars and Rachel gives her the money, the humbled Maria then backs down again. The two women continue to talk at cross-purposes, revealing intimate details of their lives. The scene ends on an anticlimactic note when Maria thanks Rachel for the money and leaves abruptly to go into the delicatessen.

The scene between Maria and Rachel turns out to be important for another reason, namely, it motivates one of the film's two subplots. During their conversation, we've watched a Biker Mom park a baby stroller in front of the store and go inside. When Maria enters, the Biker Mom talks on the pay phone. Maria tries to buy a six-pack of beer, but the clerk asks for proof of her age, and then lures her into the back room. After the clerk tries to molest her, Maria sticks a lit cigarette in his eye and manages to escape. Once Maria is outside, the Biker Mom screams that someone has stolen her baby, but Maria runs off quickly when the clerk stumbles out of the store.

The two separate story lines involving Maria and Matthew intersect at the first turning point when the two characters get together at approximately twenty-nine minutes. After Matthew discovers Maria huddled in the corner of an abandoned house, she initially tells him to get lost, but then admits to him that she needs a place to sleep. Maria wakes up the next morning in Matthew's bedroom. She first boasts of being a murderer, then confesses that she's thinking of killing herself. He reciprocates by showing her his hand grenade. After Matthew leaves, Maria makes a mess in the kitchen, but she happens to see a newspaper headline: "Infant Kidnapped at Bus Stop." A ruckus ensues once Mr. Slaughter and Matthew arrive home. Mr. Slaughter slaps Matthew, removes Maria's clothes from the washer, and tosses them on the floor. Maria takes a dress from the upstairs bedroom and puts it on before heading out to find Matthew.

Matthew enters a local bar where the patrons are clearly frightened of him. He punches the deli clerk (who now has a patch over one eye) and pushes Anthony out of his way, then orders a bottle of Scotch. Maria's older sister, Peg, sits down next to Matthew and attempts to pick him up. The two trade insults back and forth before Peg asks Matthew whether he has a girlfriend. She also suggests this is the source of his problem.

MATTHEW: Do I have a problem?
    PEG: Of course you do.
MATTHEW: Oh yeah, and what do *you* think my problem is?
    PEG: I don't think you get laid enough.
MATTHEW: Is that so?

> PEG: Well, what kind of relationship could a man as
> screwed up as you possibly have?
> MATTHEW: I don't have relationships.
> PEG: You love 'em and leave 'em, huh?
> MATTHEW: I don't *love* anybody.
> PEG: You mean, you just *have* a girl.
> MATTHEW: I take what I can get. Now if you're through talking,
> do you want to go out back and fuck?
> PEG: (*Speechless*) You're talking to the mother of two. You
> know that! You can't be talking to somebody's
> mother like that. Bastard!

(MATTHEW *gives her a glass.*)

> MATTHEW: Here, have a drink.
> PEG: Oh, fuck off.
> MATTHEW: No, seriously. I mean it. Stay. (*He pours her a drink.*)
> PEG: Everything's been very screwed up since my divorce.
> He took the kids away from me like I'm unfit or
> something.[5]

The exchange of insults creates a parody of the small talk we would
expect in a typical bar pickup. Matthew has the advantage initially, but
Peg scores when she suggests Matthew's problem has to do with the
fact that he doesn't get laid enough. Matthew takes the offensive when
he states the obvious subtext: "Now if you're through talking, do you
want to go out back and fuck?" Matthew's remark offends Peg, who
guilt-trips him by declaring that he shouldn't be talking to a mother
that way, causing Matthew to offer her a drink. Peg tells him to "fuck
off," which induces Matthew to ask her to stay. Only after these rapid
shifts in each character assuming a power advantage does Peg finally
open up to Matthew, revealing that she's lost her kids in the divorce.
Maria's sudden arrival breaks off the exchange, causing the story to
take a new direction, when Maria invites Matthew to stay at their
house because she's afraid of her mother.

The middle act focuses on the complications of Maria and
Matthew's burgeoning romance. Since neither Jean nor Peg has any
money, Matthew offers to pay for the abortion, despite the fact that
he'll be forced to take a job repairing TVs. After Matthew convinces
Maria to wear her glasses, which she has avoided because they make

Matthew, Maria, and Peg at the bar

her look "brainy like a librarian," her new intellectual look creates desire in Matthew and they nearly kiss, before Matthew pulls back at the last moment. She'll wear glasses, but, in exchange, Maria asks Matthew for his hand grenade, which she puts in her desk drawer. She then writes in her notebook: "I am ashamed. I am ashamed of being young. I am ashamed of being stupid." The shameful recognition of her own naïveté and ignorance causes Maria to begin to ask more fundamental questions about her life, especially concerning marriage and whether or not she should have an abortion.

The subplot involving the stolen baby is reintroduced when Maria and Matthew meet at the train station. Remembering that Rachel mentioned that her husband carried a briefcase and smoked a pipe, Maria goes to look for him, but this describes virtually every male commuter getting off the train. A second subplot develops when Jean tries to persuade Matthew that Peg would be the better catch, especially since Maria will now have to support her as compensation for her husband's death. Matthew and Maria finally kiss, after which she tells him she's going to have an abortion the next day and he agrees to accompany her. It leads to the following dialogue:

MARIA: Why do you hang around here and look after me like
this?
MATTHEW: Somebody has to.
MARIA: Why you?[6]

This exchange, including Maria's dialogue hook, will serve as an
important reference point.

The romantic plotline between Maria and Matthew intensifies
when Matthew proposes marriage at the abortion clinic, prior to getting into a fight in the waiting room. In a parking lot near the train station, Maria questions Matthew about his proposal, thereby subverting
the conventions of what we might expect in a typical romantic scene.

MARIA: Did you mean it? Would you marry me?
MATTHEW: Yes.
MARIA: Why?
MATTHEW: Because I want to.
MARIA: Not because you love me or anything like that, huh?
MATTHEW: I respect and admire you.
MARIA: Isn't that love?
MATTHEW: No. That's respect and admiration. I think that's bet-
ter than love.

Jean threatens Maria after she returns home

Maria and Matthew discuss marriage

MARIA:	How?
MATTHEW:	When people are in love they do all sorts of crazy things. They get jealous, they lie, they cheat. They kill themselves. They kill each other.
MARIA:	It doesn't have to be that way.
MATTHEW:	Maybe.
MARIA:	You'd be the father of a child you know isn't yours.
MATTHEW:	Kids are kids, what does it matter?
MARIA:	Do you trust me?
MATTHEW:	Do you trust me first?
MARIA:	I trust you.
MATTHEW:	You sure?
MARIA:	Yes.

(MATTHEW *looks at* MARIA *and then kneels down in front of her.*)

MATTHEW:	Then marry me.
MARIA:	I'll marry you if you admit that respect, admiration, and trust equals love.
MATTHEW:	OK. They equal love.[7]

For Hartley, a marriage proposal becomes not a declaration and acceptance of romantic love, but a form of bargaining, a play on the whole notion of a marriage contract. It is emotion that creates the behavior to which the volatile Matthew so strenuously objects: the jealousy, the lying, the cheating, the murderous impulses. He argues for a more intellectual mutual understanding—respect and admiration—but Maria adds a spiritual component, "trust," by agreeing to marry him if he will admit that "respect, admiration, and trust equals love." Matthew agrees and the two of them kiss. Maria gets distracted, however, when she notices a bumper sticker advertising Cape Holiday, the vacation resort Rachel mentioned earlier. The two attempt to determine which car belongs to Rachel's husband. Maria later locates Rachel's pipe-smoking husband, Robert, who faints as she approaches. She manages to take his address label from his briefcase and, once he revives, returns the five dollars. Maria later complains that Matthew is drinking too much and that his job is making him mean and boring. After Maria goes to the store, Jean tells Matthew she wants him out of her house. Matthew challenges her to an arm-wrestling match, but Jean suggests a drinking contest.

The second turning point occurs at seventy-six minutes, when Maria meets Nurse Paine at a diner and indicates she wants an abortion, thus giving the film a three-act structure: a first act of twenty-nine minutes, a second of forty-seven minutes, and a final act of twenty-eight minutes. In the published version of the script for *Trust,* Hartley acknowledges that his films tend to have a traditional structure:

> For the most part, the feature films I've made, even up to *Simple Men,* have been based on a fairly traditional, classic narrative structure. I used to have it worked out like a map. But it's blurred now. I believe I was taught that a conventional classic American film was to have sixty-four scenes with everything in its place. Introduction, exposition, inciting incident, false climax, true climax, reversal, and denouement. It was math. A way of structuring the raw material.
>
> *Trust* was built on that structure too. But once I got the story worked out on that schema, I started screwing around with it, doing damage to it, trying to achieve, moment by moment, what it was I wanted. It's emotional from this point on. If I feel something is lagging or moving too fast, I adjust it. I add scenes. Move scenes

around. Whatever is needed to make the thing interesting. But I
have started from a fairly traditional dramatic structure on all of
my features.[8]

Hartley subsequently experimented with structural innovation, most
notably with *Flirt*.

The subplot involving Jean's desire to have Matthew marry Peg
builds in the third act. As the two drink, Jean indicates that she does-
n't want Maria to make the same mistake she and Peg have made. She
also confesses to feeling relief now that her husband is gone. Jean
asks Matthew whether he loves his father, but Matthew insists he
doesn't love anybody. Matthew compares his relationship with his
dad to the old analog technology before he passes out on the floor.
Jean manages to get Matthew upstairs and into Peg's bed. She
removes his clothes, and leaves her hair clip there. After Peg gets
home, she's surprised to find the gin bottle full of water and
Matthew passed out in her bed.

Maria runs into Anthony, who has failed his college entrance exam,
at the grocery store. He tries to kiss Maria, but she fights him off. After
Maria returns home, Jean asks her to retrieve her hair clip from Peg's
room. After a brief argument, Maria goes upstairs and gets it without
any acknowledgment of Matthew, even though we see her internal
struggle in the shower afterward. Maria does not respond to her
mother's ploy, primarily because she has been able to move beyond
such petty jealousy. As Hartley comments: "She's transcended the need
for revenge. Her mother's obsessive, petty, manipulative behavior is
the behavior of a desperately disturbed person. Why lower herself to
that level? On the other hand, why should Maria assume Matthew to
be impervious to her sister's temptations? It's humility. And it takes a
saint to maintain it."[9] Right after this, Maria gets an abortion and can-
cels their marriage plans. She does this not only for her own sake, but
to prevent Matthew from becoming exactly the kind of person he
hates. Thus, her decision to have the abortion ironically becomes a
selfless or saintly act.

After Maria has an abortion, she tracks down Robert. While Rachel
sits in the living room and appears very distraught, Robert drops a
newspaper with a headline indicating that the kidnapped baby has
been found in a phone booth. Robert informs Maria the police
received an anonymous tip and adds that the baby's doing fine.

Matthew returns to Maria's house, carrying flowers and a thesaurus. Suddenly Mr. Slaughter knocks on the door. Mr. Slaughter's cruelty toward Matthew has to do with the fact that his wife died giving birth to Matthew, a situation for which he holds Matthew responsible, even though this revelation comes rather late and never really gets developed in the film. After Matthew refuses to return home, the codependent nature of their relationship becomes obvious. Mr. Slaughter complains: "Matthew, I spent my whole life looking out for you, now you desert me." Like Jean, Mr. Slaughter's own personal problems prevent him from letting go of his child, and both parents attempt to control and manipulate their kids through the familiar tactics of guilt and blame. As Mr. Slaughter continues to criticize Maria, Matthew demands that his father admit to his fear of being lonely. The two get into an argument over Maria, which turns into a brawl. (The Oedipal nature of their conflict is reinforced by the fact that Maria wears Mrs. Slaughter's dress for much of the film.) By the time Maria arrives, the fighting has stopped. Maria informs Matthew she's had an abortion and no longer wants to get married, leaving him crushed. After Mr. Slaughter and Jean finally meet, Maria discovers that Matthew's hand grenade is missing from the drawer upstairs.

Oblivious to the danger, Maria rushes inside the deserted computer factory where she finds Matthew holding the grenade in one hand and the pin in the other. Maria takes the grenade from Matthew and tosses it; after a delayed reaction, it explodes. Peg and Jean both faint outside the factory, while Matthew and Maria lie on the ground, framed in a tight composition. The camera is above them, so that their heads are in the frame, but their bodies are pointed in opposite directions. They manage to achieve a selfless, spiritual bond:

MATTHEW: Why have you done this?
MARIA: Done what?
MATTHEW: Why do you put up with me like this?
MARIA: Somebody had to.
MATTHEW: But why you?
MARIA: I just happened to be here.[10]

The two stare at each other as two policemen drag him away and place him in a squad car. As the patrol car drives off, Matthew doesn't take his eyes off her. Maria walks after the car, puts her glasses on, and continues to stare at the car as it disappears, leaving her stranded in the road. The scene recalls the ending of Bresson's *Pickpocket* (1959), in which Michel discovers Jeanne only after the most circuitous journey.

In the interview accompanying the screenplay for *Trust*, Hartley openly acknowledges Bresson's influence:

> I am very affected by Bresson and, more and more, I am con-sciously using that knowledge—whatever that means. Sometimes it's just an emotional clarity that I sense in his films, that I try to bring to mine when I'm writing. When I'm shooting too. Bresson cuts right past everything that's superfluous and isolates an image that says exactly what it's meant to say.[11]

The scene in *Trust* in which Jean sets up Maria to discover Matthew and Peg in bed is a good example of the Bressonian strategy of paring down a scene to its most basic cinematic elements, which is evident from the script:

INT. STAIRWAY. NIGHT.

MARIA moves up the stairs toward Peg's room.

INT. MARIA'S KITCHEN. NIGHT—SAME TIME.

Maria stares at Matthew as he's taken away in a police car

JEAN doesn't blink. She waits motionlessly, her sewing frozen in her hands. She is terribly frightened.

On the stove, the kettle starts to whistle.

JEAN doesn't react. She breathes in deep, waiting.

The kettle whistles . . .

INT. STAIRWAY. NIGHT—SAME TIME.

The empty stairway. From the kitchen we hear the kettle's shrill, relentless whistle.

INT. MARIA'S KITCHEN. NIGHT—SAME TIME.

JEAN at the table, not moving; stiff as a board, waiting. The kettle is deafening. Jean's hands, with the sewing, slowly drop to the table. She hangs her head there a moment, then . . . The whistling stops.

JEAN looks up, startled.

MARIA is standing there, her hand still on the stove's burner knob.

MARIA pours a cup of tea and brings it, with the hair clip, over to the table, setting it before JEAN.

MARIA: Here you go. I'm going to bed. Good night.

(JEAN sits there, uncomprehending, as MARIA kisses her on the head and leaves the kitchen. MARIA seemed completely undisturbed. JEAN stares at her hair clip and at the tea, puzzled.)

INT. STAIRWAY. NIGHT—MOMENTS LATER.

JEAN comes quietly, but determinedly, up the stairs and moves toward Peg's room.

INT. PEG'S BEDROOM. NIGHT—SAME TIME.

JEAN opens the door slowly.

The hallway light falls over . . .

MATTHEW and PEG, asleep together on the bed.

JEAN just stares at them, dumbfounded.

INT. MARIA'S BATHROOM. NIGHT—SAME TIME.

In the shower, MARIA is pressing her forehead into the corner of the tiled wall with her eyes shut tight and her fists clenched and held up just beneath her chin. The water pours down over her head. The bathroom fills with steam.[12]

A number of things are immediately evident about the scene. For one thing, the words are laid out on the page like poetry. It also contains very little dialogue. The tension is conveyed almost entirely through images and sounds: the motionless Jean holding her sewing and the whistling kettle to which she does not respond, the dropping of her hands, and the sound of the kettle that stops abruptly. Maria seems to have no reaction, which dumbfounds her mother, but we view her inner spiritual struggle later inside the shower. The emotional turbulence is not conveyed through performance, but becomes evident instead from the cinematic details Hartley chooses: Maria's forehead against the wall, her closed eyes and clenched fists held beneath her chin, the gushing of water over her, and the steam that fills up the room.

Bresson is not the only stylistic reference. In *On Directing Film*, David Mamet argues that "A movie script should be a juxtaposition of uninflected shots that tell the story."[13] He uses Soviet montage to differentiate between what he terms "dramatic action" and "narration" in explaining an alternative approach to the protagonist-driven storytelling that dominates the American cinematic tradition. As Mamet explains:

> You always want to tell the story in cuts. Which is to say, through a juxtaposition of images that are basically uninflected. Mr. Eisenstein tells us that the best image is an uninflected image. A shot of a teacup. A shot of a spoon. A shot of a fork. A shot of a door. Let the cut tell the story. Because otherwise you have not got dramatic action, you have narration. If you slip into narration, you are saying, "you'll never guess why what I just told you is important to the story." It's unimportant that the audience should guess why it's important to the story. It's important simply to *tell* the story. Let the audience be surprised.[14]

Although Mamet seems to confuse Eisenstein with Kuleshov and Pudovkin (the more historically accurate exponents of the montage theory he invokes), his emphasis on more neutral images and cutting to convey the dramatic action of the scene mirrors Hartley's style of visual storytelling.

Hartley's stylization, like Mamet's, extends to his use of dialogue as well. Although there is minimal dialogue in the above example, this scene is somewhat atypical of Hartley, whose scripts often emphasize verbal dialogue over narrative action. Hartley's highly stylized dialogue does not conform to the naturalistic conventions advocated by the manuals. At times, Hartley resorts to obvious clichés, or aphorisms reminiscent of Godard, such as: "Television is the opium of the masses." Jean tells Matthew: "A family's got to stick together, come hell or high water." Matthew responds: "A family's like a gun. You point it in the wrong direction, you're gonna kill somebody." The exchange also highlights Hartley's use of deadpan humor. There is a musicality to his colloquial language, which creates unusual verbal rhythms through repetitions of certain words and phrases. There is a sense that Hartley enjoys playing with language, and that his dialogue provides his characters with an opportunity to indulge in the pleasures of spoken language for its own sake. When Maria talks with Nurse Paine at the diner, they discuss Matthew:

> PAINE: How is he?
> MARIA: Dangerous. But sincere.
> PAINE: Sincerely dangerous.
> MARIA: No, dangerous *because* he's sincere.
> PAINE: I see. And now he's becoming insincere?
> MARIA: Not exactly. He's just sort of numb.[15]

Conversations between characters become the occasion to explore the very meaning of words, or the concepts behind them. Even though his characters speak the same language, their words often cause misunderstandings and confusions, thus accentuating rather than closing the gap in human communication.

Hal Hartley shares with other American independent auteurs, such as Jim Jarmusch and Todd Haynes, a penchant for a strategy of narration more closely aligned with art cinema than mainstream Hollywood fare. Because of his idiosyncratic style, Hartley's films represent an acquired taste. It takes a while to become attuned to their mannered dialogue and performances, fringe characters, droll sense of humor, surprise reversals, spare mise-en-scène, and overall dramatic flatness. The rigorous stylistics of Hartley's films no doubt also account for the fact that not a single one has become a mainstream hit, including *Henry Fool*, which won the Best Screenplay Award at the 1998 Cannes Film Festival. Despite his lack of commercial success, Hartley has nevertheless had a surprisingly prolific career, even if he has been forced to produce his films on relatively minuscule budgets. There can be no denying his critical impact, however, not only as a director, but also as a screenwriter. That *Trust* turns out to be as brilliant on the page as it is on the screen is a tribute to Hartley's rare ability to mix the literary and the visual into a highly personal style. In terms of the multiple-plot film, Hartley's *Trust* creates an unusual structure in which the subsidiary plot threads, while having a thematic link to the main plot, undercut rather than enhance the dramatic impact that such devices traditionally provide. Like other strategies of independent filmmakers, such as Jarmusch's use of an ambivalent protagonist or Haynes's passive protagonist, this contributes to a deliberate flattening of the classical dramatic arc.

Chapter 5

Shifting Goals and Plotlines in *Gas Food Lodging*

A dapted from Richard Peck's novel *Don't Look and It Won't Hurt*, Allison Anders's substantially reworked script for *Gas Food Lodging* (1992) mixes Southwestern regionalism with a strong female perspective in telling the story of three women—a single mother, Nora, and her two daughters, Trudi and Shade—as they struggle to cope with life in a small desert town. Three main characters and multiple lines of action result in the intersection of three different stories at various points, which serves to complicate the plot structure. The three women, however, are not given equal weight in terms of screen time. The film clearly favors Shade, then Trudi, with Nora getting the least attention. Although *Gas Food Lodging* explores the lives of all three women, the story is narrated from the point of view of the younger daughter, Shade, who really serves as the main protagonist. Because Shade's goals change as the plot of *Gas Food Lodging* progresses, one of the more intriguing aspects of the film's structure has to do with the fact that the decisive turning points have to do with Trudi and her desire to leave Laramie and only indirectly with Shade.

Syd Field defines the concept of a turning point, or what he terms the plot point as "an incident, or event, that 'hooks' into the action and spins it around into another direction."[1] Field doesn't specifically relate first and second plot points to the goals of a protagonist, but other manual authors do. Linda Seger, for instance, lists as one of the functions of turning points: "It's often a moment of decision or commitment on the part of the main character."² Michael Hauge goes even further by equating the concept of the three-act structure and the two act-breaks with specific changes in the motivation of the protagonist. Hauge writes: "The next means of defining each act is in terms of the *outer motivation for your hero*. The three acts of the screenplay correspond to the three stages of the hero's outer motivation. Each change in the hero's outer motivation signals the arrival of the next act."³ Kristin Thompson also makes the assumption "that the turning points almost invariably relate to the characters' goals" and discusses them in terms of the protagonist.⁴ In many films, the turning points do actually involve the protagonist, but just as often this is not the case. In *River's Edge* (1987), for instance, the protagonist, Matt, tells the police where his friend Jamie's body is hidden, which serves as the film's first turning point. The second act-break, however, occurs when Feck rather than Matt takes action by shooting Jamie's disturbed killer, Samson. As we saw in an earlier chapter, neither one of the turning points in *Fargo* has to do with either Jerry or Marge. The turning points in *Reservoir Dogs*, as I will address in chapter seven, also involve actions by characters—Mr. Blonde and Mr. Orange—other than the protagonist, Mr. White. What's unusual about the structure of *Gas Food Lodging* is not that the turning points don't involve decisions or actions by the main protagonist (Shade), but rather that both of them are determined by the same character (Trudi) in a secondary line of action.

Shade does have her own goals. At the beginning of the film, she essentially wants three things: to find a man for her mother, to find her father, and to have a loving relationship with Darius, her glam-rocker friend. But none of these things actually work out for her. As a result of her sister's advice, Shade takes a risk in throwing herself at Darius and gets rejected when he turns out to be gay and unable to respond to her sexually. She sets up her mother with her old boyfriend, Raymond, but we already know that he is married to someone else, and the dinner date that Shade arranges for them marks the final end of their relationship. Shade does finally track down her deadbeat father, John, but he turns out to be a terrible disappointment as a father.

While Shade is unable to attain a single one of her original goals, she does manage to stumble into a romance with Javier, which culminates in his profession of love for her and their lovemaking in the desert. Interestingly, though, their romance becomes overshadowed by

Trudi giving birth in the hospital, her refusal to return home, and Shade's ultimate discovery of the fate of the baby's father, Dank. Although Shade fails in her efforts to find a man for her mother, Nora manages to find one (Hamlet Humphrey) on her own. Just as Shade's experience with Javier does not seem to serve the same dramatic function in the story as that of Darius—she has never really articulated a desire to have a relationship with Javier in terms of a goal—Hamlet doesn't appear to satisfy Shade's need to have a normal family. Even her final meeting with her father, John, represents a false climax largely because the events involving her sister rather than her father turn out to represent the final rupture in Shade's main quest to have a normal family. The real climax of the movie involves Shade's discovery that Dank has remained true to the end, which, at least for her, represents the thematic fulfillment of the Elvia Romero melodramas she watches, as well as her own childhood home movie.

Shade's inability to achieve any of her goals in *Gas Food Lodging* is not necessarily a defect in her character or in the script, but rather represents a deliberate attempt on Anders's part to provide a "feminine perspective" as an antidote to what she considers to be the "masculine" goal-orientated characters found in conventionally structured stories. As Anders explains in an interview in *Filmmaker*:

> I think that woman's stories have always been told, to a certain extent, but in the framework of a male dominated business. I actually think that the three act structure is totally masculine. That's not to say that women can't use that structure, but I think it doesn't allow for how most women's lives work, which is on the rhythm of process, rather than a rhythm of goals. I often find that women go for one thing and end up with something entirely different. For a man, that means he failed, he didn't achieve his goals. For a woman, that's not necessarily the case; it's like we got something else, something we never dreamed of. We have a different rhythm than men. I feel like that's a feminine perspective, that maybe we can break out of traditional structures.[5]

Anders intends her more meandering multiple-plot structure to be an alternative to the three-act paradigm. In an interview in *scr(i)pt*, Anders bristles, "If you sit down and shake the pages of the script, do the three acts fall out? What is that? It's just something someone invented. It's not a rule."[6] Anders argues for a more intuitive, idiosyncratic, and formally inventive approach, especially by a screenwriter trying to get noticed for her or his independent voice. Her criticism is aimed directly at the manuals:

> You should also tell the story the way it should be told. For the most part, the screenwriting books aren't very useful. They're most useful when it comes to getting the story out of you, but in terms of structure, they're totally useless. To have certain things that are supposed to happen on certain pages is preposterous. And when you're a voice that's never been heard, you have to find a new language to tell the stories. You basically have to invent your own language.[7]

True to her own advice, *Gas Food Lodging* attempts to differentiate itself from the conventional paradigm in a number of interesting ways.

Acknowledging the strong influence of Wim Wenders, for whom she worked as a production assistant, Anders has indicated that she is much more interested in her characters than in the actual mechanics of plot. Even in terms of her writing method, she begins with her characters:

> I start with characters because I really don't have any plots and I'm always amazed at the end of it going, "Wow, I can't believe that it works!" Plot is not one of my things. Probably a lot of it comes from Wim, because I'm not terribly interested in resolving the plot. I'm more interested in my characters resolving. Wim was always like, yeah, the story just seemed like some bothersome thing that I had to hang everything on. I think that's how I feel too. It's like a clothes line, and you've got the colorful textures, which I'm really interested in. I'm interested in what's on the clothes line, not the clothes line itself. This is pretty anti-Hollywood. For the most part, Hollywood is all about the clothes line, and they think they can just hang anything up there. Like, maybe we'll put Bruce Willis here. Maybe Arnold Schwarzenegger there . . .[8]

Anders's interest in character rather than plot certainly mimics what Jim Jarmusch had to say about his backward approach to constructing *Stranger Than Paradise*, and it's interesting to note that he also worked with Wenders prior to making his own films. The more character-driven approach of both Anders and Jarmusch is clearly antithetical to the one taken by the manuals. Although Field, for instance, admits that story can grow out of character, he nevertheless insists that you have to know the script's overall structure—the ending, beginning, and both major plot points—before you can begin to write it.

Gas Food Lodging begins with a moving point-of-view shot down a desert road. We wind up finally in the tiny oasis town of Laramie, New Mexico, an utterly desolate place. The story is narrated by a sweet-natured fifteen-year-old girl, Shade, who, teary-eyed, watches a Spanish-language melodrama in the town's otherwise empty movie theater. Shade credits Elvia Rivero, the heroine of these melodramas, with being the romantic impulse behind the events of the story. It is from Elvia that Shade gets the idea that what she needs is a man, not for herself, but for her single mother, Nora. "Then we could do all the dumb normal stuff regular families do," Shade tells us, underscoring the dysfunctional nature of her own family situation. Once this story line gets established, a romantic plotline gets introduced almost immediately. As Shade rushes down the street, she passes a vintage clothing shop, where a young man, Darius, dressed in retro clothes, calls to her. He holds up a red- and yellow-striped platform shoe and beckons for her to come inside, but Shade has to run off to meet her sister.

Trudi outside the diner

Shade's older sister, Trudi, is another story altogether. The attractive and sexy seventeen-year-old has a huge chip on her shoulder and is already intent on escaping from Laramie. As Trudi and Shade eat at the roadside truck stop where Nora slings hash, Trudi lashes out at the Mexican busboy, Javier, for knocking over a glass of soda, referring to him derisively as a "wetback." Trudi and Nora clash over her choice for dinner, causing Trudi to storm out of the restaurant. Javier also quits as a result of Trudi's insult, leaving Nora to perform double duty.

Later that night in the trailer park where they live, Shade sits in her room trying to figure out the right kind of man for her mom. We learn important exposition, as she describes some of Nora's previous choices—one violent, one rich, another very young—and takes out an old home movie from a canister. "There are so many kinds of guys," Shade says in voiceover, "but there was only one guy missing," namely, her own father. This introduces a second story line, as Shade calls El Paso information and asks for "John Evans," hoping to track him down. When she gets a number and dials, a man answers, but Nora's car suddenly pulls in the driveway, causing Shade to slam down the receiver.

Nora's conflict with Trudi escalates when she discovers that Trudi has been staying out late with guys and also skipping school. As a result of their heated late-night argument, Trudi quits school and takes a job as a waitress at the same truck stop. On her first day, Trudi seems more interested in primping in the bathroom than in serving customers, but she meets a handsome English rock hunter as a result of bringing him the wrong burger. Shade meanwhile discovers that Javier works as a projectionist at the Spanish-language theater where she watches the Elvia Romero melodramas, but hard feelings remain between them over the diner incident.

Unbeknownst to Shade, Nora already has a secret boyfriend, but we learn about the relationship just as it is ending. As Nora leaves work, she meets Raymond in the parking lot. "I think," Nora tells him, "we've been over this about a hundred times too many." Raymond persists, telling her, "We never hurt nobody." But Nora insists that she needs to serve as a role model for her two daughters. Before they separate, Nora kisses Raymond passionately before letting him go, flip-flopping between her conflicting emotions. Shade's own romantic plotline begins to develop in the next scene, as she sits on the top of a bunk bed listening to music with Darius, a glam-rocker with dark fantasies about pushing beyond the boundaries. He explains the meaning of the Olivia Newton-John song they're listening to:

> DARIUS: It's like Adam and Eve. He was fine grooving in Paradise, but Eve wanted something scary. She wanted the fucking edge. She wanted to jump off cliffs just so she could see what it was like to fall. Risk. That's what this song's all about, Shade. That's what Eve wanted. That's what Olivia wants. That's what I want.

It's obvious from the scene that Shade has a terrible crush on him.

Trudi's initial romantic plotline ends unexpectedly. As a bunch of high school kids ridicule her for being a slut, Trudi asks them if they've seen Brett, her date from the night before, but he turns out to be at the truck stop with someone else. The rock hunter, Dank, sits in his Jeep studying a map, but he can't help but notice the distraught young waitress through the window of the diner. After Dank inadvertently leaves his coffee Thermos on the fender of his Jeep, Trudi chases after him, and accepts his offer of a lift home. During the ride, Trudi expresses her reservations about men, while Dank discusses his enthusiasm for rocks. When they arrive at her trailer park, she kisses him aggressively, then stops and apologizes: "Look, that's the best I can do. I'm tired."

In terms of the overall structure of *Gas Food Lodging*, the first turning point occurs when Trudi accepts a ride from Dank at twenty-six minutes. This event marks the start of their relationship, which will dominate the middle act. The story line involving Shade's desire to find someone for her mother resurfaces as she sees the perfect man in the form of a cowboy standing in front of a bar. In voiceover, Shade says, "It was like he walked straight out of an Elvia Rivero movie." The guy turns out to be Nora's old flame, Raymond. Trudi accompanies Dank up to the caves to look for fluorescent rocks, and the two end up passionately making love. After Dank takes Trudi home the next morning he tells her he has to go away for a few days to explore a mineshaft near Carlsbad and that he will be back on Wednesday. Completely smitten now, Trudi sulks at first, then melts when he gives her a rock as a token of his sincerity. He tells her solemnly, "I'll dream about you. Dream for me, Trudi." Nora has had it with Trudi, however, and gives her a month to find her own place. Nora tells her, "Pay your rent alone. See how dandy that is." But Trudi boasts to Nora that she's found someone and won't end up being left alone like her mother.

The two sisters later get a chance to have an intimate talk. As they lie in their beds, Shade tells Trudi that she doesn't want her to move out. Trudi shows Shade the rock and tells her about Dank and the desert. She also encourages her younger sister to make the first move on Darius. Decked out to look like Olivia Newton-John, Shade then visits Darius and mimics his earlier lines about wanting to "go to some scary dark place." But Darius, who is clearly gay, is unable to respond to her sexual advances. He insists, "It's not you. It's me." Shade counters, "That doesn't help."

The end to Shade's romantic plotline involving Darius comes as something of a surprise, mainly because its demise comes so abruptly in the middle act. Almost immediately, however, a new romance figure materializes in the form of Javier, a character who has already figured in two previous scenes. Shade surprises Nora by fixing dinner and inviting Raymond. Afterward, our expectations of a rekindled romance subside when they say goodbye privately. As Wednesday arrives, Trudi becomes overjoyed with anticipation at seeing Dank again, but he winds up being a no-show. Trudi lapses into a depression, and eventually does not even bother to get out of bed. Thus, all three characters suffer broken relationships in the middle act.

Trudi's broken relationship, however, has the most dramatic complications because she's managed to become pregnant. Nora wants her to get an abortion, but Trudi stubbornly refuses, guilt-tripping her mom by telling her, "I bet you probably even tried to abort me, didn't you?" Trudi insists on having the baby and giving it up for adoption. Shade and Nora accompany her to the bus station. Still angry, Nora waits in the car, but then finds it within herself to give Trudi a hug and some money. Before she leaves for Dallas, Trudi tries to reassure Shade that Darius was just scared. The second turning point occurs when Trudi leaves the family for Dallas at sixty-three minutes. *Gas Food Lodging* has a first act of twenty-six minutes, a second act of thirty-seven minutes, and a third act of thirty-four minutes.

Trudi's departure impacts Shade's family life significantly. As Shade and Nora eat dinner together, Shade asks what they are going to do now without Trudi there, since they don't really talk to each other very much. At Tanya's party, Shade attempts to rescue her friend from one of the guys from Los Angeles, but he becomes more assertive and tries

Shade's surprise dinner for Nora and Raymond

to push her back inside. When Shade attempts to protect Tanya, his aggression shifts to her. A liquor delivery person grabs the guy by his long hair and pushes him away forcibly, ending the confrontation. This turns out to be John, the man who earlier had lent Shade money to buy fabric softener. As he drives Shade toward the trailer park, John refers to her by name and asks about her sister and mother, and acknowledges that he's her father.

Shade's unexpected meeting with John has repercussions. Although Nora seems surprised, she has only critical things to say about him. Shade breaks into tears, blaming Nora for the fact that they don't have a normal family and accusing her mother of hating men. After watching another Elvia Rivero movie at the local movie theater, Shade visits her father in a run-down place where he's living with a woman named Kim. She asks him for fifty dollars in order to buy a nightgown for Trudi, but the request results in a bitter argument between John and Kim that causes her to leave. As Shade walks down the road, John comes after her in his pickup truck and gives her the money. He also makes a lame attempt to explain his failure to be in contact with them. Shade's fantasy about her caring father—the one who holds her in the home movie from her childhood—collapses

Trudi argues with Nora about having the baby

rather undramatically under the weight of her dad's basic character flaws, bringing an abrupt end to this plotline.

The film shifts to the romantic plotline involving Javier after Shade visits him and apologizes for Tanya's refusal to let him come to the party. Shade meets Javier's mute mother, Lucille, who dances to the vibrations of music pulsating from the floor. Javier and his mother dance, and Lucille gets Shade to participate. Shade winds up later in Javier's arms, where—like in an Elvia Rivero matinee—he tells her she's beautiful and professes his undying love for her in Spanish. In the desert, Shade discovers her soul mate in Javier and, in the process, herself. Shade later goes bowling with Nora and her new boyfriend, Hamlet. He refers to Shade as "one of those matinee junkies" and wins her over by imitating the out-of-sync dialogue of Spanish-language movies. Afterward, Shade and Javier watch Shade's home movie from the projection booth of the movie theater. An image of John holding Shade as a baby flickers on the screen.

Nora and Shade are both at the hospital when Trudi labors to give birth, along with Hamlet who takes snapshots. Dank's last words reverberate in Trudi's mind as she groans and pushes to get the baby out. The birth of Trudi's little girl soon gives way to sadness, as the adoptive mother looms in the background. As they stare at the baby behind glass, Shade's narration laments the fact that the baby will share their features, but will never actually know them:

> SHADE: The baby had lips just like Trudi. Maybe she would have her same smile. Or maybe she would have Dank's eyes. Or maybe she would have raised her eyebrows just like my mom. Maybe when she started to talk . . . her voice would sound like mine. She'll grow up with her new mom in Dallas. And she will never see where any of her features came from. She will never know Laramie . . . or the desert where she was conceived. She will never know us.

Trudi, however, has not changed much as a result of the experience. She introduces Shade to a new friend, Ivy, a model with whom Trudi plans to share an apartment in Dallas. Shade tries to persuade Trudi to come back home. The story climaxes at ninety-three minutes when Trudi refuses to return to Laramie, thus severing ties to her family.

The resolution follows as Hamlet drives Nora and Shade back in his pickup truck. Shade sees a sign advertising "Natural Day-Glo Rocks—2 Miles Ahead." Shade convinces Nora and Hamlet to drop her off there. Shade accuses the guy of ditching her sister, but it turns out to be a case of mistaken identity. From Cecil and his girlfriend, Shade learns that they obtained the rocks from a British rock hunter, whose abandoned Jeep they had recognized. In a flashback, we see Dank's death in a landslide of dust. Cecil tells Shade that the authorities sent his body and possessions back to England, except for the rocks. When Shade tells them "his girlfriend just had a baby girl," Cecil gives Shade a rock that has four different colors. Shade puts the rock in her purse and walks away into the desert. In voiceover, she poetically sums up the situation:

> SHADE: He didn't leave her. And now, after all that has happened . . . it was the single gesture . . . the one true heart which has already changed the paths of daughters not yet heard from, those not yet born. He was hers till the end. And I'll tell her in time.

The image of Shade, receding into the background, dissolves to black.

Although the three women's stories in *Gas Food Lodging* run on parallel tracks for the most part, their lines of action do intersect

Shade, Nora, and Hamlet return home from the hospital

periodically, largely as a result of coincidence, a strategy more typically found in art cinema. Shade, for instance, first gets to know Javier as a result of Trudi's racist outburst in the diner. She later meets him again in the projection booth of the Spanish-language movie theater as a result of technical problems. She also happens to run into him on the street with his friends after the embarrassing incident with Darius. Shade sees Raymond outside a bar and tries to fix him up with her mother, unaware that her mother's been having a secret affair with him. Shade, however, never meets Dank, the person who figures so prominently in Trudi's life and in the drama of the film. Nevertheless, she turns out to be the only one who finds out the truth about his fate. Shade also runs into her father by accident in a convenience store, then, even more improbably, gets rescued by him at the party. After Shade tells her mother about her discovery, Nora expresses no interest in him.

Even though the stories only overlap intermittently, Shade's deeply sensitive narration really provides the unifying thread in the larger family narrative. Shade's character benefits from two distinct perspectives: her own birth order and the Spanish-language melodramas she sees at the local movie theater. As the younger child, she is able to watch the mistakes of her older sister and learn from them. Not surprisingly, the only advice she receives from Trudi turns out to be misguided, and ends her relationship with Darius. Nora is so preoccupied with her problems with Trudi that she basically ignores Shade.

Shade's visits to the Spanish melodramas, however, provide her with a more idealistic perspective that allows her to look beyond life's disappointments. Both Nora and Trudi have been wounded by previous experiences with men. As a result, they clash with each other throughout the film. Nora breaks off her affair with Raymond because she feels an obligation to be a better role model. She worries about Trudi becoming sexually active, but what she doesn't know is that Trudi has already been damaged by an unreported gang rape. Except for the moment when Trudi reveals this intimate secret to Dank after they have had sex in the ultraviolet light of the cave, neither she nor Nora appear to be very reflective about their lives. Shade, in fact, is the only one who seems capable of providing the proper perspective and understanding about the events that are happening to them, which is why she serves as the film's narrator.

Nora's story revolves around her relations with men, specifically John, Raymond, and Hamlet. But none of these relationships really involves a dramatic conflict. Nora has already decided against Raymond because he's married to someone else, and Hamlet more or less falls into her bed without obstacles or any sense of dramatic struggle. Nora experiences very little conflict whether to pursue the relationship with Hamlet because Hamlet's statement that he's "in it for the long haul" stands in direct contrast to Raymond's and John's transient affections. Nora thus manages to solve her own relationship problems without Shade's help. Although there are no conflicts regarding her romances, Nora's major dramatic conflict actually involves Trudi, whose sexual promiscuity has become a source of concern for her. The conflict between Nora and Trudi centers on the fact that Trudi is obviously repeating the same mistakes as her mother. Trudi presents Nora with a mirror reflection of herself, which is why the two of them cannot get along with each other.

Trudi is not a completely likeable character. She has a negative attitude and proves to be a racist when she calls Javier a "wetback." Trudi also gives Nora and Shade a hard time. She gets her comeuppance when Brett dumps her and the other high school kids ridicule her for being a slut, but the lovemaking experience in the cave manages to soften her. The next morning, Trudi confesses to Dank that her promiscuity results from being gang raped in her first sexual encounter. This revelation provides motivation for her behavior and turns her into a much more sympathetic character.

> TRUDI: But I've been thinking about it a lot lately and think-
>   ing about why I can't say no . . . and why I have to
>   always do it. And I think it's because of my first time.
>   These guys just did what they wanted.
> DANK: What are you saying?
> TRUDI: They pulled a train on me. They gang-banged me. I
>   didn't report it. Are you crazy? Let the whole town
>   know about it? I never told anyone. Not even my
>   mom. I knew their names. Two of them were broth-
>   ers . . . Sonny and Dan Richardson, and Ralph Elli-
>   son. A guy they called Tex. I never saw them again.

Dank moves closer to comfort her.

> TRUDI   (*cont.*): Don't . . . After that, I never said no again.
>   Why bother? They just do it anyway. This was the
>   first time I really wanted to do it. It was the first time
>   I felt anything.

This is exactly the type of scene that Todd Haynes wanted to avoid with Carol White in *Safe* because it provides the audience with a psychological explanation of character. Yet this scene between Trudi and Dank is compelling precisely because of the detachment in Ione Skye's performance. Anders had actually written this direction into the script: "She continues to talk, detached, as if she were talking about something that happened to someone else."[9] In an interview about *Gas Food Lodging*, Anders explains this aspect of the scene: "That's because there's an odd detachment with most survivors of rape and sexual abuse. You have to be detached, otherwise you'll be in a state of hysteria all the time and you won't survive. So I wanted a very detached reading. Ione read the script, saw that and did it just beautifully. She gave Trudi this numbed-out quality which was just right."[10] Anders has also indicated that the scene is autobiographical, and, in fact, that she deliberately chose to use the real names of her actual rapists.[11]

Trudi has become transformed by her brief relationship with Dank, but after he does not return and she discovers she is pregnant, she reverts back to her previous behavior. Trudi squabbles with Nora over how to deal with the situation. Her decision to have the baby and give it up for adoption rather than to have an abortion seems to be a spiteful gesture aimed at her mother, rather than a rational choice. Trudi's desire to stay in Dallas with her new friend, Ivy, only indicates that her pregnancy has not changed her substantially. If anything, it has only cemented her cynicism, as evidenced by her superficial new friend and interest in pursuing a career in modeling.

Gas Food Lodging explores the wounds of a broken family, especially the impact it has on children. Whereas Trudi winds up replicating the mistakes of her mother, Shade develops the mentality of a survivor.

> SHADE: Things don't always work out like you want them to, and in my experience, it almost never does. A lot of people say you're stupid to have expectations on anything. But they're just afraid of disappointment. Me . . . I guess I'm more afraid of not having any daydreams left. I mean, disappointment is easy. You can get over it. But what do you do with yourself, if you can't imagine the future the way you want it to be?

The Mexican melodramas she watches in the rundown Spanish-language theater provide her with a romantic antidote to her own dysfunctional family situation. A husband can threaten to leave his wife, but he cannot actually follow through on it because of the young baby the wife clutches in her arms. This presents a striking contrast to Shade's own family experience. Throughout the film, Shade continues to hold onto the home movie, which shows her as a baby in her father's arms.

Georgia Brown describes *Gas Food Lodging* as a "road movie *négatif*," by which she means that it is the men who get to have the adventures in typical road movies, while it is the women who get stranded by the wayside.[12] In this sense, the title of the film becomes a metaphor for the situation of women, which is to service men's needs at the various rest stops during their journeys. As such, *Gas Food Lodging* is both a family melodrama as well as a contemporary women's picture. This female perspective makes the film both unusual and interesting, even if the women here nonetheless remain romantically attached to men:

> NORA: I can't get it through your head that you're not the
>   only one with a family to protect. My girls are grown
>   up now. I can't be messing with a married man. I got
>   to set some kind of example.
>
> RAYMOND: It seems to me that if I make you feel good that's the
>   type of example that would mean something to your
>   girls. Better than their role model of being a lonely
>   woman.
>
> NORA: Yeah, I get lonely. I do. So, big deal. Women are
>   lonely in the '90s. It's our new phase. We'll live . . .
>   I've been lonelier.

In spurning an affair with Raymond, Nora knows this option only too well, since her last line presumably alludes to the period after John deserted her and their two kids.

All three women in *Gas Food Lodging* end up lonely at one point or another in the film. Trudi winds up in tears after Brett rejects her after their sexual encounter. After Dank forgets his Thermos of coffee on the fender, he tells her, "My mind just walks away sometimes." Trudi responds, "Yeah that's what men do, they walk away." A short time later, after she accepts a ride from Dank, Trudi gets an opportunity to explain the remark further: "Their emotions walk away. Their minds walk away. Everything they say to you walks away. . . . Their promises walk away." Her romantically charged lovemaking with Dank gives Trudi reason for optimism temporarily, but Dank—through no fault of his own—does not return, leaving her ultimately heartbroken and alone. Shade also winds up dejected when Darius completely ignores her after she makes a fool of herself, but Shade manages to recover somehow and to grow as a result of the experience. Shade finds a better relationship with Javier and Nora finds more stability with Hamlet, but neither brings the type of catharsis one might expect. Todd Haynes sees this as being emblematic of melodrama:

> For, despite whatever we might imagine as "melodramatic" con-
> tent, these are really just stories about people falling out of love,
> about marriages and families in struggle, about social regulation
> and desire. In other words, these are stories about most of *us*. And

unlike more respected dramatic forms that hinge on catharsis and breakthrough, classic melodrama is not about overcoming. The women in these films never transcend their conditions, either in thought or in deed. Rarely are we even sure what it is they learn from their struggles. That's because, despite its narrative overdetermination and simplicity, classic melodrama is not prescriptive. If it has a message to proclaim it's always, at the very least, a supremely mixed one.[13]

In *Gas Food Lodging*, the adoption of Trudi's baby seems to overshadow everything else. As such, as Haynes suggests, it represents a continuation rather than rupture or break with the family pattern.

As a contemporary woman's picture, *Gas Food Lodging* is an attempt to provide an intimate glimpse into the lives of women. An example of this occurs in the scene where Shade and Trudi strip the beds and get the clothes together for the ritualistic trip to the laundromat. As the two young women do this, Nora sits on the toilet, complaining, "And who used all the tampons and didn't buy a new box?" Trudi responds, "Not me. I'm the dominant female in this house. You're both following my cycle." Just as Nora folds toilet paper to use in place of a sanitary napkin, Shade announces that she has bought some. Trudi then grabs Shade's metal canister containing her home movie, teasing her that it contains birth-control pills. After Shade demands it back, the two get into a shoving match in which Shade gets hurt. When Trudi laughs, this upsets Shade even more. As the sisters each blame each other for starting the ruckus, Nora enters and comments to Trudi, "I can always depend on you to cause trouble." Such a scene neither expands character nor advances the plot. It is not even expositional because it fails to provide us with any new information— we already know that there is tension between the sisters and that Trudi causes Nora trouble. Nor does the scene have multiple functions in the way Seger advocates. But rather the purpose of this scene is to provide a sense of the texture of the daily lives of this all-female household, which includes petty squabbling and mundane talk of such female things as stockings, sanitary napkins, and birth-control pills.

Nora's love scene with Hamlet also discusses sex from a decidedly female perspective. After they make love, Hamlet questions his performance. Nora tells him it was great. Still insecure, he offers to make it better.

> NORA: It was fine. It really was. I think it has to do with get-
> ting used to a man . . . getting used to his body . . .
> position . . . the size. Oh, the size is great. The body's
> great.
> HAMLET: That just leaves position.

Lovemaking thus becomes a means to discuss gender issues about performance anxiety in men, penis size, female orgasm, and position—all
from a woman's point of view.

As the above two scenes should indicate, not all scenes function to
advance the plot, nor do the characters in *Gas Food Lodging* have the
clearly defined goals found in most conventional screenplays. The film
has a great deal of romance, but is very short on actual conflict since it
lacks a clearly defined antagonist other than fate. The richly drawn
female characters do change, but it is difficult to talk about a "transformational arc" (Seger's term) or "character arc" (McKee's term)—in
other words, plotted changes in character—when the goals of the
characters are continually shifting. Nora does find an available and
good-natured man in Hamlet and Trudi does wind up escaping from
Laramie, but Shade's overriding goal of having a normal family never
works out. At the end of the film, Trudi has given her baby away and
refuses to return home, thus putting an end to Shade's familial dream.
Shade uncovers information about the fate of Dank, but there is not a
real sense of closure or resolution in the end. Shade's final narration is
extremely ambiguous. It does not really serve to tie up the loose ends
of the story proper, but instead projects Dank's true heart onto the fate
of future daughters.

Gas Food Lodging privileges romance over dramatic conflict.
Anders provides an interesting twist on the road movie, switching the
emphasis of the genre from one of movement to one of stasis. The film
also shifts the inherent gendered point of view of the road movie from
the men who take the journeys to that of the women who get left
behind. Anders does succeed in continually shifting the goals of her
characters along with the various plotlines she sets up. This not only
undermines the whole notion of the goal-driven protagonist, but also
results in a more open-ended, multiple-plot structure. Together with
its uniquely female perspective, it is exactly these twists and turns away
from classical narrative convention that help Anders to establish the
film's highly personal and distinctive tone.

Chapter 6

The Ensemble Structure of *Me and You and Everyone We Know*

In her first feature, *Me and You and Everyone We Know* (2005), which won major awards at both Cannes and Sundance, Miranda July employs a particular form of the multiple-plot film, which is often referred to as the "ensemble" film. Instead of focusing on a single protagonist, ensemble films disperse the narrative through various separate story lines involving multiple characters. In such a structure, it is often difficult to isolate a main protagonist because the various characters are frequently accorded equal weight and screen time, and they function as protagonists in their own separate lines of action. The various lines of action proceed in parallel directions, which then intersect and crisscross— sometimes only tangentially—at strategic points in the story, and reinforce each other through overt thematic links. Although multiple-plot films, and ensemble films in particular, are by no means a contemporary development, such structures have become increasingly popular in recent years despite most manuals' fixation on stories that involve only single protagonists.[1] Robert Altman's *Nashville* (1975) is generally regarded as a classic example of an ensemble film, but many independent films—from *Happiness* (1998) and *Thirteen Conversations About One Thing* (2001) to *Me and You and Everyone We Know*—employ this type of structure.

Ensemble films differ from classical Hollywood films in several important ways. The setup of an ensemble film often takes much longer to establish the numerous main characters, as well as their various lines of action. Because such a structure necessitates that a large number of characters need to be introduced rather quickly, we often get snapshots of the characters rather than the type of gradual character development and detailed exposition more typically found in both classical and art cinema. The quick portrait employed in ensemble films also provides less opportunity to motivate the behavior of the different characters. Todd Haynes, for instance, uses a sense of duration derived from art cinema to construct a portrait of Carol White through a gradual buildup of the texture and details of her sanitized life. The Coens spend a good deal of time motivating Jerry's behavior in the first act of *Fargo*, especially when we meet his father-in-law and view his family situation. In contrast, many ensemble films rely on sketches of more recognizable character types. July's *Me and You and Everyone We Know* features the kooky artist, the uptight museum curator, the jilted husband, two Internet-fixated kids, an adult who flirts dangerously with sex-obsessed teenagers, a ten-year-old enraptured with consumer products, and a love-struck elderly man.

Simple multiple-plot films such as *Trust* and *Gas Food Lodging* have two or three main characters, but *Me and You and Everyone We Know* actually involves ten different main characters, as well as nine separate lines of action. Todd Solondz explains the ensemble structure of *Happiness*, a film which has an equally large number of story lines, in practical terms: "I had a bunch of different story ideas, and I couldn't make up my mind which one I wanted to make a movie about. I wasn't willing to do one over the other, so I figured out a way to combine them, hoping that they would cohere and play off each other."[2] Even the three Jordan sisters, Solondz maintains, became a plot contrivance "to thread different stories together." For him, the thematic links between the different story strands were of greater importance. July describes the process of writing her script as accumulative or accretive. Rather than thinking of the screenplay in terms of dramatic conflict and the intricacies of plot, July conceived of it as building "an ensemble cast" of characters:

> The main thing was sort of like, "Oh, if I were to ever write a feature, probably for my first one it would be best to just not come up with a plot that I'd have to fill out," given that I have no idea how to write a screenplay. It's better to just make a space where I could just keep writing stuff every day, based on what I was feeling that day. And keep adding characters and learn as I go how to make it become a single story.[3]

In her preference for character over plot, greater concern for texture and detail, and her "connect-the-dots" approach to story structure, July, of course, sounds very much like Jarmusch and Anders, but she deviates from them by opting to make an ensemble piece.

Unlike Jarmusch, Haynes, or Anders, July's characters have clearly defined goals that remain consistent throughout the film. Christine Jesperson (Miranda July) has two intersecting goals that reinforce each other. She wants to get her performance video shown at the local art museum and she develops an instant crush on Richard Swersey, a shoe salesman she meets at the department store. From the moment Christine meets Richard, she becomes so smitten by him that she verges on becoming a stalker; whereas, because his recent separation from his wife, Pam, causes him to suffer a loss of self-esteem, Richard is understandably ambivalent about starting a new relationship with a stranger. Christine receives encouragement from Michael, her Elder Cab client, who insists on her being assertive in the pursuit of what she really wants in life, thus reinforcing her goal-driven behavior.

In a major gender reversal, the women in *Me and You and Every One We Know* tend to be the main instigators or initiators of the film's action. Not only does Christine charge after Richard impetuously, but Heather and Rebecca engage their fourteen-year-old classmate Peter in a contest to see which of them is better at fellatio. They are the ones fully in control of the sex act, as they order him to get washcloths, a towel, sweets, and mood music (which they provide when he doesn't have the CD). In addition, they set the boundaries of his behavior, forcing him to lie passively with a pillow over his head, while a young neighbor, Sylvie, lurks voyeuristically outside the window. Heather and Rebecca also provoke the sexual fantasies of Andrew, Richard's neighbor and coworker, who tacks obscene notes about them on his apartment windows. When the two girls later decide to lose their virginity with the older man, Andrew panics and hides from them. Nancy Herrington, the stern museum curator, also engages Richard's kids in an Internet chat room by sharing her sexual fantasies, including Robby's childlike one involving the exchange of poop, and she eventually entices him to meet her on a park bench. In July's film, it is the kids, rather than the adults, who turn out to be even more intrigued and obsessed by the mystery of sex. Such a view reverses and, hence, subverts the prevailing myth of childhood innocence that so permeates contemporary American culture. In this respect, *Me and You and*

Everyone We Know tackles taboo subject matter previously explored by Todd Solondz in such films as *Welcome to the Dollhouse* (1995) and *Happiness*.

The pedophilic content of *Welcome to the Dollhouse* somehow managed to be overlooked by both critics and the moviegoing public, but Solondz's next effort, *Happiness*, made such denial impossible by turning it into a central trait of his main character, Bill Maplewood. Despite winning the International Critics Prize for Best Film at Cannes, *Happiness* was dropped by its distributor, October Films, after receiving pressure from its parent companies, Universal and Seagram, prior to commercial release. Recent changes in pornography laws brought about by the pervasive influence of the Internet made the film's original distributors extremely apprehensive about handling such risky material. In the case of *Happiness*, as well as with films such as Harmony Korine and Larry Clark's *Kids* (1995) and David Cronenberg's *Crash* (1996), the issue was not government censorship, but really "self-censorship" on the part of the film's production and distribution company, or more specifically, its more image-conscious parent companies. Ron Meyer, Universal's chief executive officer, reportedly fumed about *Happiness*: "I don't want to understand the mind of a pedophile. I don't want that to be part of this company."[4] Yet such a view clashes with the admitted intentions of the film's coproducer, Christine Vachon, who defended the independent film precisely on the grounds of its subversive content. "*Happiness*, like all groundbreaking films," she insisted, "is provocative and cutting-edge."[5]

James Schamus, the executive producer of *Happiness*, offers his own interpretation of why Seagram was worried about its subsidiary distributing the film:

> While Universal executives were pleased with the overwhelming positive response to *Happiness* at Cannes, word of the film's potentially controversial subject matter was causing concern. Seagram is a publicly traded corporation whose primary business at the time of the screening was in the "consumer goods" sector—in this case, the tricky alcoholic beverage market. With significant regulatory legislation pending in the United States, and with a stock share price deflated by worries on Wall Street about the wisdom of the company's entry into the entertainment business (Seagram had partially financed its purchase of MCA/Universal with the sale of the stock in DuPont—stock that subsequently skyrocketed in

value while Universal's value stayed relatively flat), executives were feeling vulnerable to the possibility that right-wing and Christian organizations might target the company's products for a consumer boycott should the film incite much controversy.[6]

October found itself in an awkward and difficult situation vis-à-vis its parent company, and eventually made a deal for the production company Good Machine to distribute it instead. As *Variety* commented about October's decision not to release *Happiness*, a film that it financed: "In this era of proliferating studio-owned indies, the move points up the hazards that independents face from studio corporate culture with the often-dicey content and subject matter of their pics."[7]

By flirting with taboo subject matter, *Me and You and Everyone We Know* ran into similar difficulties in attempting to obtain financing. According to July:

> I know now that it's sort of like an indie success story in that it took us nine months. But those were nine really hard months of really going to everyone and everyone passing. Everyone other than the two companies that made it passed. And that's a lot of rejection everyday. The reasons people passed were so obvious. I wouldn't attach stars. I wanted to play the lead, a child's sexuality, an ensemble cast. It's just endless the excuses you could have to not make it.[8]

Despite the fact that July's film includes pedophilia, coprophilia, voyeurism, and the sexuality of children, there's an innocence to the way *Me and You and Everyone We Know* handles the material that's very different from Solondz's more cynical treatment. For one thing, Bill Maplewood is an unrepentant sexual predator in *Happiness*. With Solondz, there is a deliberate attempt to be provocative, whereas July disarms the shock and impact of sex in an Internet chat room, teenage fellatio, or adult fantasies about children with both sympathy and humor. While indulging in sexual fantasies with teenagers, Andrew is acting inappropriately and illegally, but the girls initially pursue him, and he never follows through once the opportunity arises. When Richard tells him that it takes a village to raise a child, Andrew punctures that platitude by raising the specter of junkies and child molesters in the community, even though, on the latter issue, he might be alluding to himself. Nancy's meeting with Robby is sad and touching, especially when she gives him a kiss. She naively expects that she's been communicating with an adult in the chat room. Nancy's not really a sexual predator, but rather a sad and lonely single woman.

Miranda July's previous video shorts, which were screened largely within an art world rather than a commercial context, are actually more provocative and disturbing than her first feature. *Nest of Tens* (2000) and *Getting Stronger Every Day* (2001), for instance, both deal with the issue of child molestation.[9] The latter video involves a narration by a man named Stephen. He discusses two separate TV movie story lines—one about a child named Stephen being molested, and the other about a child being abducted by aliens—in which the two kids have difficulties being reintegrated back into their families. As Stephen narrates the two stories, a woman lies on a bed with a huge cat and a little girl lies on the floor of the bathroom with a stuffed animal over her face. It seems to be a dysfunctional family, in which no one talks to each other. All three of them appear to be under the spell of a mysterious outside and elusive force in the form of a mutating shape that casts a bright light on them. Stephen returns to the story of the molested child, who marries someone from his second-grade class. Confusing the actress with the character, he describes her drowning in milk inside a huge Cheerio in *Honey, I Shrunk the Kids* (1989). He indicates that Stephen is a very messed up man, who "just needed love from someone his own age." The film ends with an image of the woman, whose body is covered by the huge, fluffy cat, whose tail covers her genital area. Unified through cutting and Stephen's narration, the characters remain separate spatially. The film is deliberately ambiguous, but a viewer can't help but wonder whether this Stephen is the same person described in the TV movie. The connection between the twin themes of child molestation and alien abduction bears a striking resemblance to Gregg Araki's indie feature *Mysterious Skin* (2005), which was based on Scott Heim's novel of the same title.

Nest of Tens creates a parallel structure between the four lines of action. One involves a young girl named Molly who discovers that her mother has brought home a strange man. Molly's mother and new boyfriend, Steve, sit in a living room, and try to arouse each other sexually, while the little girl watches television. This clearly causes Molly to feel insecure and uncomfortable. A second story line involves a developmentally disabled man's public reading and discussion of various phobias. When a woman in the audience asks him about mistaken identity, his examples revealingly suggest that molestation can result from confusing your mother with another woman. This connects with

July's reference to *Psycho*, which introduces a third plotline about a boy in a blue shirt. His bizarre ritual involves a naked baby girl who lies on a blanket, with her genitals and buttocks exposed, as if she's ready to get her diaper changed. The boy performs a cleaning ritual and writes down zeroes and ones on a piece of paper, which he tapes to the arms of an office chair. As heavy music blares on the soundtrack, the boy presses the numbers on the paper as if he's controlling the baby's bodily movements.

In the fourth line of action, a young girl at the airport reverses the power relations between adults and children, especially in sexual matters, by twice simulating a vagina with the folded skin on her arm, and by demanding that a business traveler named Helen (played by July) acknowledge what it looks like, as well as indicate her preference for the first or second one. The girl takes one of Helen's hairs from her head and blows it into the air. White lines appear over images of people moving about the airport, as if charting out the path of the hair, eventually forming the shape of a heart. The white line seems to follow a man as he walks outside, before heading into space.

Through voiceover and intercutting between the four story lines that comprise *Nest of Tens*, July creates thematic and associative connections between and among the various characters. Otherwise the film's plotlines remain separate and don't intersect and come together in terms of the interactions of any of the characters. A simple parallel structure is much less conventional than the type of ensemble structure July employs in her first feature. *Nest of Tens* utilizes incident, but it doesn't have an overarching plot, which pushes it closer to being an experimental film. Despite the difficulties in raising financing for the film, July's experience at both the Sundance Writing Institute and Sundance Directing Workshop might account for the fact that *Me and You and Everyone We Know* employs a three-act structure, extensive use of motifs, genre elements, and a happy ending as concessions to both commerce and convention. In *Me and You and Everyone We Know*, art, sex, and the Internet provide the connecting links between July's various characters. They provide us with a composite view of a neighborhood, which Peter demonstrates at one point through the symbols of his digital aerial diagram. As Peter tells Robby: "This is me and you and everyone we know," suggesting that the film will be a "network narrative" or "web of life" plot, two other terms that have been applied to the structure of the ensemble film.[10]

Christine makes her video

Me and You and Everyone We Know begins with Christine, who is video recording the voiceover for a photographic still of a couple on the beach at sunset: "If you really love me, then let's make a vow, right here, together, right here. Okay? I'm going to live each day as if it were my last. Fantastically. Courageously. With grace." Christine not only says the lines, but also assumes the role of an imaginary male partner in repeating them. Meanwhile, Richard, who is separating from his wife and moving out of the house, approaches Peter and his seven-year-old brother, Robby, and asks whether he looks "like a guy who might have a wife and kids and stuff?" From Christine reciting her monologue—"And in the dark of the night, and it does get dark, when I call a name. It'll be your name"—the camera pans outside to Richard, who, in an attempt to get his kids' attention, pours lighter fluid on his hand and sets it on fire. When Christine later asks him what happened to his bandaged hand, Richard offers two versions. She first opts for the longer explanation, in which he explains, "I was trying to save my life, and it didn't work." When she then asks for the second, he simply tells her, "I burned it."

In the first act, we're introduced to the various characters. Besides Christine, Richard, Peter, and Robby, we meet Michael, who's madly in love with a woman named Ellen. As Richard and his kids carry empty cartons out of their new house, we glimpse ten-year-old Sylvie, spying on them from next door. At the shoe store, we meet Andrew. After Richard sells Michael a pair of blue sneakers, he talks Christine into buying pink shoes, despite her complaints about having "low ankles," which cause her feet to hurt. He tells her, "People think foot pain is a fact of life, but life is better than that." Michael chimes in, "Your whole life could be better. Starting right now."

As they drive home, Christine regrets buying the shoes, but Michael soon notices that a father and his daughter have left a newly purchased goldfish in a plastic bag of water on the hood of their car. Christine wants to get the man's attention, but Michael argues that doing so will cause it to fall off. Recognizing the goldfish's impending doom, Christine offers some last words: "I didn't know you, but I want you to die knowing you were loved. I love you." The car slams on its brakes, causing the goldfish to fly off the roof and onto the back hood of another passing car. Michael pulls in front of the car in order to keep it at a steady speed as the father and his daughter watch in horror from behind, but the inevitable happens. The three-minute sequence does not serve to develop the plot, but it nevertheless emphasizes the fragility of life and creates a thematic link to Christine's desire to live it to the fullest, and to Richard's and Michael's similar life-affirming

Richard talks with Peter and Robby

statements at the shoe store. The death of the goldfish, and Christine's desire to love it, even though a stranger, will reignite her desire for Richard, a person whom she doesn't really know either.

As Richard discusses his marriage with Andrew, he has an epiphany similar to the one Christine expressed in her video.

> RICHARD: I don't want to have to do this living. I just walk around. I want to be swept off my feet, you know? I want my children to have magical powers. I am prepared for amazing things to happen. I can handle it.

At Michael's instigation, Christine attempts to submit her video directly to the curator at the museum, Nancy Herrington, who refuses to accept it, even when Christine drops it on the floor in the elevator and it ends up in the assistant curator's hands.

Christine's visit to the art museum provides July, a highly accomplished and well-known multimedia and performance artist, with an opportunity to parody the art world. The local museum of contemporary art has an exhibition of forty years of war photography, entitled "Shock and Awe." After Christine leaves, Nancy and her assistant visit a gallery where an artist is installing a new show. Nancy stares at a hamburger wrapper on the floor, admiring how "real" it looks. The artist responds, "Oh, that wrapper is real." He claims that he always mixes in a few real objects in order to "cast a glow over the plaster objects." Nancy picks up a coffee cup that has a picture of a cat and insists it's hers, but the artist responds: "No, I made that." Later, in the middle act, when Nancy and her assistant are judging Christine's submission, she asks, "Is she of color?" Her assistant answers: "No. But she's a woman." When she realizes it's Christine's piece, she asks, "Didn't we already show a local person this year?" She then rejects it, and discusses her criteria for the slides: "All right, what we need to ask ourselves about each one of these is: Could this have been made in any era, or only now?"

Epiphanies continue to drive the characters in the first act. While retrieving his morning newspaper, Andrew runs into Heather and Rebecca, who pretend to be eighteen-year-old lesbian sisters:

> ANDREW: I would love to believe in a universe where you wake up and you don't have to go to work and you step outside and meet two beautiful eighteen-year-old sisters, who are also girlfriends and . . . are also very nice people.

Heather asks him what he'd do if they actually were eighteen. He says, "I can't talk dirty to you because then I'd be a pervert and probably even a pedophile too, so . . ." After Andrew, who doesn't have to work until the afternoon, goes inside, he watches them from his window. Heather waves, turns around, lifts her skirt, and exposes her under-pants. She suggests to Rebecca that Andrew's probably masturbating. When Rebecca asks how she can tell, Heather indicates the huge crack in the building beneath his window. She says, "See that crack? That's where his hard-on is." The two teens then kiss to try to excite him even more. They also later taunt Peter on the way home, but then see Andrew's sign taped to his window, "First I would tell you both to take off your shirts so I could get a look at your sweet little nipples."

The pedophilic theme gets reinforced as Peter and Robby respond to someone in an Internet chat room, who writes, "I'm wearing pants and a blouse." Robby, of course, is too young to understand, but Peter tries to set him straight by suggesting that gender is a very fluid con-cept in cyberspace. Peter tells him: "So imagine a fat guy with a little wiener." In what has become one of the most hilarious scenes in any recent contemporary film, Robby offers up his own sexual fantasy involving the back-and-forth exchange of poop, forever. To Peter's sur-prise, the fantasy gets the person on the other end very aroused.

Christine returns to the shoe store and attaches socks to her ears in an effort to get Richard's attention. When Richard leaves work, Chris-tine chases after him. Their walk to their respective cars turns into a metaphor for their imagined relationship, after she learns that he's recently separated from his wife. The point where they'll part, Tyrone Street, becomes an important marker. He suggests that it represents twenty years, but she trumps him: "Okay. Well, actually I was thinking Tyrone is, like, when we die of old age. And this is, like our whole life together, this block." After this, an awkwardness sets in, similar to what occurs between Willie and Eva in *Stranger Than Paradise* and, when Christine and Richard reach Tyrone, they go their separate ways. Richard drives off, but Christine suddenly appears and hops into his car. He freaks out: "What are you doing in my car? No, I don't know you, and you certainly don't know anything about me. I mean, what if I'm a killer of children?" Richard objects to her fairy-tale conception of him. Christine is devastated by this turn of events, as he demands: "Can you get out of my car now?" At thirty-five minutes, this signals the first turning point, which represents both the beginning and end of

Richard and Christine walk toward Tyrone Street

their relationship—all of which, rather bizarrely, occurs within the span of five minutes.

Besides the two plotlines involving Christine's career and romantic ambitions, six other plot threads have been introduced in the first act. These include Richard's struggle to be a single father and relate to his estranged kids, Michael's desire for Ellen, Andrew's fascination with Heather and Rebecca, the two girls' harassment of Peter, Peter and Robby's escapades in the Internet chat room, and Robby's fascination to find the source of a mysterious sound. One other new plotline gets introduced in the middle act, and this involves Peter's infatuation with Sylvie. Following his sexual experience, which has caused him to reflect on the picture of his once happy family, somewhat surprisingly, Peter has no further contact with either Heather or Rebecca. Although Sylvie watched Peter receive oral sex from outside the window, she never reveals this secret. After Peter later gets sick and Richard is too busy at work, Sylvie's mother picks him up at school. When Sylvie gets home, she finds Peter sleeping on the couch. The framing of her entrance suggests that Sylvie is attracted by his genitals, but she leaves abruptly. While at her house, Peter learns that Sylvie, who earlier played the role of a mother bird feeding worms to her babies, has a hope chest full of consumer products she's been accumulating for her future husband and daughter. Toward the end of the middle act, Peter asks her about her hope chest in front of two friends, but Sylvie feigns ignorance.

As the sheer number of actions in *Me and You and Everyone We Know* indicates, ensemble films have a somewhat different structure than the one suggested by the traditional three-act paradigm. For one thing, there are enough significant events occurring at regular intervals to maintain audience interest over the course of a film. The chief means of sustaining that audience interest occurs through the repeated use of what Kristin Thompson refers to as a "dangling cause," which she describes as "information or action which leads to no effect or resolution until later in the film." As Thompson argues, "Many such dangling causes typically stitch a classical narrative together," but their use becomes even more exaggerated in ensemble films.[11] A dangling cause becomes a very useful device for cutting away from a story line at a particularly suspenseful moment, as we see in July's handling of Heather and Rebecca's decision to have sex with Andrew, Robby's rendezvous with the mysterious person on the Internet, or Michael's revelation to Christine about Ellen.

In a romantic comedy, such as *Me and You and Everyone We Know*, the middle act usually provides the obstacles that will prevent the two lovers from coming together, but that doesn't happen here because Richard's separation from Pam makes him available, even if he's hesitant to become involved with Christine initially. Michael, for instance, asks Christine about the shoe salesman, but she tells him: "It turns out he's a killer of children. So, oh, well." She nevertheless returns to the shoe store, gets Richard to help her repair her compact mirror, and after he suggests going for coffee sometime, gives him her Elder Cab card. As Christine's romantic plotline reopens, the one involving her career appears to end as her video piece is rejected by Nancy at the museum. Richard actually dials Christine's number, but, when Andrew asks whether Robby's old enough to walk home alone, Richard hangs up and rushes home, only to find both of his kids already there.

Christine's career plotline shifts unexpectedly, as Nancy re-watches her video, which addresses the curator by name. Christine assumes that Nancy has a successful personal life—family, kids, and a dog—and makes her piece "interactive" by asking Nancy to call her and say "macaroni" to indicate that she's actually viewed it. As Christine stews about Richard and waits to hear from him, Nancy calls and

says the code word. Christine learns from Michael that Ellen has broken up with him because she's going to die. As the two discuss it,
Michael tells her, "I've long since stopped trying to make people do
things they don't want to do." Christine protests, "But she's the love of
your life. You're just going to let her go?" Michael's revelation provides the motivation for Christine to return to the shoe store. When
she sees Richard and Pam conversing, Christine jealously shoves a
talking picture frame that says "I love you" at Pam, before storming
off. The picture frame connects to a self-affirming shirt of Pam's that
Richard earlier found annoying. Christine curses everyone, including
old people, children, and peace, as she drives through the neighborhood with "Fuck" written on the front windshield of her car. At seventy minutes, her failure to reconnect with Richard represents the
second turning point.

Linda J. Cowgill suggests: "In ensemble films, the strongest climax
often comes at the end of Act Two instead of Act Three."[12] In Solondz's
Happiness, for instance, the second turning point occurs when Johnny
Grasso's rape is confirmed by his father's outburst at the hospital.
From this point on, it is only a matter of time before Bill Maplewood
will be caught. Even though Bill strikes again by stalking and raping
Ronald Farber after this, the confirmation of the first rape serves as a
much stronger climax than the one at the end of act three, when Bill
admits to his son what he has done. While Cowgill's point applies to
Happiness, it is only partially true in the case of *Me and You and Everyone We Know*. Christine achieves success in her career plotline at the
end of the second act, but not in the romantic one. *Me and You and
Everyone We Know* is eighty-six minutes long, excluding the final credits, and turns out to have a first act of thirty-five minutes, a second act
of thirty-five minutes, and a very short third act of sixteen minutes.
The first act takes longer than in most films because so many different
characters have to be introduced. The middle act is short because there
are not the usual escalating obstacles blocking the characters' desires.
Besides its focus on Christine's career ambitions and the rekindling of
her relationship with Richard, the middle act simply develops the plotlines of the other characters, including Peter's new fascination with
Sylvie.

The various plotlines resolve rather quickly in the third act.
Andrew hides from Heather and Rebecca, who turn up at his house
intent on losing their virginity. Estranged from his two kids after

Peter and Sylvie

yelling at them over the scare involving Robby, Richard takes off his
bandage; Peter and Robby accompany him on a walk through the
neighborhood and end up singing a religious hymn. After Peter buys
Sylvie a present for her hope chest, she lays him down on the rug and
offers her vision of her future family life. Nancy finally meets her
cyberspace partner, who turns out to be Robby. Michael accompanies
Christine to her show at the museum. Earlier, Christine had borrowed
a photo from Ellen, which she uses to create a piece based on Michael's
desire to take her to see Mayan ruins. In the video, she plays Ellen and
it becomes a eulogy for the deceased woman. While at the museum,
Richard finally calls and invites Christine to meet his sons. She asks,
"Can we do that right now?" The film climaxes as the two of them
finally get together. It resolves when Robby discovers the source of the
strange tapping noise.

   Visual and verbal motifs, as Kristin Thompson points out, are
devices whose function is to provide "overall unity and clarity" in classical storytelling.[13] This is another example of how July creates a delicate
blend of both conventional and unconventional elements in *Me and You
and Everyone We Know*. The notion of touching, for example, becomes a
crucial way of connecting the various characters. In Christine's initial
video, she says: "All right. Now let's kiss to make it real, okay?" She kisses

her own hand to simulate the kiss, which causes her to feel even more frustrated. When Christine first meets Richard at the shoe store, he insists to Michael that he never touches the customer's feet anymore.

> RICHARD: No. No, we don't touch the foot anymore. If you notice, we spend a lot of time touching the shoe—lacing the shoe—then we just put it on the ground and watch you try to get your foot in. We can hand you tools—a shoehorn, a nylon sock—but we will never touch your foot with our hand. Now, I'll tell you what I can do. I can press on the shoe to see if it fits.

Christine, who's been watching, encourages him to touch Michael's foot through the prophylactic blue sneaker. Richard, of course, has a bandage on his hand from burning it, so he can't really touch anyone with it either, which becomes another motif. During the fellatio contest between Heather and Rebecca, touching once again becomes an issue. Like a professional prostitute, Heather outlines the rules: "You can't touch us. You can't touch our heads. And we're not going to touch each other." Rebecca adds, "And you have to tell us when you're going to 'scooch.'" Heather also washes Peter's penis before performing oral sex. When it's Rebecca's turn, she insists that it be wiped off to avoid being exposed to Heather's germs.

In Christine's video of the two pink shoes, one representing "me" and the other "you," she films her feet tentatively touching each other. When Nancy judges the submissions for her digital show, she stares at her coffee cup that's being used by the artist installing his new show. Her assistant is also skeptical about a piece that obviously references AIDS by suggesting that they already have photos of e-mails. Nancy responds: "E-mail wouldn't even exist if it weren't for AIDS. Fear of contamination. Fear of bodily fluids." In the Internet chat room, the person, later revealed to be Nancy, comments that Robby's mention of excrement makes her want to touch herself. His diagram of the bodily exchange of poop provokes her to want to meet him. Later, she'll ask him again, "Are you touching yourself?" Robby looks at his two thumbs that happen to be pressed together, and answers, "Yes." After Nancy discovers she's been chatting in cyberspace with a young child, their kiss will soften Nancy and provide her with a title for her show: "Warm: 3-D and Touch in the Digital Age." Finally, after Richard calls Christine, she places her hand on his formerly bandaged one. Interestingly, the two don't kiss, as usually occurs at the end of a romantic comedy. She positions herself behind him rather than facing him. Their clothed bodies press against each other, and their eyes close, referencing Richard's earlier description of the early stages in his marriage, when he and Pam would simply sleep like babies. Andrew also appropriates this fantasy in his obscene posting to the teenage girls.

Birds serve as another prominent motif. In the first act, a bird links Christine and Richard. Christine uses seagulls on the soundtrack of her sunset fantasy, while Richard stares at a bird on a tree branch as we hear Christine's romantic voiceover narration. Richard's wife, Pam, gives Richard a framed photograph of a bird, which Robbie will later scribble on. Sylvie plays a game in which the other neighborhood kids lie on the ground in a circle. She asks Robby, "You want to be a little bird and get a little worm? Just lie down and peep." Robby does this, but, as soon as she gives him the treat, he gets up and flies away. As Richard straightens up the house after he's called and invited Christine to meet his kids, he tries to hide the bird photo in the bushes, but Christine catches him and suggests inserting it into a nearby tree.

July also uses circular shapes as a visual motif. In the middle act, as Richard stares at the moon, Christine reflects a moonlike beam from her compact mirror at the various displays in the shoe store, where she imagines Richard standing with his bandaged hand. As she manipulates the compact, the mirror falls to the ground and bounces on the floor of the shoe store during the daytime. Robby also provides Richard with an elaborate verbal description of the circular metal chore wheel they have at his mom's house. Peter will serve Heather and Rebecca two round peppermint candies on towels prior to the fellatio contest. Peter depicts Robby and him as two round dots in his digital rendering of their neighborhood, and Christine will draw circles around individual letters in a book, spelling out the word "ring," as she desperately waits for Richard to call her. Throughout the film, Robby has been perplexed and mesmerized by a tapping sound he hears. His father dismisses it as something that occurs early in the morning, only Robby's never been up to hear it. His mother tells him, "It's the lights, Robby. See these street lights. They're run by a big computer that tells them when to go on and off. That's what that sound is." Robby finally investigates on his own. It turns out to be a nervous commuter banging a quarter on the metal street sign. Robby asks, "What are you doing that for?" The man responds, "I'm just passing the time." The rising sun showers his face with a warm glow. As the bus arrives, the man hands him the circular quarter. Robby looks at the sun and bangs the coin against the street sign as the sun continues its morning ascent.

While many independent filmmakers employ realism as an alternative to the staged contrivance of classical Hollywood, July's characters are rooted not in realism but in a kind of surrealism that owes a debt to the cinema of Luis Buñuel. In terms of motivation, for instance, it's never very clear what attracts Christine to Richard, other than the fact that she might have a Buñuel-like shoe fetish, she identifies with his wounded hand, or he happens to be the first person she meets after making her inspirational video. Her desire for some type of intimacy is so intense and profound that, like her surrealist forbears, Christine seems to represent an unrepressed id. In the scene where Christine and Richard imagine their lives together as they head toward Tyrone Street, she's dressed in a striped outfit that recalls the striped box carried by the bicyclist in Buñuel and Dalí's surrealist classic *Un Chien Andalou* (1928). There is no coyness, no attempt on her part to hide her attraction, no superego ready to intervene, so that she comes to embody our own most secret desires. July's obsessed characters verge on being lunatics—human beings responding to mysterious impulses beyond their rational control—whether it be Richard setting his hand on fire, Christine eulogizing a dead goldfish, Andrew writing obscene notes to teenagers, or Nancy sharing porn fantasies in an Internet chat room. However, it's really the elaborately intricate and flexible ensemble structure of *Me and You and Everyone We Know* that allows July to present a broad spectrum of characters within a neighborhood. Despite having to juggle so many different characters, the film's ultimate strength lies in its ability to create a composite portrait of this group of lonely adults and children who flounder about in search for some type of intimacy and human connection in an otherwise impersonal digital age.

Part Three

Temporal Structures

Chapter 7

The Flashback Structure
of *Reservoir Dogs*

Quentin Tarantino has criticized the notion of cinema's inherent linearity, arguing that he's simply applying techniques of the novel to film. Rather than employing flashbacks, Tarantino claims to be reshuffling the sequence of the narrative events in his films:

> It's *not* a flashback. Novels go back and forth all the time. You read a story about a guy who's doing something or in some situation and, all of a sudden, chapter five comes and it takes Henry, one of the guys, and it shows you seven years ago, where he was seven years ago and how he came to be and then like, *boom*, the next chapter, *boom*, you're back in the flow of the action. Is that a flashback? . . . It's like they apply terms to movies that they don't to novels. It helps put handcuffs on movies . . . I like the revealing of information and deciding what I'm gonna reveal and when I'm gonna reveal it. I think a certain suspense comes from that."[1]

Tarantino's argument seems to be aimed at the fact that flashbacks are traditionally motivated as character memory, as happens in *Memento* when Leonard Shelby talks about his deceased wife or Sammy Jankis. What Tarantino criticizes as "putting handcuffs on movies" is actually the negative associations the term "flashback" has taken on in the manuals, which often refuse to acknowledge that a film, like a novel, also has the ability to switch and mix tenses. Yet this is exactly what Tarantino does so masterfully in his directorial debut, *Reservoir Dogs* (1992), a postmodern amalgam of Hong Kong cinema–inspired violence, pop culture references, and gangster-genre poetics reminiscent of Jean-Pierre Melville. Tarantino's scrambled-time structure adds greater complexity to the narration of *Reservoir Dogs* by finding a more inventive way to tell this story than through strict linear progression.

Reservoir Dogs ignores many of the supposed rules of good screenwriting, especially concerning the use of flashbacks. Syd Field, for example, acknowledges the device can be "used to expand the audience's comprehension of story, characters, and situation" but he nevertheless considers it "a dated technique." Field maintains that "Your story should be executed in action, not flashback."[2] He considers it a technique to avoid unless a really creative way can be found to employ it. Richard Walter has similar mixed reactions to the flashback, which he considers "a much abused screenwriting conceit."[3] Linda Seger's strong objections to the flashback center on it as a technique for revealing character motivation. She writes:

> Flashbacks as a means to explain motivation rarely work well. This is true for a number of reasons. First of all, motivation is meant to push the character forward. Flashbacks, by their nature, stop the action because they find the motivation in a distant past, rather than in the immediate present. If the motivation really happened long ago, the character would have been in the story long ago. Real motivation happens in the present time. It might be the last in a series of incidents that happen, but motivation happens when the character is ready. It happens now. It's imminent. It's present.[4]

Despite her reservations, Seger concedes: "Some flashbacks are necessary for thematic purposes or to serve the style of the film."[5] To his credit, Robert McKee takes the most open stance on the issue of flashbacks, pointing out that they can be employed either well or poorly. He cites *Reservoir Dogs* as an example of a film that utilizes the technique for dramatic effect, comparing Tarantino's design to that of an Agatha Christie murder mystery.[6]

Reservoir Dogs' scrambled-time structure adds an element of unpredictability to the story that manages to keep the audience off balance. According to Tarantino:

> Pretty much nine out of ten movies you see let you know in the first ten minutes what kind of movie it's going to be, and I think

the audience subconsciously reads this early ten-minute message and starts leaning to the left when the movie is getting ready to make a left turn; they're predicting what the movie is going to do. And what I like to do is use that information against them.[7]

Tarantino makes a deliberate attempt to undercut and subvert audience expectations, a strategy he has described elsewhere as "fucking up the breadcrumb trail."[8] In *Reservoir Dogs*, Tarantino chooses not to show what most people would consider the most crucial event in the story, the diamond heist, and to concentrate instead on what happens afterward. Tarantino's decision to withhold certain critical information represents a storytelling strategy for maintaining viewer interest because, as McKee suggests, the mystery of not knowing what happened arouses our curiosity about what has transpired previously.

In an issue of *Creative Screenwriting* devoted to Tarantino's work, Mary Dalton and Steve Jarrett argue that *Reservoir Dogs* has an unconventional dramatic structure:

> *Reservoir Dogs* clearly does not conform to a traditional dramatic format, certainly not a three-act structure nor even a progression of exposition, complication, climax, and denouement. Instead, the script seems to be organized into two large sections—the first before we know Mr. Orange is an undercover cop and the second after we learn that piece of information. It's almost as if Tarantino tells us the story up to the point of that revelation then goes back and retells the story in light of this new information.[9]

By suggesting that *Reservoir Dogs* has a two-act rather than a three-act structure, Dalton and Jarrrett clearly overstate the case, but their contention that there is not "even a progression of exposition, complication, climax, and denouement" seems even more puzzling upon closer analysis.

Reservoir Dogs turns out to have a three-act structure, but the flashbacks tend to obscure our sense of it, primarily because Tarantino returns to previous events at crucial dramatic moments. When Mr. White asks Mr. Pink how he managed to get away, we get a flashback sequence of Mr. Pink running down the street in the immediate aftermath of the diamond heist with the police in hot pursuit. The flashbacks also provide background information about the major characters. Such information would normally be provided in the first-act setup, but Tarantino parcels it out in each of the acts. After Mr.

Pink suggests that Mr. Orange may be the rat, Mr. White defends him, triggering the chapter on Mr. White. When Mr. Blonde later shows Mr. White and Mr. Pink the cop stuffed in his trunk, this cuts directly to the background story on Mr. Blonde, which shows his steadfast loyalty to Joe Cabot and Nice Guy Eddie. After Mr. Orange shoots Mr. Blonde and reveals he's the undercover cop, we then get a long section about him. We learn about his infiltration of the gang, watch his acting preparation for the role, and see him right before and after the heist, which ends with him wounded in the back seat. We then follow Eddie, Mr. White, and Mr. Pink back to the warehouse where they discover that Mr. Orange has killed Mr. Blonde. Joe's arrival results in the climax and denouement.

Woven into the film's overall structure is the interplay between violent action and more static scenes of characterization that are largely dependent on talk. Tarantino has written some of the most exciting dialogue in contemporary American cinema. His dialogue takes pleasure in talk for its own sake. As Sarah Kozloff points out in *Overhearing Film Dialogue*, it is also the specialized language of a particular genre, namely, the gangster film.[10] The dialogue in *Reservoir Dogs* is vernacular as well as profane. It aims to shock the audience through its sheer vulgarity, as his characters routinely spew offensive words—faggot, bitch, nigger, and Jap—and lines that are intended to insult and stereotype nearly all groups, including gays, women, African-Americans, Asians, and Jews. Confronted with Mr. Pink's refusal to leave a dollar tip for the waitress, Nice Guy Eddie comments, "I don't even know a fucking Jew who'd have the balls to say that."

Reservoir Dogs involves six major characters: Joe Cabot, Nice Guy Eddie, Mr. Pink, Mr. Blonde, Mr. Orange/Freddy, and Mr. White, and each of them seems to be given nearly an equal amount of screen time. This suggests that the film has multiple protagonists, especially since the story is not filtered through any of their points of view. But when we ask which of them has a dramatic conflict that lies at the core of the film, the choice immediately narrows to Mr. White, since he is the only one who is forced to navigate between various and conflicting loyalties. He must decide whether to get Mr. Orange medical attention or to let him die, and whether to defend him when accusations are made that he's actually an undercover cop who has infiltrated the gang. Without Mr. White, *Reservoir Dogs* would lack a dramatic center.

The first ten minutes of *Reservoir Dogs,* which serves as a long pro-
logue, are no doubt intended to confound the viewer, a strategy which
runs counter to the advice found in the manuals. According to Field:
"You've got ten pages to establish three things: (1) *who* is your main
character? (2) *what* is the dramatic premise—that is, what's your story
about? and (3), what is the dramatic *situation* of your screenplay—the
dramatic circumstances surrounding your story?"[11] For the initial
eight minutes of *Reservoir Dogs,* eight men—six in identical black suits
with skinny ties—sit in a diner and engage in digressive chitchat. They
discuss such topics as the lyrics of pop songs and whether or not to tip
waitresses. Nothing is clear at this point. Not only is the protagonist
unclear, but we're also unsure about either the dramatic premise or the
dramatic situation. Although the men could be gangsters—there are
several joking references to shooting Mr. White for stealing Joe's telephone book—there are no hints in the conversation that these men are
about to commit a diamond heist. For an additional two minutes, we
watch them leave the restaurant and strut down the street in slow
motion during the credits.

Tarantino's dialogue in the opening scene violates traditional
screenwriting conventions. Not only is the dialogue not concise, but it
fails to advance the plot. Because it is hard to get a handle on who's
actually speaking, the overlapping dialogue cannot be said to provide
characterization, except for Mr. Pink. It also misleads us at times. Mr.
Brown (played by Tarantino) does a lot of the talking. He's the one who
theorizes that Madonna's song "Like a Virgin" is about making love to
someone with an oversized penis, but Mr. Brown turns out to be a very
minor character. Ironically, it is Mr. Blonde who interprets the song as
being about a vulnerable girl meeting a sensitive guy. Some dialogue,
however, turns out to be related to someone's specific character. Mr.
Blonde, for instance, offers to kill Mr. White for keeping Joe's address
book—which would certainly be keeping in character—while both Mr.
White and Mr. Orange share a bond in not being huge Madonna fans.

The ambiguity of the opening diner scene teases the viewer to
speculate about the identity of these men. Our suspicions that they
might be criminals get confirmed soon afterward. Following the credits, the screen fades to black, and we hear someone scream in agony
and indicate he's dying, as we cut to the inside of a moving vehicle,
where Mr. Orange (Tim Roth) lies in the back seat, covered with
blood. Mr. White (Harvey Keitel), the driver, takes him to an empty

warehouse in order to wait for Joe, who will get a doctor. Suddenly the door bursts open and Mr. Pink (Steve Buscemi) heads toward them, yelling, "Was that a setup or what?"

Tarantino's characters often engage in the kind of lengthy monologues condemned by manual writers such as Richard Walter, who insists that movies should have "natural sounding, quick, short, to-the-point dialogue with lines that link, interlock, intertwine, and bounce up and back like a Ping-Pong ball among the characters."[12] Mr. Pink is especially loquacious—it actually becomes part of his character that he talks as much as he does. When Mr. White asks him whether he thinks they were set up, Mr. Pink responds:

> MR. PINK: You even doubt it? I don't think we got set up, I know we got set up! I mean really, seriously, where did all those cops come from, huh? One minute they're not there, the next minute they're there. I didn't hear any sirens. The alarm went off, okay. Okay, when an alarm goes off, you got an average of four minutes response time. Unless a patrol car is cruising that street, at that particular moment, you got four minutes before they can realistically respond. In one minute there were seventeen blue boys out there. All loaded for bear, all knowing exactly what the fuck they were doing, and they were all just there! Remember that second wave that showed up in the cars? Those were the ones responding to the alarm, but those other motherfuckers were already there, they were waiting for us. (*pause*) You haven't thought about this?[13]

Walter claims that studio readers would flag such extended speeches as "amateurish," but Tarantino's background in acting has been a strong influence on him:

> Look I never went to writing school: "Write a Screenplay in 27 Days," Robert McKee or any of that nonsense. Everything I learned as an actor I completely applied to writing and one of the things you get taught as an actor is, when I'm writing, I just get the characters talking to each other—whatever happens is what happens and what they say is what they say.[14]

When Tarantino's characters talk, they have a tendency to say a great deal.

Mr. Pink's revelation at sixteen minutes that there must be a rat among them functions as the inciting incident, thereby providing both a sense of mystery and dramatic tension. After Mr. White asks how he got out, Mr. Pink indicates that he managed to escape by shooting his way out, which triggers the film's first flashback. We hear a store alarm and sirens as we see Mr. Pink, carrying a satchel, being chased down a busy sidewalk by three cops. As Mr. Pink darts into the street, he gets hit by a car, which sends him crashing into the windshield. He picks himself up, breaks the side window with his gun, drags the woman driver out of the car, and gets into a shooting match with the cops. He shoots one and then another before he's able to drive off, as the lone surviving cop gives chase on foot. When we return to the present, Mr. Pink indicates he "tagged a couple of cops." Mr. White, in turn, reveals he killed a couple as well.

The discussion between Mr. Pink and Mr. White shifts to Mr. Blonde's insane behavior, causing the two to wonder how Joe could have possibly hired him. As Mr. Pink continues to speculate about the identity of the rat, the two men accuse one another, as well as the injured Mr. Orange, whom Mr. White defends. The tension only subsides when Mr. Pink heads off to find the commode. Mr. Pink's departure leads to a second flashback, which begins with a digression. The scene shifts to Joe Cabot's office where Joe asks Mr. White about his crime partner, Alabama (who turns out not to have any bearing on the story), but Mr. White tells him he hasn't seen her for a year and a half. The digression has another purpose. The discussion about certain details of Mr. White's personal life emphasizes the sense of familiarity that exists between Mr. White and Joe. A title card formally introduces "Mr. White." The ensuing scene provides basic exposition, as Joe lays out the plan to rob a diamond wholesaler on the day of a scheduled shipment from Israel.

Back at the garage, Mr. Orange has passed out, forcing Mr. Pink and Mr. White to deal with the sensitive issue of what to do with him. Mr. Pink suggests dumping him at a hospital, but Mr. White confesses that he has told Mr. Orange his name and where he's from. (Mr. Orange has several times called him "Larry.") Mr. Pink, who prides himself on his professionalism, explodes over this. Mr. White defends himself by saying that Mr. Orange was dying in his arms. After Mr. Pink decides they won't be taking him to the hospital now, Mr. White punches him in the mouth and kicks him across the room. Mr. Pink pulls out his gun and Mr. White does likewise. The camera tracks back from the standoff to reveal the notorious Mr. Blonde, who leans against the post drinking a fast-food beverage through a straw.

Mr. White discusses the robbery

The appearance of Mr. Blonde, at thirty-three minutes, represents the first turning point and leads to the short middle act. Mr. White and Mr. Blonde get into an argument over Mr. Blonde's behavior during the robbery, but Mr. Pink gets them to calm down. Mr. Blonde asks Mr. White, "I bet you're a big Lee Marvin fan, aren't you?" After Mr. White laughs, Mr. Blonde remarks, "Yeah, me too. I love that guy." He tells them to follow him out to his car, where he opens the trunk to reveal a handcuffed cop inside. Mr. Blonde suggests that maybe they can find out some information from the cop while they wait for Nice Guy Eddie.

A title card, "Mr. Blonde," triggers another expository flashback scene. We learn not only Mr. Blonde's proven loyalty to Joe and his personal friendship with Nice Guy Eddie, but also how he came to be included in the heist. Like the digression about Alabama in the chapter on Mr. White, the chapter on Mr. Blonde gets sidetracked into a wrestling match between Vic Vega (Mr. Blonde) and Eddie that has strong homoerotic overtones. Afterward, Eddie complains to Joe:

> EDDIE: Daddy, did you see that?
> JOE: What?
> EDDIE: Guy got me on the ground, he tried to fuck me.
> VIC: You wish.
> EDDIE: You sick bastard, Vic. You tried to fuck me in my father's office. Look, Vic, whatever you wanna do in

> the privacy of your own home, go to it. But don't try
> to fuck me. Man, I don't think of you that way. I like
> you a lot, but I don't think of you that way.

VIC: Eddie, if I was buck cowboy, I wouldn't even throw
you to the posse.

EDDIE: No, you wouldn't, you'd keep me for yourself. You
know, four years fuckin' punks up the ass, you
appreciate a piece of prime rib when you see it.

VIC: I might break you in, Nice Guy, but I'd make you my
dog's bitch.

EDDIE: Ain't that a sad sight, Daddy? Man walks into prison
a white man, walks out talkin' like a fucking nigger.
You know what? I think it's all that black semen been
pumped up your ass so far. Now it's backed into
your fucking brain, and it's coming out your mouth.

VIC: Eddie, you keep talkin' like a bitch, I'm gonna slap
you like a bitch.[15]

The scene's significant humor rests on the fact that it is hard to imagine
that a son would ever engage in such sexually charged banter in front of
his own father, never mind one who's also a crime boss. It turns out to
be simply Tarantino's way of showing the two men are friends, because
nothing comes of this latent homoeroticism in terms of the plot. Afterward, Joe and Nice Guy Eddie attempt to find a solution to Vic's parole

Standoff between Mr. Pink and Mr. White

problem by getting him a job as a dock worker. Eddie then suggests to Joe that Vic be included in the jewelry heist.

The middle act continues with a shot of Eddie talking on the phone as he drives toward the warehouse, which intercuts with the guys beating up the cop at the garage. After more verbal sparring between Mr. White and Mr. Blonde, Eddie orders Mr. White and Mr. Pink to accompany him to get rid of the cars, leaving Mr. Blonde behind. As soon as everyone's gone, Mr. Blonde lives up to Mr. White's worst fears. He makes the cop squirm by aiming a gun directly at his face. He takes a straight razor from his boot and begins torturing the cop to the sounds of "Stuck in the Middle of You," by Steeler's Wheel. As he dances to the music, Mr. Blonde slashes off the cop's ear. The camera follows Mr. Blonde as he gets a can of gasoline and splashes it all over the cop. As he lights a match, the cop begs him to stop, but Mr. Blonde suddenly takes a couple of bullets in the chest. Tarantino cuts to a shot of Mr. Orange, who empties his gun. Mr. Orange asks the cop his name (Marvin Nash), and reveals that he's also a cop.

The revelation, at sixty-one minutes, that Mr. Orange is actually an undercover cop represents the second turning point. Since the film is roughly ninety-five minutes (not including credits), this would create a first act of thirty-three minutes, a short second act of twenty-eight minutes, and a third act of thirty-four minutes.[16] As Marvin cries over his disfigurement, Mr. Orange tells him to hold on—police officers are positioned a block away and are waiting to move in. Marvin cries out, "I'm fucking deformed!" Mr. Orange screams back, "Fuck you! Fuck you! I'm fucking dying here! I'm fucking dying." He insists the cops won't make a move until Joe Cabot shows up.

The second turning point pushes the film in a new direction. After another title card, "Mr. Orange," the film moves back in time to show his connection to the heist. Inside a diner at night, Mr. Orange, whose real name is Freddy Newendyke, announces to a black undercover cop named Holdaway that Joe Cabot's planning a new job, and that he's gotten "inside." Holdaway asks him: "Use the commode story?" In flashback, Holdaway coaches Freddy how to tell a convincing story. We watch as Mr. Orange memorizes a scene about selling pot during the Los Angeles marijuana drought of '86, so he can prepare for his under-cover work like an actor playing a role. He practices in his apartment, in front of a graffiti-covered building outdoors as Holdaway looks on, and we later see him telling the story to Joe, Nice Guy Eddie, and Mr. White in a club.

Freddy discusses making a pot delivery at the train station, when he suddenly has to urinate. We see a flashback, as Freddy walks into the bathroom and confronts four L.A. County sheriffs and a German shepherd. The cops stop their conversation; the dog barks. As the camera tracks around him in the bathroom, Freddy sets up the intense drama of the situation. Freddy's monologue (the rest of which he delivers in the bathroom) segues into a monologue by one of the sheriffs who tells a story about nearly shooting a guy who was only reaching for his registration, as Freddy goes over and stands at one of the urinals. While the sheriff continues his story, Freddy washes his hands and uses the hand dryer, which drowns out the sheriff. Tarantino cuts between slow-motion shots of Freddy drying his hands and the stares of three different cops, as well as the German shepherd, whose bark is barely audible. After the dryer turns off and we hear the sheriffs talking once again, Freddy walks out nonchalantly. Back in the club, Joe Cabot comments, "You knew how to handle that situation. You shit in your pants, and dive in and swim."

The aforementioned scenes involve long, extended monologues, including monologues within monologues, but Tarantino's dialogue is so lively and entertaining—he's such a good storyteller himself—that he manages to hold our interest through what are essentially static passages. Part of the trick is that Tarantino creates a dramatic and suspenseful context for his characters to talk, which gives what they say a certain urgency. As Charles Deemer points out: "Indeed, when the rhetorical energy gets high in a Tarantino script, either something terrible is about to happen—or something just has, from which we need recovery."[17]

On the day of the diamond heist, Freddy gets a call from Eddie that it's "showtime." Before he leaves, he looks in the mirror and says, "Don't pussy out on me now. They don't know. They don't know shit. You're not gonna get hurt. You're fucking Baretta. They believe every word, cuz you're super cool." From an unmarked police car, we see Freddy get into Eddie's car. As the car heads toward the warehouse, Eddie, Mr. White, Mr. Pink, and Freddy discuss the difference between white women and black women. Eddie tells a funny story about a black woman named Elois, whom he likens to the woman on the TV show

Beleaguered crime boss Joe Cabot

Get Christie Love, at one point confusing her with the blaxploitation star Pam Grier before Mr. Orange sets him straight.

At the warehouse, Joe comments, "You guys like to tell jokes and giggle and kid around, huh? Giggling like a bunch of young broads in a school yard." He then chastises them, sets out the ground rules, and assigns them their aliases. In one of the funniest scenes in the film, Mr. Pink questions his moniker and a humorous discussion ensues about the code names, an idea that Tarantino borrowed from *The Taking of Pelham One Two Three.* The humor helps to provide a much-needed release from the film's extreme violence:

> MR. PINK: Why am I Mr. Pink?
> JOE: Because you're a faggot, all right?

Everybody laughs.

> MR. PINK: Why can't we pick our own colors?
> JOE: No way, no way. Tried it once, it doesn't work. You get four guys all fighting over who's gonna be Mr. Black. But they don't know each other, so nobody wants to back down. No way, I pick. You're Mr. Pink. Be thankful you're not Mr. Yellow.
> MR. BROWN: Yeah, but Mr. Brown? That's too close to Mr. Shit.
> MR. PINK: Mr. Pink sounds like Mr. Pussy. How about if I'm Mr. Purple. That sounds good to me, I'll be Mr. Purple.

JOE: You're not Mr. Purple. Some guy on some other job is Mr. Purple. You're Mr. Pink!

MR. WHITE: Who cares what your name is?

MR. PINK: Yeah, that's easy for you to say, you're Mr. White and you have a cool-sounding name. All right, look, if it's no big deal to be Mr. Pink, you wanna trade?

JOE: Hey, nobody's trading with anybody! This ain't a goddamn fuckin' city council meeting, you know! Now listen up, Mr. Pink. There are two ways you can go on this job, my way or the highway. Now what's it gonna be, Mr. Pink?

MR. PINK: Jesus Christ, Joe. Fuckin' forget it. It's beneath me. I'm Mr. Pink, let's move on.[18]

Joe, who stands in front of a blackboard like a harried school teacher, is unable to assign code names without being challenged by his unruly group of gangsters. In the earlier scene where Mr. Blonde and Nice Guy Eddie end up wrestling on the floor, he yells: "All right, enough of this shit. Break it up. This ain't a playground." Eddie reinforces the notion that he's a child by constantly referring to his father as "Daddy." Surrounded by a bunch of children, the traditional authoritarian crime boss has become a beleaguered figure, so much so that, as we observed in the opening diner scene, leaving a tip for a waitress can become a site of contention. Even Mr. Blonde scoffs at the notion of having a "boss" in the scene where he tortures the cop. He tells his victim: "One thing I want to make clear to you. I don't have a boss. Nobody tells me what to do."

After Mr. White and Freddy stake out the jewelry store and go over the details, Tarantino cuts to right after the robbery, allowing us to see the events prior to Freddy getting shot. A car comes around the corner and crashes into a parked vehicle. Mr. White and Freddy jump out, but Mr. Brown, his face bloodied, remains in the driver's seat. Freddy watches as Mr. White shoots up a patrol car containing two cops. After they determine that Mr. Brown is dead, Mr. White leads Freddy down an alley as police sirens blare, and then stops an oncoming car by pointing a gun. Freddy heads for the driver's side, but the woman occupant pulls a weapon from the glove compartment and shoots him in the stomach, knocking him to the ground. Instinctively, Freddy returns fire. As Mr. White drags Freddy out of the frame, we cut to the same scene as earlier in the film, but this time the camera remains fixed on Freddy, who moans, "I'm sorry. I can't believe she killed me . . ."

Nice Guy Eddie, Mr. White, and Mr. Pink return to the warehouse to find Mr. Blonde dead, the cop slumped in a chair, and Mr. Orange (Freddy) crumpled at his feet. Eddie runs over to his dead friend, Mr. Blonde. Eddie could care less about the cop and proves it by shooting him right on the spot. Mr. Orange insists that Mr. Blonde planned to kill them when they returned and to steal the diamonds, but Eddie refuses to buy the story. He demands to know what really happened, when suddenly we hear Joe's voice ask, "What the hell for? It would just be more bullshit." Joe identifies Mr. Orange as an undercover cop.

The climax of the film comes once Joe exposes Mr. Orange as the rat. When Mr. White continues to challenge him, Joe takes out a revolver and points it at Mr. Orange, but Mr. White counters by aiming his at Joe. Eddie points his weapon at Mr. White in order to defend his father. Mr. Pink reminds them they are supposed to be professionals, but Joe suddenly fires at Mr. Orange, causing a chain reaction, which leaves both Eddie and Joe dead. Mr. Pink snatches the bag of diamonds and hustles out the door. As sirens sound, Mr. White crawls over to Mr. Orange, who is still breathing. He tells him: "Sorry kid. Looks like we're doing a little time." Mr. Orange admits that he's a cop. Cradling Mr. Orange, Mr. White aims his gun directly at Mr. Orange's mouth. Off-screen voices order Mr. White to drop the gun, but he

Freddy (Mr. Orange) and Mr. White stake out the jewelry store

pulls the trigger, and then gets blown out of the frame as the police open fire.

Tarantino's reworking of the gangster film stands the genre on its head by creating characters whose human flaws make them the perfect embodiments of our own anti-heroic time. The criminals and cops in *Reservoir Dogs* struggle to live up to the codes of professional conduct demanded of them, even as they fall hopelessly short when put to the test. Anyone who shows a human side—Mr. White, Joe, Freddy—ends up dead. Only Mr. Pink, whose loyalty extends no further than himself, has a fighting chance at survival. That's the cynical subtext of *Reservoir Dogs*, which creates an amusing portrait of both gangsters and cops, whose self-consciousness about their own image has been gleaned from the numerous films, TV programs, and pop music they've consumed previously. The same could be said about Tarantino, who, in his revision of the gangster genre, creates a masterful pastiche of elements he borrowed freely from some of his favorite movies, including Kubrick's *The Killing* (1956), *The Taking of Pelham One Two Three* (1974), and Hong Kong director Ringo Lam's *City of Fire* (1987).[19]

Tarantino manages to create memorable characters in *Reservoir Dogs* by cleverly working against genre stereotypes. Tarantino portrays these modern gangsters as being completely immersed in popular culture—from Madonna songs to TV shows to blaxploitation stars, such as Pam Grier. Joe Cabot is hardly your typical crime boss. Joe projects a gruff exterior in an effort to exert control over the motley group he has assembled to pull off the diamond heist, but he makes a fatal mistake of judgment. When Joe figures out that Mr. Orange is the rat, he explains, "He was the only one I wasn't a hundred per cent on. I should have my fucking head examined going ahead when I wasn't a hundred per cent."[20]

Mr. White suffers from a similar character flaw. Torn between his allegiance to the gang and his compassion for his wounded crime partner, Mr. White struggles with a moral dilemma: He feels responsible for the dying Mr. Orange. As he tells Mr. Pink, "That bullet in his belly is my fault. Now while that might not mean jack shit to you, it means a helluva lot to me." Mr. White's sentimentality proves to be his downfall. Mr. Pink, on the other hand, provides a striking contrast by refusing to allow such emotions to interfere with his personal or professional conduct. When he balks at tipping the waitress, Mr. Blue counters that "they're counting on your tip to live." But Mr. Pink rubs his fingers together, and tells him, "Do you know what this is? It's the world's smallest violin, playing just for the waitresses." Mr. Pink's loyalty goes only so far, so that when things go awry, he tells Mr. White, "I say the plan becomes null and void once we found out we got a rat in the house." Mr. Pink's attitude serves him well since, at the film's end, he's the only one left standing.

Mr. White's sentimentality is never fully explained in the film. There is no backstory to provide us with insight into his personal psychology. He's simply a tragic hero, who goes down for his mistaken beliefs. Besides his own guilt over Mr. Orange getting shot, there is something else that leads him to believe that Mr. Orange could not possibly be the rat. Mr. White sees Mr. Orange retaliate against the woman who wounds him during the car jacking. If he were really a cop, how could he gun down an innocent bystander by callously shooting her? As Holdaway tells Freddy, "It's the details that sell your story," and that singular detail is what convinces Mr. White to believe in Mr. Orange. After Mr. Orange confesses to Mr. White at the end that he is in fact an undercover cop, Mr. White admits his personal betrayal and pays a price for giving in to such emotion. Confronted with his own fatal error of judgment, Mr. White has no choice but to shoot Mr. Orange, in turn causing his own death.

Although the media attempted to portray Tarantino as an overnight success, this was hardly the case. Tarantino had spent six unsuccessful years trying to interest production companies in allowing him to direct either *True Romance* or *Natural Born Killers*, the first two screenplays he had written, both of which he hoped would be his first films. No matter how brilliant the scripts were judged by some readers, they were considered much too violent and offensive for mainstream taste, causing Hollywood to pass on the work of the wannabe director. The most controversial aspect of *Reservoir Dogs*, in fact, had to do with its excessive violence. Despite his genuine enthusiasm for the film, Harvey Weinstein, who picked up the domestic distribution rights for Miramax, had strong reservations about the incredibly brutal scene where Mr. Blonde tortures a cop and ends up slicing off his ear as pop music blares in the background. According to Jami Bernard, Weinstein reportedly told Tarantino, "If you cut out the ear scene, you have a popular hit. If you leave it in, you lose the women. Thirty seconds would change the movie in the American marketplace."[21] But Tarantino was adamant about keeping the scene, which was his favorite in the movie. He considered it to be a kind of signature scene, much like the Coen brothers' shot of the hand impaled on the knife in *Blood Simple.* "If violence is part of your palette," Tarantino told one of his interviewers, "you have to be free to go where your heart takes you."[22]

The controversial scene appears in the film with only minor changes from the original screenplay:

MR. BLONDE   *(off)*: Now I'm not gonna bullshit you. I don't really care about what you know or don't know. I'm gonna torture you for awhile regardless. Not to get information, but because torturing a cop amuses me. There's nothing you can say, I've heard it all before. There's nothing you can do. Except pray for a quick death, which you ain't gonna get.

He puts a piece of paper over the cop's mouth.

COP'S POV

Mr. Blonde walks away from the cop.

MR. BLONDE: Let's see what's on K-Billy's 'super sounds of the seventies' weekend.

He turns on the radio.

Stealer's Wheel's hit 'Stuck in the Middle with You' plays out the speaker.

Note: This entire sequence is timed to the music.

Mr. Blonde slowly walks toward the cop. He opens a large knife [razor in completed film].

Mr. Blonde just stares into the cop's/our face, holding the knife [razor], singing along with the song.

Then, like a cobra, he lashes out.

A slash across the face.

The cop/camera moves around wildly.

Mr. Blonde just stares into the cop's/our face, singing along with the seventies hit.

Then he reaches out and cuts off the cop's/our ear.

The cop/camera moves around wildly.

Mr. Blonde holds the ear up to the cop/us to see.[23]

There is no question that the scene deliberately pushes the limits of good taste in terms of its violence. Mr. Blonde admits that he intends to torture the cop not to extract information, but for the pure thrill and enjoyment it will give him. Tarantino thus announces Mr. Blonde's avowed sadism as a prelude to the action. He then ups the ante by having Mr. Blonde turn on the radio, so that the act of torture will have musical accompaniment. The script also indicates in a note: "This entire sequence will be timed to the music." The effect is to suggest that the violence will also be choreographed, and indeed Mr. Blonde not only sings but he does a dance step to the music prior to lopping off the cop's ear. But Tarantino goes even further by describing his intention to implicate the viewer in the violence by placing the audience in the masochistic position of also being the victim. Although brief, the scene manages to create a sense of sheer visceral horror.

Todd McCarthy's Sundance review of *Reservoir Dogs* in *Variety*, although extremely positive, hinted at the effect the film's excessive violence might have on audiences by predicting that "this piece of strong pulp will attract attention but looks like a modest box-office performer." McCarthy mentioned the Sundance viewers who fled the screening and concluded that "it's still a needlessly sadistic sequence that crosses the line of what audiences want to experience."[24] Ella Taylor's piece in *LA Weekly* had a genuinely positive tone as well, but she also took exception to the ear scene by criticizing it as "designer brutality." She writes: "The torture scene infuriates me because it has no point other than to show off its technique, and to jump-start our adrenaline, which takes some doing these days; we've grown so numb to images of brutality that they have to be jacked up to fever pitch to stir us at all."[25] Despite such reactions, *Reservoir Dogs* went on to become a huge hit at Cannes, Toronto, Telluride, and the New York Film Festival, generating tremendous critical response despite its violence, which was commented on in nearly every review. The film wound up grossing $2.8 million domestically—substantially less than it might have generated without the ear scene—but achieved even greater commercial success in the home video market, where it shipped nearly one million copies. Marketed as the work of a major auteur, *Reservoir Dogs* did even better overseas, becoming a cult hit in France and especially England, where it grossed nearly $6 million theatrically after censorship problems held up its release on video.

Although *Reservoir Dogs* achieved notable critical success, Tarantino's next effort, *Pulp Fiction* (1994), parlayed another unusual story structure, big-name stars (Samuel L. Jackson and John Travolta), pop-culture quotation, and pure visual style into a major coup at the box office by grossing over $100 million domestically, as well as an equal amount overseas. The film received the top prize at Cannes and ended up being nominated for seven Academy Awards. For some observers, *Pulp Fiction*, and its subsequent marketing effort by Miramax, represented the co-option of the indie movement by mainstream interests. Yet *Reservoir Dogs* has had an equally profound influence on subsequent American independent films by creating an appetite for edgier fare. The work of Neil LaBute, Todd Solondz, Kimberly Peirce, Darren Aronofsky, and Miranda July—to cite several examples—owes a tremendous debt to *Reservoir Dogs*, which serves as a model for their own attempts at pushing against the boundaries of acceptable content and taste. It is nevertheless Tarantino's inventive use of the flashback—a technique that has been dismissed by several manual writers—to create an alternative temporal structure that marks his real achievement in *Reservoir Dogs*.

Chapter 8

The Temporal Complexity
of *Elephant*

Jonas Mekas's desire to shoot all screenwriters had to do with the fact that they "perpetuate the standard film constructions, dialogues, plot" by following "their textbooks of 'good' screenwriting."[1] The issue of even whether to use a screenplay in making an independent film goes back to the controversy surrounding John Cassavetes' first feature, *Shadows*. Appearing on the Jean Shepherd radio show *Night People* to promote Martin Ritt's *Edge of the City* (1957), in which he acted, Cassavetes boasted that he could make an even better film if he only had the funds.[2] The gesture elicited $2,500 in contributions from listeners. This unexpected response led Cassavetes to attempt additional fund-raising, which resulted in his securing an initial film budget of $20,000. He managed to get together an ensemble group of actor friends, and they began work on the project. Cassavetes describes his working methods: "*Shadows* from beginning to end was a creative accident. We got the things we did because we had nothing to begin with and had to create it, had to improvise it. If we had had a writer, we would have used a script. I invented or conceived the characters of *Shadows*, rather than the story line."[3] Cassavetes went on to add: "The script, as such, did not exist until after the film was over. Then we made one up just for copyright reasons."[4]

Shadows was released in two different versions. The 1958 version was based on improvisation, but, according to Ray Carney, the 1959 version was actually scripted because Cassavetes believed the earlier improvised film had been a failure.[5] Not everyone, however, was pleased with the "new and improved" second version. Mekas, who was then editor of *Film Culture* magazine, as well as film critic for the influential *Village Voice*, felt betrayed. He had effusively praised the first version, which he had called "the most frontier-breaking American feature film in at least a decade."[6] *Film Culture* had awarded *Shadows* its First Independent Film Award in early 1959 for being "able to break out of conventional molds and traps and retain original freshness" and lauded its sense of "improvisation, spontaneity, and free inspiration."[7] To Mekas, the scripted version was "just another Hollywood film." For him, it was the first version of *Shadows* that represented an important and radical breakthrough. "Rightly understood and properly presented," he wrote in his *Village Voice* column, "it could influence and change the tone, subject matter, and style of the entire independent cinema."[8]

Gus Van Sant has suggested that abandoning the use of a traditional screenplay in *Elephant* (2003) provided him with a greater sense of freedom during the actual production. He told *Screenwriter Magazine*:

> For me, the screenplay's always been something that you work on in private, and then you use that on the set. You basically copy it. You transfer it, and in that transferring period, you're very busy interpreting the actual screenplay and there's not a lot of room for extra stuff—the *fun* stuff—that's outside the screenplay. So when I got rid of the screenplay, I found that there was only the fun stuff.[9]

The fun stuff includes being able to improvise scenes that rely on what Van Sant calls "ordinary conversations rather than scripted conversations."[10] The elimination of scripted dialogue permitted him the flexibility to approach the narrative in more formal and visual terms. According to Van Sant, his written outline gradually transformed into a map: "The sentences became, actually, lines on a map. And the map was the footprint of the school."[11] In order to create his structural blueprint, Van Sant drew heavily on an Eastern European art-cinema tradition of utilizing long takes and intricate camera movements found in films by Miklós Jancsó and Béla Tarr. For much of *Elephant*, Van Sant uses extended tracking shots to follow his teenage characters as they traverse the seemingly endless and intersecting corridors of a suburban high school. These tracking shots provide the formal basis for temporally linking together the various scenes that comprise the story of two youths who methodically gun down their unsuspecting high school classmates.

Van Sant had been interested in making a film about the Columbine shootings ever since the tragedy occurred on April 20, 1999. He had initially approached Harmony Korine to write a screenplay for a fictional film that dealt with Columbine and the issue of high school violence, but Korine wound up getting side-tracked by other projects and never actually produced a script. Van Sant then turned to the novelist JT LeRoy, whose first novel, *Sarah* (2001), he was also attempting to make into a film.[12] In developing the script for what would become *Elephant*, LeRoy conceived of the Home Box Office–produced film as "a series of interconnecting vignettes, with one story leading to another."[13] Van Sant describes the end result:

> What he [LeRoy] wrote was not even about a school shooting, it was about different types of high school violence. There was some bullying, there was a kid carrying around a gun in a book. There was a girl who had been cutting her legs and her arms, so she wore these long pants to gym class and the teacher was angry with her for wearing long pants. There were flashbacks to Indian torture and things like that that this girl had in her head. There was a huge piece in the middle, like a 30-minute scene of a very animated teacher who gets the class into a huge discussion about school violence.[14]

With pressure coming from the film's producer, Diane Keaton, to begin production on the project, Van Sant told *Filmmaker* that he didn't think he could proceed with "this particular script."[15] Consequently, he decided to abandon LeRoy's screenplay in favor of a more improvisational and structural approach to the Columbine material, one that he had already experimented with in his previous film *Gerry* (2002). Instead of a script, Van Sant relied on a written outline: "I pretty much had it in my head, but there was [an] outline. But the outline [of] the day's shooting would be something like a sentence, maybe a few sentences, and not a number of pages."[16] In addition, Van Sant allowed his nonprofessional cast of Portland teenagers to improvise their lines, thereby collapsing the divide between actor and role—a technique pioneered by John Cassavetes in *Shadows* and later utilized by Richard Linklater in *Slacker*. He also created an intricate and complex temporal structure that weaves together the lives of the various characters, sometimes repeating the same event from another character's perspective in a manner similar to what occurs in Doug Liman's *Go* (1999).

Go has often been described as a youth culture version of *Pulp Fiction*, largely because it employs a structure that loops back on itself to explore the same event from the perspective of three different characters. John August, *Go*'s screenwriter, had originally written the film as a narrative short, but he expanded the first section about Ronna, Claire, and Manny into a feature by filling in the missing information about the other characters. The idea for *Pulp Fiction* was also to combine three different stories, but *Pulp Fiction* actually employs a far more complicated narrative structure. Both films use what amounts to framing devices involving a coffee shop: the holdup in *Pulp Fiction* and Claire's unexpected meeting with Todd Gaines in *Go*. But whereas *Pulp Fiction* reshuffles the chronology of events to create an additional conceptual puzzle for the viewer, *Go* simply retraces the same events from the perspective of the different characters: Ronna and her friend, Simon, and Adam and Zack. When we return to the opening scene in *Go*, the film ties up the loose ends involving what happened to Simon and Ronna. The drug dealer, Todd Gaines, serves a similar role to Marsellus Wallace because both men turn out to be the forces connecting the various characters and incidents.

Elephant combines aspects of both *Pulp Fiction* and *Go*. The sheer complexity of its temporal structure becomes one of Van Sant's devices for maintaining audience interest in a story whose tragic outcome has already been predetermined by the historic events of the infamous shootings at Columbine High School, in Littleton, Colorado, where Eric Harris and Dylan Klebold killed twelve classmates and a teacher, while wounding scores of others. Rather than turning *Elephant* into a fictional character study of its teenage killers, such as Ben Coccio does in *Zero Day* (2003), another film about the Columbine tragedy, Van Sant creates snapshot portraits of their potential victims in the first act as we are introduced to John, Elias, Mr. Luce, Nathan and Carrie, Michelle, Acadia, Jordan, Brittany, and Nicole.

Elephant begins with a fixed-shot time-lapse of electrical poles and speeding clouds, over which we hear the sounds of a pickup football game. The shot gradually darkens from day to night during the opening credits, which indicates the time span of the film. This is followed by a moving shot of autumn trees from a car, which weaves erratically down the street, sideswiping parked vehicles and nearly running over a bicyclist, before screeching to a halt. John, a blond-haired teenager, gets out of the car, assesses the damage, and insists on taking over the wheel from his drunken father. This first scene, in which the peaceful tranquility of a beautiful autumn day becomes ruptured by drunken driving, foreshadows the sudden chaos and unexpected horror that will be unleashed upon this suburban community later that day.

It is actually John, rather than the two teenage shooters, Alex and Eric, who becomes the key figure in the film, in the sense that he provides a connecting link between and among the various characters in what can be viewed as a structural "web-of-life plot" or "network narrative." John also serves as the pivotal character in deciphering the chronology of events that occur over the course of twenty-four hours within a two-day period. The elaborate temporal structure of *Elephant* moves backward and forward in time, but it also creates a Cubist sense of the simultaneity of various events in the process. For instance, while John has to take over the driving for his drunken father and ends up in Mr. Luce's office, Eli presumably photographs the punk-looking couple in the park. Michelle meanwhile appears in the scene of the football game, just prior to our being introduced to Nathan. In a long tracking shot, he walks inside past Jordan, Brittany, and Nicole, causing Jordan to react to his good looks. After Nathan meets Carrie, they go to the principal's office to sign out. In this shot, we can barely make out John walking on the left-hand side of the frame. This shot cuts to the earlier reaction shot of Mr. Luce. He tells John, "Get to class. Don't be late for detention." This slight temporal overlap creates a linkage between the two scenes, as we suddenly become aware of the simultaneity of the two story lines—the one involving John, and the other involving Nathan and Carrie. John comes out of the office and leaves the car keys for his brother at the front desk, as the camera tracks over to Nathan and Carrie, who start to leave the office as the camera then moves past them to catch a teacher as he heads into another room, where two people yell, "Surprise!"

After John leaves the office, he cries in an empty room, presumably because of the incident with his father and the subsequent detention. A young woman named Acadia happens to pass by. She walks over to him and lifts his flat blond hair to see his face:

Acadia kisses John

> ACADIA: What's wrong?
> JOHN: Nothing
> ACADIA: You're crying.
> JOHN: *(shrugging)* Yeah.
> ACADIA: Is it something bad?
> JOHN: I don't know.

The young woman kisses John on the cheek, but then indicates that she has to go to a "Gay-Straight Alliance" meeting.

The film picks up with Nathan and Carrie again, and the simultaneous temporal connection once again is reinforced by the fact that we hear the off-screen voices yelling "Surprise!" Nathan, the handsome jock, and his attractive, highly jealous girlfriend, Carrie, could easily be the prom king and queen, but she has an appointment later that afternoon to find out whether she's pregnant. Nathan, however, seems more fixated on having a blast with his buddies that afternoon. The film cuts to Eli as he strolls down the school corridor with his camera. Someone says, "Hey, Eli," and he responds, "What's up, John?" After they do an elaborate handshake greeting, Eli asks John if he can take his picture. As he snaps one, the school bell sounds, which causes Michelle to run past them. The two teens shake hands again, and John asks Eli whether he's going to the concert that night. He responds, "No, my parents are being bitches." The camera follows John down the corridor and outside. He calls to a dog. The dog runs over and John gets the dog to jump in the air before running into Alex and Eric, who are walking into the building with their arsenal of weapons.

In terms of *Elephant*'s overall structure, the introduction of the two teenage assassins actually serves as the film's first turning point at twenty-two minutes, when Alex and Eric, dressed in paramilitary outfits and carrying heavy equipment bags, inadvertently pass John on their way into the school building. The brief dialogue exchange provides a foreshadowing of their violent intentions:

> JOHN: Hey, what are you guys doing?
> ALEX: Get the fuck out of here and don't come back. Some
>   heavy shit's going down.
> JOHN: What are you doing?

As John stares in disbelief, Alex and Eric continue on their way inside.

Rather than creating a series of obstacles in the middle act, as would be typical in a conventional dramatic structure, Van Sant extends the initial setup by providing exposition about Alex before continuing with the vignettes of the other characters. We cut from the

Eli photographs John as Michelle heads down the hall

above scene to physics class the previous day, where Nathan and several classmates ply Alex with huge spitballs. After Alex goes to the
men's room to clean up, he scopes out the cafeteria and takes notes. A
female student asks him what he's writing in a notepad. Alex tells her,
"It's my plan." When she wants to know for what, he indicates, "Oh,
you'll see." As evidence of his tenuous psychological state, the lunch-
room sounds gradually intensify, causing Alex to hold his head with
his hands.

Following this, the second act moves back in time in order to show
the events involving Eli and Michelle just prior to the crucial scene
where Eli meets John in the hallway and Michelle runs to her job in the
library. We return first to the story line involving Eli, who walks into
the crowded school building, presumably after photographing the
punk couple in the park. He greets several students as he walks down
the long hallways into the photography room. Once Eli disappears into
the darkroom, we hear the name "Michelle," which also appears as an
intertitle. A woman says, "Michelle, look, we've got to talk about this
gym clothes problem." She responds to her gym teacher, "I don't want
to talk about it." After the gym teacher insists that Michelle has to wear
shorts, the camera follows Michelle as she enters a large gymnasium.
The film returns to Eli, who emerges from the darkroom, develops the
film, hangs it to dry, and snips a section of it, before cutting back to the
women's shower room, where Michelle enters and changes, and we
hear the voices of other students ridiculing her for being a nerd.

Van Sant, however, creates additional confusion in the viewer's
understanding of the film's temporal structure by then cutting to the
shot of Alex returning home from school on the previous day. In this
brief scene, he goes directly to the refrigerator in the kitchen, takes a
couple of swigs from a gallon bottle of milk, and then heads down the
stairs to the basement. Positioned as it is between the parallel and
chronological story lines involving Eli and Michelle, the temporal shift
to Alex disrupts the pattern of temporal continuity that's been established. In effect, it adds an element of complexity to the overall structure because it keeps the structure from becoming both obvious and
predictable. We return to the darkroom, where Eli talks to another student photographer about her photo. He leaves his print of the punk
couple to dry before heading out and down the long corridor. John
walks up to him and the two greet each other—it's the same scene we
have seen earlier, but this time from Eli's perspective. The scene, which

will be repeated three times and from the perspective of three different characters—John, Eli, and eventually Michelle—turns out to be absolutely crucial to an understanding of the temporal structure of *Elephant*. We watch as Michelle runs by once the bell sounds, and then follow Eli as he walks into the school library. We hear the librarian give instructions to someone about books that need to be re-shelved. As Eli crosses the library, Michelle passes behind him, pushing a cart full of books.

The film moves back in time once again to the earlier scene of Nathan passing Brittany, Jordan, and Nicole on his way to the main office, but this time we see the scene from their, rather than his, point of view. The extended take of Brittany, Jordan, and Nicole from behind walking down the hall and into the cafeteria is one of the most formally spectacular shots in the film. It begins as the three walk down the food line and choose their lunch. The camera accelerates and then follows one of the cafeteria workers who veers off into the kitchen in order to light up a joint with one of the dishwashers. The camera then follows another worker, switches to a third who picks up a stack of trays, and ends up back on the three young women as they traverse the crowded cafeteria and take seats at a table by the window. The camera moves to the window. One of the women asks, "Is that John?" We, in fact, see John walking outside. Brittany, Jordan, and Nicole discuss the fact that he has a dog with him, thus connecting it time-wise to the scene where John then bumps into Eric and Alex. The camera moves around them as Nicole declines an invitation to go shopping because of her boyfriend, which causes jealous resentment in Jordan. The three eventually pick up their trays and leave. The camera follows them and then focuses on a skinny young woman who has trouble understanding why someone would say she was a bad singer. The camera moves past her and picks up Brittany, Jordan, and Nicole as they head down the hallway and into the bathroom. This extended, carefully choreographed tracking shot that ends on the women's restroom symbol lasts over six minutes. The three walk into the bathroom and each go into three separate stalls. We hear the sounds of vomiting, followed by flushing toilets, which indicates they all suffer from eating disorders.

The long tracking shot described above confirms one of the startling and largely unrecognized aspects of *Elephant*'s time frame, namely, that what we've been watching—at least in terms of the events

Nathan walks through the school grounds

we witness just prior to the shootings—closely approximates real time. This aspect has been reinforced by the fact that Van Sant presents large chunks of the action in continuous-take tracking shots, thus emphasizing an almost Warholian sense of duration to the events that are depicted. In the case of Nathan, for instance, the camera originally follows him in a wide shot from the football field, as he heads toward the school building and goes inside. It proceeds to follow him from behind in a closer shot as he walks down long hallways, up the stairs, back outside past some kids playing hacky sack, and into another wing of the school. As in Warhol's cinema, invariably something interesting happens in the two extended tracking shots from the perspective behind Nathan. The irony of the lifeguard emblem—the cross pattern—on the back of his bright red sweat shirt, as it bobs up and down, is its resemblance to the crosshair in the weapon of the video game that Eric will play in Alex's basement later on. In a similar manner, the simulated targets in the game are all shot from behind as they move away, much like Mr. Luce will be gunned down in the third act. Nathan, along with Carrie, will end up cornered by Alex in the cafeteria meat locker as the film ends. Van Sant comments on another effect of long, extended takes: "The unwaveringness of the camera has an interesting effect on what you're accepting as fabrication vs. reality. Losing the device of cutting starts to make it less display-oriented and more of an account. Even though you know the camera is there, somehow the way you absorb information becomes more devastating."[17] Not surprisingly, Van Sant's theoretical position here mimics that of André Bazin. In *Elephant*, however, real time becomes extended into cinematic time through the depiction of the simultaneity of events, which has been created by repeating the same event from the perspectives of multiple characters.

Eric, Alex's sidekick in the planned massacre, does not reappear until near the end of the second act. As Alex plays Beethoven on the piano in the basement, a figure appears at the window as the camera tracks around the room, revealing typical high school art work—an expressionistic, graffiti-based painting and numerous drawings, including one of an elephant. It moves past Alex to Eric, who stands at the doorway and comments about his music: "It's awesome. What's up?" Eric makes himself comfortable on the bed and grabs a laptop.

Eric and Alex

The camera tracks from Alex back toward Eric, whom we watch play a video game in which he systematically guns down simulated human targets. As he aims at the backs of two more targets on the video monitor, Van Sant cuts to a shot from behind Alex as he continues to play classical music. The camera holds on the back of Alex's head for well over a minute until he finally ends the Beethoven piece on a discordant note and gives "the finger" to the sheet music with both hands. Alex gets up and sidles next to Eric on the couch. Eric playfully tells him, "You suck," as Alex grabs the laptop and searches for Web sites that sell weapons, ending up on one entitled "GunsUSA." The film cuts to an extended time-lapse of clouds in the sky gradually darkening as the sound of wind turns into the crackle of thunder.

The film cuts from the shot of the dark clouds to a blue-filtered night image of Alex asleep on the bed with his clothes on. As we hear the sound of thunder in the distance, the camera tracks to a shot of Eric asleep on the couch. At breakfast the next morning, Alex sits at the table as his father presumably leaves for work. The camera tracks over to reveal Eric drinking orange juice. The ensuing brief dialogue exchange, in which Eric makes a snide remark about Alex's mother, reveals a negative side to Eric's character.

> ALEX: What's that smell?
> ERIC: That's just your mom.
> ALEX'S MOM: You know, you could find other places to eat. I'm sure there are better restaurants in town.
> ERIC: Nah, you're the best.

Alex's mother heads out.

ALEX'S MOM: Lock the door!

The two teens then watch a program about Nazi propaganda on TV in the living room. Rather than embodying their belief system—the way the media attempted to portray the Columbine killers as neo-Nazis—the program instead suggests Alex and Eric's naïveté about the Nazis, including the fact that Eric is not even sure what Hitler looks like. After a package arrives, Alex removes what appears to be some type of automatic weapon, and the two teens head into the garage to test its firepower.

The film cuts back to a long tracking shot behind Michelle as she trudges down the long corridor. We hear the same dialogue that we've heard previously, as Eli greets John and takes his picture. As the bell sounds, Michelle begins to run and we follow her as she passes them. Her pace slackens as she turns down another corridor and enters the school library. She walks into an office, signs in, and heads out with the Asian-American librarian, who tells her to take a cart of books and re-shelf them in the nonfiction section. As Michelle pushes the cart that makes a creaking sound, Eli passes by. Michelle begins to stack books, but the loud click of an automatic weapon causes her to look toward the source. This occurs at approximately sixty minutes, thus providing the second major turning point in the film.

Elephant has a three-act structure—a first act of twenty-two minutes, a second act of thirty-eight minutes, and a short final act of eighteen minutes, which focuses almost entirely on the immediate prelude to the shootings and then the actual massacre. There are less than one hundred shots in the entire film. The shot breakdown turns out to be equally revealing. There are roughly twenty shots in the first act, twenty-nine in the second act, and forty-nine in the third act. In other words, the third act contains as many shots as the first two acts combined.

As the above shot breakdown indicates, the pace of the film accelerates dramatically in the third act. The click of the automatic weapon creates a sound bridge to the opening of the shower door, as Alex enters and turns on the water. The camera holds on Alex taking a shower. Eric appears naked and enters the shower stall. Eric tells him, "I guess this is it. We're going to die today." After a muffled inaudible response, Eric comments, "Yeah, I've never even kissed anybody. Have you?" Eric then kisses Alex and the two engage in a long embrace. Afterward, as they dress, Eric makes small talk before the scene cuts to a plan of the building. While Alex explains the details, we see proleptic (flash-forward) shots of them driving toward school, walking toward the entrance of the building in para-military outfits, passing through the language lab, standing in the hallway, and then opening fire as their fellow students scatter in a shot that mimics the placement of the weapon in the earlier video game. We see shots of Alex firing his weapon in the school library, and of Eric standing over Mr. Luce, who cowers on the ground. Alex continues detailing his plan to hit the best targets: "dumb-ass jocks and shit." Alex then lists his arsenal:

ALEX: Because we'll have a fucking field day down there. I mean, come on. You got your Tec-9 and your rifle and I've got my shotty and my .223 on my back. And I got a couple of pistols and a knife. We have enough explosives to last us almost a day. Most importantly, have fun, man.

The two teens load their weapons into their car and drive to school. During the drive there, we hear the sound of heavy, nervous breathing in the car. As Alex and Eric walk toward the building, they run into John. The same conversation that we've heard earlier gets repeated, but this time from the reverse angle.

Not only does Van Sant play with the notion of simultaneous real time in the first two acts, but once Alex and Eric begin their carnage, the film nearly approximates the actual time frame of the events of the Columbine shootings, which occurred over the course of fifteen minutes. In *Elephant,* the carnage lasts roughly twelve minutes. The violent segment begins with a shot of Alex and Eric, as they stand in the hallway waiting for the bombs to go off. After nothing happens, the two teens stroll through the hallways with their weapons and proceed to walk into the library, where Eli snaps a picture of Alex at the moment he suddenly fires at Michelle, causing blood to splatter over the books behind her as her body slumps out of the frame. He shoots another student, which causes pandemonium. The gunfire registers on Nathan and Carrie in the hallway outside.

The achievement of *Elephant* rests on Van Sant's ability to create dramatic expectations through his highly structural approach without having to rely on standard Hollywood conventions. Whereas Van Sant's earlier film *Gerry* did not succeed, largely because it failed to engage the viewer through either character or its slight semblance of a narrative, *Elephant*'s loaded subject matter almost guarantees the viewer that there will be a significant dramatic payoff. The last segment fulfills that promise, as the film shifts from being nonlinear to linear, and Alex and Eric proceed to wreck havoc on those who happen to cross their paths. The extremely slow buildup, in fact, only heightens viewer expectations, knowing full well where the story is heading, which commences with the violent shooting of Michelle in the library.

In the scene in *Reservoir Dogs* where Mr. Blonde slices off the cop's ear with a razor blade, Tarantino's use of music and choreography turns violence into a form of entertainment. Van Sant, in contrast, carefully avoids turning violence into spectacle for its own sake. In fact, Michelle is the only one of the two main characters who we actually watch get gunned down in the third act. As is symptomatic of news and documentary photographers, Eli chooses to photograph the murder rather than to intervene. Alex traps Brittany, Jordan, and Nicole in the bathroom, but Van Sant chooses to cut away from the scene rather than to depict the actual violence. We nevertheless witness Eric brutally shoot Mr. Luce after first appearing to show the principal mercy. He also shoots Benny, the seemingly fearless African-American student, who, although we see him earlier playing football with Nathan, isn't formally introduced as a character until very late in the film. Van Sant teases us into believing that Benny will prove to be the film's missing hero, but he then rather quickly deflates this expectation. In terms of the other major characters, we watch Benny earlier escort the traumatized Acadia out the window to safety. Alex, in effect, warns John about what is about to transpire, presumably because John is a nice guy. The film ends with Alex taunting Nathan and Carrie in the meat locker, at least leaving their fate in question.

The ambiguity of the fate of Nathan and Carrie, as well as Brittany, Jordan, and Nicole, is countered by the fact that we actually see twelve students either shot or about to get shot in the film. Alex shoots Michelle as well as three other kids in the library. We also see the student in the GSA meeting get killed, as well as Benny. When Alex enters the cafeteria, we glimpse the body of one of the cafeteria workers on the floor. If we add Nathan and Carrie and the three female friends, Brittany, Jordan, and Nicole, that equals twelve shooting deaths— either witnessed or implied. It seems entirely plausible that the bad singer who hides in one of the bathroom stalls would elude Alex.

One of the major surprises of the third act involves the moment when Alex unexpectedly shoots Eric, but like most of what we see in *Elephant*, the motivation for his behavior is not readily apparent, and therefore remains open to speculation. Does Alex shoot Eric out of mercy? Does he shoot him because of the earlier kiss in the shower? Does he shoot him as a result of a pathology that is hinted at by the heavy breathing we hear when he opens the package containing the automatic weapon, drives toward school in the car, and as he sits in the cafeteria before rising to gun down his friend. The soundtrack—the intense sound of birds, which seems to reference *Psycho* (a film Van Sant re-created shot for shot in 1998)—does seem to indicate Alex's unbalanced mental state.

Six years after Columbine, it is now assumed that Dylan Klebold was hot-tempered, suicidal, and depressive, while Eric Harris was clearly a psychopath.[18] What Van Sant gives us in the film then is not necessarily a true portrait of the actual Columbine killers, but rather fictional representations of them as they were portrayed by the media, especially in the immediate aftermath of the event. As Van Sant himself suggests of *Elephant*: "It has elements of Columbine. But we never really tried to get at who these people were. We sort of invented our own."[19] The very title, in fact, alludes to the discrepancies five blind men might have in attempting to describe an elephant. Van Sant explains: "You know, for five blind men the elephant is like a wall to one, a rope to another, a tree to another, a snake to the fourth one. . . . It's an unanswerable question."[20] For Van Sant, the events of Columbine continue to remain an enigma. For instance, in various media coverage, especially after the event, Klebold and Harris were reported to be gunning for jocks, blacks, and nerds. Alex even mentions "dumb-ass jocks" in detailing his plan. Van Sant plays with these notions, but in the end shows that such individuals, rather than being singled out as deliberate targets, were more or less random victims of an original plan gone hopelessly awry.

Van Sant offers very few character traits for the killers. They play video games and surf the Internet, practice classical piano, get pummeled by spitballs, watch a documentary film about the Nazis, quote Shakespeare, and kiss in the shower before heading off on their rampage. Because he is an openly gay director, Van Sant's inclusion of the extended shower kiss proved controversial for gay audiences, who believed that it played into one of the worst possible stereotypes. But *Elephant*, unlike many independent films, is ultimately not character-driven. Like Haynes's treatment of Carol White in *Safe*, Van Sant sticks to surfaces rather than attempting to provide psychological motivation for any of his characters. Instead, his formal strategy of employing extended tracking shots allows us to scrutinize the faces of the characters without being able to penetrate the surface. As Kent Jones points out, "*Elephant* seems like a study in how much faces *don't* give away about people, how much *can't* be gleaned from studying them. The film is perfectly built around behavior as the containment of emotions rather than their revelation—in other words, adolescence."[21] Yet, just as often, Van Sant places his camera behind his adolescent performers, thus preventing us from even having access to facial cues.

The teenagers depicted in *Elephant* have typical problems. John's struggle with his alcoholic father in the opening scene creates sympathy for him, largely because of the reversal in roles. Two of the other characters also allude to problems with their parents. Jordan, for instance, complains that her mother has been going through her stuff at home, while Eli blames his parents for his not being able to go to the concert. Issues involving possible pregnancy, eating disorders, bodily inhibition, possessive friendships, bullying, and the appearance of gayness all surface at various points in the film. Van Sant shows us that high school helps to create emotional disconnection rather than connection for these teenagers. At the principal's office, Mr. Luce simply stares at John, before dismissing him by saying, "Get to class. Don't be late for detention." When John cries afterward, Acadia briefly comforts him, but she immediately has to run off to the GSA meeting. Carrie might be pregnant, but the ramifications of this don't seem to register on her jock boyfriend, Nathan, who appears to be more preoccupied with having a good time with his friends later that afternoon. Van Sant relates this to the film's sense of realism: "Things don't have beginnings and ends in our lives, and if you want to make storytelling lifelike, you have to play by the rules of reality, which is that nothing is connecting, nothing is making sense. It's like a Hobbesian world of people striving to get to their next meal."[22]

Van Sant's use of extended tracking shots through the maze of long corridors goes even further than this by implying that this disconnection is inscribed in the very architecture of the prisonlike school building. The film shifts the focus to high school's inherent regimentation and social control. The viewer spends much of the time engaged in real-time observation of these high school students as they shuffle between classes and respond instinctively to class-period bells. With time and space so heavily regimented and controlled, the fragmented quality of their interactions could hardly be otherwise. Van Sant comments:

> But I find it interesting that there's one thing no one has mentioned about the film. The thing you're actually watching all the time is a dislocation and nonconnection. It's visible, it's in the representation. It's what the film represents. The connections aren't there between the students or between the students and the authority figures. It's all askew and whacked out. I tend to think our life is like that, and that's why I think the answers lie within us.[23]

Such dislocation becomes the defining aspect of the high school experience, where social interaction gets relegated to the random time between classes—in other words, the school hallways, bathroom, and cafeteria.

In its representation, the film privileges visual over verbal information by minimizing the amount of spoken dialogue. This allows the viewer an even greater freedom to contemplate and speculate about the events that are occurring. Yet the biggest criticism lodged against *Elephant,* which won the Palme d'Or at the 2003 Cannes Film Festival, has been that it fails to provide answers about the Columbine shootings. Van Sant, however, takes issue with such criticism:

> The way I thought the film is supposed to work is that it leaves a space for you to bring to mind everything you know about the event. It doesn't give you an answer. There's no one-stop solution. And if you think there's an answer you can isolate—maybe it's video games, maybe it's the parents—then that lets you think that the problem is somewhere else and that you aren't part of it. And that's a mistake, because we all are part of it.[24]

Elephant refuses to provide viewers with either easy answers or the sense of closure we find in classical cinema.

Although the film employs a three-act structure and builds suspense through its slow buildup to the explosive third act, *Elephant* does not make many other concessions to dramatic storytelling conventions. After achieving mainstream success with *Good Will Hunting* (1997) and *Finding Forrester* (2000), Van Sant claimed to be bored with the standard way of making films, and thus turned to art cinema for inspiration. He moved away from the dialogue-driven screenplay toward a greater concern for realism and visual storytelling. One of the more astonishing aspects about *Elephant,* in many ways, turns out to be its pared-down and elegant simplicity. How can shots of teenagers walking down long corridors manage to keep us absorbed for so long? Yet *Elephant*'s remarkable achievement depends largely on Van Sant's imaginative temporal structure. More than anything, this succeeds in transforming what otherwise might seem utterly mundane into a highly complex and engaging story.

Chapter 9

Memento as Puzzle Film

Tarantino's tense switching in *Reservoir Dogs* provided an alternative storytelling strategy, but critics and audiences certainly had no difficulty understanding the various shifts in time as flashback sequences that served an expository and dramatic function. As independent screenwriters and directors gradually began to experiment more freely with temporal elements in the 1990s, however, audiences sometimes struggled to follow the basic spine of the story. Alain Resnais's *L'Année dernière à Marienbad* (*Last Year at Marienbad*, 1961) served as a prototype for this development. This art-film classic created a highly formal dramatic puzzle that rests on the issue of whether its two central characters actually had a romantic relationship with each other previously. Not even the screenwriter, Alain Robbe-Grillet, or the director could agree on the issue. Whereas illegibility and lack of clarity were always considered a defect in the classical storytelling model, a shift began to occur, as films such as Christopher McQuarrie and Bryan Singer's *The Usual Suspects* (1995) began to be appreciated for the deliberate ambiguity of their narration. Originally used to designate a subgenre of the thriller film, the term "puzzle film" began to be applied to all films that create intellectual conundrums for the viewer, often as a result of their imaginative temporal play.

The narrational instability caused by Leonard Shelby's anterior-grade memory loss in Christopher Nolan's neo-noir *Memento* (2001) provides the basis for what is generally considered to be one of the most original puzzle films in recent years. Based on a short story, "Memento Mori," by Jonathan Nolan, *Memento* debuted at the 2001

Leonard Shelby

Sundance Film Festival, where it won the Waldo Salt Screenwriting Award, but failed to find a major distributor. After subsequently being released by its production company, Newmarket, *Memento* went on to achieve unexpected box-office success, garnering over $25 million in its domestic release.

Nolan's second feature shares a number of similarities with Christopher McQuarrie's Academy Award–winning screenplay for *The Usual Suspects*, which also employs a flashback structure and an unreliable narrator. Leonard Shelby's unique mental condition, however, makes him unaware of his own deceit, in striking contrast to Verbal Kint's deliberate and calculated con-artistry as the narrator of *The Usual Suspects*. Both films play mind games with the viewer in the process. *The Usual Suspects* uses the unknown identity of the master criminal, Keyser Söze, as the film's framing device and as its major narrative question mark, whereas *Memento* begins with a murder and then proceeds both backward and forward in an effort to unravel the mysterious circumstances that led up to this event. Like all good mysteries, the two films provide many false and contradictory clues along the way, and each manages to withhold the most important exposition until the very end. *The Usual Suspects* and *Memento*, along with films such as David Lynch's *Lost Highway* and *Mulholland Dr.*, *Donnie Darko* (2001), *Primer* (2004), and M. Night Shyamalan's more mainstream *The Sixth Sense* (1999), rely on the type of ambiguity more typically associated with art cinema to create elaborate puzzles for the viewer. In many ways, *Memento* represents one of the purest examples of a "puzzle film" because it engages the viewer not only through the intricate labyrinth of its story, but also through a cognitive foregrounding of the heightened paranoid mental state of its disturbed protagonist and by engaging the viewer directly in the process of deciphering the film's rather confounding structure.

Linda Seger cites *Memento* in her manual *Advanced Screenwriting* as one of two examples of a storytelling pattern she refers to as a "reverse structure." Seger writes, "Some films are structured so that the whole film is a flashback—beginning at the present and working backward to a key incident from the past. We see this in *Betrayal*, based on a Harold Pinter play of the same name, and in *Memento*, written by Christoper Nolan."[1] Although one of the formal hooks of the film is clearly its reverse chronology, the actual structure of *Memento* turns out to be a great deal more complex than it has been described by various commentators, including Seger. There are really two parallel stories that run simultaneously throughout the film. Some parts (the incidents involving Teddy and Natalie, the scene with the prostitute, and so forth) are presented in color, while others (Leonard's phone calls, presumably from Teddy, the flashbacks about Sammy Jankis and his wife, as well as his meetings with Teddy at the motel and then Jimmy at the abandoned building) appear in black and white. The color sections unfold in reverse chronology, but the black-and-white sections are shown in chronological order. This becomes especially apparent if we think about the incidents involving Sammy Jankis and his wife, which Leonard narrates on the phone and which are also presented in various flashbacks. After Leonard gets the phone call from Teddy arranging the meeting with Jimmy, the story proceeds forward in linear progression, first in black and white, and then in color.

Christopher Nolan comments on this aspect of the film's structure in an interview with Annie Nocenti in the *Independent*: "Because the black-and-white footage goes forward, and then it meets the color footage at the end, so the shape of the script is a kind of U-turn, or a hairpin turn. They meet at the point where it changes from black-and-white to color."[2] The point where it literally changes from black and white to color occurs as Leonard watches the Polaroid of Jimmy's slain body develop. From that point on, the color section progresses forward until Leonard, dressed in Jimmy's clothes and driving his stolen

Jaguar, screeches to a halt in front of Emma's tattoo parlor. So in terms of the film's overall shape, we have two plotlines—the main one in color, and the secondary one in black and white—which head in counter chronological directions. One moves backward, the other forward, until they overlap—what Nolan calls "a U-turn or a hairpin turn" is only partially accurate—at the pawnshop to form a short loop (the extended last scene) that connects at the developing Polaroid. As James Mottram puts it, "In many ways you could also think about the film's two time-lines as being pulled together, folding in on each other and imploding."[3]

What is especially intriguing about *Memento* is not simply its unusual structure, but how perfectly it fits this particular story, about someone suffering from short-term memory loss. Nolan argues that the film's reverse structure works far better as a storytelling device than if it were told going forward:

> It's not that it doesn't work forwards, because it does. Technically it works, logically it works. It just becomes unbearable to watch. It becomes this horrible portrayal of this guy being abused and abused. The only way to get around that is to prevent the audience from seeing that abuse until much later in the film. People still seem to sympathize with him, they still want to view him in the way he views himself, which is as this kind of heroic avenging figure.[4]

Nolan's point is an important one because, as he rightly points out, the overall structure does have a significant impact on the viewer's emotional identification with the protagonist. Leonard, of course, prefers to see himself as a victim rather than as a perpetrator. He even tells Teddy as much when he steals Jimmy's Jaguar. Two different murders, both committed by Leonard, provide the bookends to the main story, but shifting the reverse chronology would make it more difficult for us to identify with Leonard because his motivations would become immediately transparent as a result of Teddy's revelations. The central mystery is not that he kills Teddy, but why?

Buried motivation turns out to be a consistent trait in the independent films I've been discussing in this book. Willie's ambivalence in *Stranger Than Paradise*, Carol White's unexplained passivity in *Safe*, Christine's impetuous obsession with the shoe salesman, Richard, in *Me and You and Everyone We Know*, Mr. White's sentimental attachment to a dying man in *Reservoir Dogs*, and Alex and Eric's erratic and homicidal behavior in *Elephant* are all examples of reluctance on the part of independent screenwriters to explain and motivate all aspects of their characters, thus preserving the more inscrutable and unpredictable elements of human behavior.

In *Memento*, forward chronology would make Leonard's actions seem inevitable, thus eliminating the major surprise. Despite its reverse chronology, Nolan insists that *Memento* remains an extremely linear film. As he told Nocenti, "Underneath it, it's very conventional—it has a three-act structure, in terms of the emotional arc. That was absolutely vital, I felt, in making that backwards structure work."[5] Told chronologically, *Memento*'s story is actually quite simple. The setup occurs in the black-and-white sequence as Leonard relates the story of Sammy Jankis to someone on the phone. That person turns out to be a crooked cop named Teddy who sets up the memory-challenged Leonard to kill Jimmy Grantz during a drug deal in order to steal a large sum of money. The inciting incident occurs at fifteen minutes, when Leonard ignores the advice tattooed on his arm and answers the phone. Teddy manages to convince Leonard that his wife's killer and the source of his memory problems is a drug dealer named Jimmy Grantz. Leonard's murder of Jimmy at an abandoned building causes the film to shift permanently to color, as Leonard watches the Polaroid of Jimmy's body develop, at twenty-five minutes. This serves as the first turning point. The long middle act involves the ramifications of Jimmy's murder. Angry at figuring out that his victim is not his wife's killer, John. G., Leonard decides to copy down Teddy's license plate number in order to prevent him from manipulating him again. He then proceeds to steal Jimmy's identity—his designer clothes, fancy Jaguar, and large stash of money. Shortly afterward, Teddy tries to convince Leonard at a tattoo parlor to leave town, but Leonard escapes out the window. Leonard finds a beer coaster in the pocket of Jimmy's jacket, which leads to an involvement with Jimmy's girlfriend, Natalie. She tricks Leonard into believing that Jimmy's business partner, Dodd, is responsible for her injuries, thus revealing that Natalie secretly harbors her own revenge plans. Natalie proceeds to manipulate Leonard into eliminating Dodd, who has come looking for the money. As the relationship between Natalie and Leonard becomes more intimate, she then offers to help him find his wife's killer, causing Leonard to write on her picture: "She has also lost someone. She will help you out of pity." This serves as the second turning point, at eighty-three minutes. Natalie then provides Leonard with the evidence that links Teddy to John G. in the third act, which culminates in Leonard killing Teddy.

In discussing her two examples of a reverse structure, *Memento* and *Betrayal*, Linda Seger writes: "Both of these films use a three-act structure. If their stories were told chronologically, each film's beginning would be the end of its story. The first turning point of the story, if you played it forward, is the second turning point of the story when it's played backwards."[6] Contrary to Seger's claim, *Memento* is not actually a palindrome that plays the same way both forward and backward. The reverse chronology, in fact, serves to complicate the story by altering the viewer's understanding of the various elements, including the major turning points. Reversing the chronology changes the viewer's comprehension of the story in a number of other ways. It serves to transform Leonard into a more likeable protagonist throughout most of the film, primarily because of his unswerving devotion to the memory of his murdered wife. This is especially evident in the first scene between Natalie and Leonard in the restaurant where she gets him to talk about his wife and he describes his terrible sense of loss. Later, when he comes to her house trying to find out about Dodd, Leonard lapses into intense melancholy over his current condition: "She's gone and the present is trivia, which I scribble down as fucking notes." As he lies in bed in Natalie's apartment, his personal agony becomes even more apparent. His inconsolable pain and sadness are also obvious in the scene where he burns a number of his wife's possessions. These scenes, however, have an additional effect. They allow us to believe that Leonard's romance with Natalie holds the possibility of some kind of redemption for him, or for the two of them together, because they both suffer from such intense personal loss. Whereas the reverse chronology (the plot) foregrounds the romance element, the chronological telling (the story) makes it clear that Natalie actually despises Leonard because he has stolen and assumed the identity of her missing boyfriend, Jimmy.

Memento's central puzzle rests on a question: Is Leonard a heroic figure seeking to avenge his wife's killer, or a homicidal killing machine fulfilling the will of others? Despite highly contradictory evidence, the answer does seem to hinge on the believability of the explanation given by Teddy at the film's end. After Teddy fails to convince Leonard that Jimmy Grantz is actually his wife's killer, he then provides interesting new information, which is corroborated by a Polaroid of Leonard:

TEDDY: That's right. The *real* John G. I helped you find him over a year ago. He's already dead.

LEONARD: Don't lie to me anymore.

TEDDY: Look, Lenny. I was the cop assigned to your wife's case. I believed you, I thought you deserved the chance for revenge. I'm the one that helped you find the other guy in your bathroom that night, the guy who cracked your skull and fucked your wife. We found him. You killed him. But you didn't remember. So I helped you start looking again, looking for the guy you already killed.

LEONARD: Oh yeah. So who was he?

TEDDY: Just some guy. I mean, does it even matter who? No reason, Lenny. No conspiracy. Just bad fucking luck. Couple of junkies, too strung out to realize that your wife didn't live alone. But when you killed him, I was so convinced you'd remember. But it didn't stick. Like nothing ever sticks. Like *this* won't stick.

Leonard looks at the Polaroid of himself.

I took that picture . . . just when you did it. Look how happy you are. I wanted to see that face again.

LEONARD   (*sarcastic*): Oh, gee, thanks.

TEDDY: Fuck you. I gave you a reason to live, and you were more than happy to help. You don't want the truth. You make up your own truth. Like your police file. It was complete when I gave it to you. Who took the twelve pages out?

LEONARD: You, probably.

TEDDY: No, it wasn't me. See, it was you.

LEONARD: Why would I do that?

TEDDY: To create a puzzle you could never solve. Do you know how many—how many towns? How many John G.'s or James G.'s? I mean, shit, Lenny, I'm a fucking John G.[7]

Although Teddy's stated reason for helping Leonard in his continued pursuit of John G. after he has already been found and murdered seems a bit disingenuous, Teddy does appear to be telling the truth about Leonard, because none of the people we see Leonard eliminate—Jimmy, Dodd, and, least of all, Teddy—could possibly be his wife's killer, thereby lending credence to the thesis that Leonard has become a delusional murderer. Leonard's decision to take down Teddy's license plate number and write "Don't believe his lies" actually changes our perception of Leonard because he does it as an act of revenge against Teddy. It sets up the trajectory for Teddy to be eliminated, not because he's John G., but because Teddy's version of Leonard's identity differs so radically from Leonard's own conception of himself. There is also the somewhat inexplicable image at the film's end, where we see Leonard in bed with his wife after he has avenged her killing. Since this image cannot possibly be a flashback, we can only really interpret it as a deranged fantasy on the part of Leonard.

Interestingly, Teddy and Natalie each warn Leonard that the other is using him, and they clearly are, given their own personal agendas. We certainly see Teddy play tricks on Leonard, just as we watch Natalie abuse Leonard because his memory problems make him so vulnerable to manipulation. Even the hotel clerk, Burt, cannot help taking advantage of Leonard by charging him for an extra room. Natalie seeks revenge for what has happened to Jimmy, and thus plots to have Leonard eliminate both Dodd and Teddy. Teddy, on the other hand, cannot resist using Leonard in a scheme to rip off a drug dealer. Each recognizes that there is a highly dangerous side to Leonard, who, in his heightened paranoid state, is like a pet cobra coiled to spring at the slightest provocation. Leonard becomes the weapon of choice in the ensuing battle between Teddy and Natalie after the drug deal provides the link between their characters.

Then there is Sammy. Is Sammy Jankis an obsession born of guilt—a projection of Leonard's own troubled psychic state? Are we to believe, as Teddy suggests, that there are things that Leonard refuses to remember, especially about his wife? When Leonard challenges him on the subject, Teddy responds, "I don't know. Your wife's surviving the assault. Her not believing your condition. The torment and pain and anguish tearing her up inside. The insulin." It is certainly true that when we do witness the actual attack on Leonard's wife firsthand, we see her eye blink after the assault. At the film's end, Teddy also insists that Sammy was simply a con man who Leonard exposed as a fraud. Teddy claims that Sammy didn't have a wife, but rather that it was Leonard's wife who had diabetes. He also suggests that Leonard's wife did not actually die in the assault, but rather as a result of being given repeated doses of insulin by Leonard in a test similar to the one involving Sammy's wife. Leonard himself panics about this possibility when he talks with the cop (Teddy) on the phone. "You could do anything and not have the faintest idea ten minutes later. Like Sammy. I could have done something like Sammy." He says this right before we watch the scene of Sammy repeatedly administering insulin injections to his wife. While it is impossible to say conclusively that Leonard has murdered his own wife, it would be difficult to explain the film's insistence on this parallelism otherwise, both in terms of its structure and Leonard's obsessive preoccupation with Sammy Jankis, whose insurance claim Leonard was responsible for turning down prior to his head injury. "Remember Sammy Jankis" remains permanently tattooed on the back of his hand, and every personal encounter becomes an occasion for Leonard to retell the story of Sammy, whose short-term memory problems seem to mirror his own. Leonard indicates that Sammy ended up "in a home ever since." When we see Sammy sitting in the institution, Sammy transforms momentarily into Leonard, thereby suggesting the possibility that *Memento*, in a manner similar to *The Cabinet of Dr. Caligari* (1919), represents the tale of an institutionalized madman.

The reverse shift in temporal chronology of the color sequences has the effect of delaying the viewer's understanding of the context of each new scene, thus allowing the enigmatic nature of events to be viewed as they appear to the distorted mind of Leonard Shelby, who suffers from an inability to create new memories. Not only can we not trust the film's narrator because of his memory problems, but nothing we see or hear subsequently can be taken at face value either. As a result of the film's utterly subjective viewpoint, virtually every situation in *Memento* becomes charged with an extreme underlying paranoia that has become a hallmark of the film noir genre.

Memento begins with a series of images projected backward, as we move from a Polaroid of a grisly murder (as the image fades back to white) to the desperate face of the film's protagonist, Leonard, right through to the point when he pulls the trigger and the face of Teddy re-materializes for a brief moment. The inciting incident occurs at fif-

Leonard shoots Teddy

teen minutes, when Leonard believes he has found his wife's killer. He checks the facts contained on his tattoo-covered body against the information listed on the driver's license and car registration. Leonard concludes, "It's him." He stares at the photo of Teddy and mutters to himself, "I found you, you fuck." He writes on the Polaroid, "He is the one." He starts to put on his shirt, then opens it as he stands in front of the mirror. Across his chest is written, "JOHN G. RAPED AND MUR-DERED MY WIFE." He buttons his shirt, then goes over and adds the words "Kill him" to the Polaroid of Teddy. Leonard loads his gun—a shot we have seen earlier—as the scene fades into a black-and-white sequence, in which Leonard talks on the phone about his condition and Sammy Jankis. He insists that "Sammy's story helps me under-stand my own situation." Unlike Sammy, who became mixed up because he lacked organization and a sense of purpose, Leonard believes that his own need to revenge his wife's rape and murder pro-vides him with the necessary focus and determination to go forward.

Right after this, we are introduced to Natalie in a restaurant. Leonard's notes on her indicate that "She has also lost someone, she will help you out of pity." When Leonard joins her in a booth, Natalie, an attractive woman who's wearing sunglasses and has bruises on her lip and cheek, also refers to him as Lenny. Natalie tells Leonard that the license number he gave her belongs to a man named John Edward Gammell, the "John G." he's been looking for. Despite her warning that he probably will not remember his act of revenge, Leonard insists that his wife's murder demands vengeance. Leonard remarks, "Just because there are things I don't remember doesn't make my actions meaningless. The world doesn't just disappear when you close your eyes, does it?"

A romantic link between Leonard and Natalie becomes established when he wakes up in bed next to her. After Natalie discusses getting information about John G.'s license plate from her friend, Leonard expresses his appreciation. Natalie, however, suggests that she's simply returning the favor. She asks Leonard, "So next time you see me, will you remember me?" After Leonard shakes his head no, the two of them kiss and Natalie insists he will. Lenny leaves Natalie's house, gets in his car, and starts the engine, but Teddy blocks his movement. In the black-and-white sequence, Leonard discusses the conditioning tests he gave Sammy in order to determine whether Sammy could learn to avoid electrified objects through instinct rather than memory.

The first turning point occurs at thirty-two minutes, when Leonard arrives at Natalie's house, shows her a Polaroid of a gagged and bloodied man, and demands to know, "Who the fuck is Dodd?" Natalie assures the panic-stricken Leonard that he agreed to help her after seeing what Dodd had done to her, but Leonard tells her, "I think someone's fucking with me. Trying to get me to kill the wrong guy." As Natalie starts to undress Leonard, she discovers the tattoos that cover his body. She then tells him about the person she has lost, Jimmy, and shows Leonard a picture of the two of them together. Natalie explains that Jimmy went to meet a guy named Teddy and never came back. She asks Leonard what he's going to do to the guy who murdered his wife. Leonard tells her, "I'm going to kill him." Natalie suggests that she might be able to help Leonard find the murderer. In bed, Leonard obsesses about his wife, wondering aloud, "How am I supposed to heal if I can't feel time?" Back in the living room, Leonard stares at the photo of Natalie and Jimmy. He takes out his Polaroid of her and writes on the back, "She has also lost someone, she will help you out of pity." When the scene shifts to black and white, Leonard discusses that Sammy's tests indicated that his problems were psychological rather than physical, allowing his insurance company to reject Sammy's claim "on the grounds that he wasn't covered for mental illness." Leonard tells the person on the phone, "His wife got stuck with the bills, and I got a big promotion."

Teddy and Leonard at the motel

The middle act focuses on the romance between Leonard and Natalie, as well as the threat posed by Dodd. After Leonard awakens from a nightmare about his wife's murder in a strange motel room, Teddy shows up, only to discover a bloodied man bound and gagged in the closet. The man turns out to be Dodd, although Leonard cannot remember how he's gotten there. On Dodd's Polaroid is written, "Get rid of him. Ask Natalie." Teddy helps Leonard escort Dodd to his car and the two of them dispose of Dodd at a remote location. We gradually learn that Dodd, a business partner of Natalie's boyfriend, Jimmy, has come after Leonard in an attempt to recover missing drug money. Leonard ignores Teddy's attempts to warn him about Natalie.

Several scenes toward the end of the middle act confirm Natalie's duplicity, but not her motivation. They also raise additional questions about Leonard's character. As Leonard struggles to write something down in order to remember it, Natalie, bruised and bleeding, arrives home and informs him that Dodd has beaten her up. After Leonard gets her some ice, Natalie tells him she took his advice and told Dodd that she didn't have "any of Jimmy's money or the drugs, and that this Teddy must have taken everything." She tells him that Dodd has threatened to kill her. Leonard offers to pay Dodd a visit, but Natalie responds, "Ah, he'll kill you, Lenny." She suggests that Dodd will probably find him now that he knows about Leonard's car. When Leonard asks her for information about Dodd, Natalie writes it down. In the black-and-white section, Leonard tries to follow the advice on his tattoo by not answering the phone. He calls the front desk and asks the clerk to hold his phone calls.

A key scene, involving Natalie, follows. As Leonard sits in the living room, Natalie arrives home and warns Leonard that Dodd is coming after them because of Jimmy. As she hides all the writing utensils in her handbag, Natalie claims that Jimmy had gone to meet Teddy with a lot of money and never returned. Now that Dodd is after the money, she begs Leonard to kill him. Leonard acts shocked, but his response elicits an angry one from her. Natalie tells him she's going to use him, and insults Leonard and his wife, which provokes Leonard to give her a bruised lip and knock her down. Natalie storms out, while Leonard looks frantically for a pen to make a note of this. Moments later, Natalie walks back in the door and blames Dodd for her facial injuries, while in the black-and-white section, Leonard has become extremely paranoid.

Back in color, Leonard and Natalie (who doesn't have any bruises) walk into her apartment. She asks Leonard how long it's going to take him to find his wife, and he then tells her the story of his wife's murder. In a flashback, we see Leonard wake up, get a gun, and head into the bathroom. As his wife gasps for air underneath a clear plastic shower curtain, Leonard shoots her assailant, but he gets hit from behind by a second man. We see his head crash into the bathroom

A key scene involving Natalie

mirror and blood start to ooze from it on the tile floor. Contrary to the police report, Leonard insists there had to be a second man, but that John G. made it appear otherwise. He tells her, "I was the only guy who disagreed with the facts, and I had brain damage."

Natalie offers to let him stay at her house for a few days. He takes a Polaroid of her and writes her name on it. As Leonard sits in the living room, Natalie rushes in and closes the curtains. In the black-and-white section, the phone rings in Leonard's room as he sits on his bed and refuses to answer it. An envelope is slipped under his door. On the envelope are written the words "Take my call." Inside is a Polaroid of Leonard, who is bare-chested and smiling. He points to the area without a tattoo above his heart—the place he's reserved for when he finds his wife's killer.

The second turning point occurs at eighty-two minutes, when Leonard makes the mistake of answering the phone. In doing so, he disregards the freshly tattooed note on his arm that tells him explicitly, "Do not answer the phone." In black and white, Leonard, now agitated, talks on the phone with a cop. Leonard tells him, "I don't know. Something bad, maybe. Why are you asking me? I can't remember what I've done." He alludes to his memory loss, and once again connects it with Sammy. Leonard's answering the phone has the effect of shifting the emphasis from Natalie to her boyfriend, Jimmy, thus providing us with the real motivation for her actions, as we soon view the events that lead to Leonard's murder of Jimmy, his confrontation with Teddy, and his own deliberate self-deception. Given the film's total length (excluding credits)—approximately 110 minutes—*Memento* breaks down into a first act of thirty-two minutes, a second act of fifty minutes, and a third act of twenty-eight minutes.

All the major characters in *Memento* represent familiar genre types: the protagonist who inadvertently becomes a victim of corrupt or criminal circumstances, the duplicitous femme fatale, and the crooked cop. As is also typical of neo-noir, all of them suffer from serious character flaws.[8] Natalie starts off as an extremely likeable and sympathetic character, but she gradually transforms into a classic femme fatale, as she connives to provide Leonard with confirmation about the identity of Teddy. Although Natalie shifts between seeming concern and sheer cunning, her motivation remains completely consistent. When she offers to pay Leonard to kill Dodd, he becomes shocked at the thought of killing someone for money. But Natalie pounces on Leonard for such hypocrisy: "What then? Love? What would you kill for? You'd kill for your wife, wouldn't you?" Natalie turns from heartfelt concern to sheer nastiness, yet her motivation turns out to be exactly the same as Leonard's, only hers is clearly more justified. In an attempt to provoke a response from Leonard, Natalie focuses on Leonard's biggest vulnerability, namely, his deceased wife. Citing venereal disease as a major cause of short-term memory loss, Natalie tells him, "Maybe your cunt of a fucking wife sucked one too many diseased cocks and turned you into a fucking retard." His violent response turns out to be exactly what Natalie wants, since she can use the bruises as evidence to convince him about Dodd, thus proving, contrary to Leonard's assertions, that "facts" can be as deceiving as memory. Earlier, Natalie uses humor to ridicule Leonard's disability: "Must be tough living your life according to a couple of scraps of paper. You mix your laundry list with your grocery list, and you'll end up eating your underwear for breakfast." It's one of the best zingers in the film.

While Natalie is consistent in terms of her motivations, Teddy proves to be a much more inscrutable character. Except for the badge and the gun, nothing about him suggests that he's really a cop, except that we recognize the figure of the crooked cop as a convention of the genre. When Teddy lets Leonard take him to the abandoned building and turns his back on him, this seems especially naive on the part of a professional lawman. In the scene where Leonard calls Teddy to come to Dodd's hotel, Leonard suggests taking Dodd outside with a gun to his back. Teddy asks, "Why would I have a gun?" Why does he need to keep up this particular charade? After they dispose of Dodd, Teddy also regrets that they didn't steal his car. In fact, the questions about Teddy only multiply. Why would Teddy allow himself to get pistol whipped by Leonard after he kills Jimmy Grantz? Or, for that matter, why would Teddy let Leonard keep his gun and the stolen money? Teddy suggests initially that Jimmy Grantz is John G. He tells Leonard, "His name's James F. Grantz, John G.," but Leonard's not stupid, and James and John are hardly the same names, nor are they interchangeable. Teddy's point, we can only surmise, is that for someone lacking a memory, they might as well be. It really makes no difference, if you can't remember your actions. He tells Leonard:

> TEDDY: Cheer up, there's plenty of John G.'s for us to find. All you do is moan. I'm the one that has to live with what you've done. I'm the one that put it all together. You, you just wander around,

you're playing detective. You live in a dream, kid. A dead wife to pine for. A sense of purpose to your life. A romantic quest that you wouldn't end even if I wasn't in the picture.[9]

But Teddy hardly seems troubled by Leonard's actions. Taking Teddy's own behavior at face value, his rationale for helping Leonard track down his wife's murderer is explained by his statement "I believed you, I thought you deserved the chance for revenge." Teddy's vigilantism might cut it once, but it hardly explains why he would then implicate Leonard in the drug deal with Jimmy. If he's doing it strictly for money, which seems to be the case, why does he let Leonard take off with the bounty? In addition, Teddy knows full well what Leonard will do to Jimmy, so why does he feign surprise at what amounts to an arranged execution? Since there is no corroborating evidence for anything Teddy says, he proves to be just as unreliable a source as Leonard. In some ways, the main story involving Teddy and Natalie is itself a red herring because the mystery of who killed Leonard's wife, even by generic conventions, would point toward our protagonist, which is why Teddy even suggests at one point that Leonard really ought to be investigating himself.

In *Memento*, truth becomes impossible to distinguish from fiction precisely because, by the very terms of the film, Leonard's problem ends up becoming our own. *Memento* succeeds in placing the viewer into the damaged mind of its protagonist, allowing us to experience the perceptual shift by which his questionable actions are made to appear perfectly logical. Despite Leonard Shelby's insistence that an objective world exists outside his own mind, *Memento* revels in a sinister relativism, where the truth of what we are seeing remains up for grabs. This seems to have been a deliberate strategy on the part of the film's makers. As Christopher Nolan told *Entertainment Weekly*: "We always intended that there would be multiple interpretations that conflict and that the audience would have to choose what they want to believe."[10]

Nolan's desire to create a completely open-ended text, where viewers would be able to create their own individual readings of the film, has been echoed by a number of other screenwriters who seek to create cinematic puzzles for the viewer. Christopher McQuarrie, for instance, took a similar stance toward *The Usual Suspects* in wanting it to remain open to individual interpretation. McQuarrie insists, "To me, a film that answers all of your questions is pointless."[11] Richard Kelly, the screenwriter/director of the enigmatic *Donnie Darko,* also balks at the idea of narrative closure by referring to it as a "Hallmark greeting-card solution." Kelly admits: "I couldn't possibly answer or completely solve the riddle of this film [*Donnie Darko*]. It would mean I have all the answers and I don't."[12]

Shane Carruth's *Primer,* an ultra-low-budget science-fiction film that won the Grand Jury prize at the 2004 Sundance Film Festival, might have succeeded in pushing the puzzle film to its outer limits. In the film, two young men in white shirts and striped ties, Aaron and Abe, split from their startup-business partners to develop a low-tech, time-travel box. The film skips basic exposition almost entirely as it proceeds to explore the philosophical paradoxes of time travel, including key issues, such as cause and effect and individual identity. The two entrepreneurs create multiples of themselves, scheme to exploit their new invention for monetary gain, and attempt to alter real-life events, before the time machine ends up destroying their friendship. Little happens in the film in terms of action. Most of the scenes simply consist of the two young inventors talking to each other, but most of their dialogue consists of opaque scientific jargon that is nearly impossible for most viewers to decode. The same holds true for the intricacies of the sci-fi story as well, which, like *Memento,* is meant to be as perplexing as the mystery of time itself.

Narrational devices such as deliberately employing ambiguity and creating an open text are considered attributes of art cinema rather than of classical cinema, which is why such strategies generally are criticized and discouraged by manual writers. Linda Seger faults *Memento* precisely on the grounds that the very characteristics of this puzzle film violate the clarity and unity demanded by classical cinema. Seger writes of *Memento,* "However, even though a film followed a very tight three-act structure, for me, it really didn't answer its central question: 'What is the truth?' Was the truth clear to you at the end? Did the ending confuse you? Did it fascinate you? Did you like its ambiguity? Or did you want clarity from the only truth-teller we had—Teddy?"[13] American distributors obviously thought that audiences would likewise demand such clarity from Nolan's narrative Rorschach test, which is why they uniformly passed on the opportunity to pick the film up for commercial release when it played at Sundance. That so many major distributors were proven wrong simply confirms the fact that independent films often confound conventional assumptions about both audiences and narrative.

Independent films always need some type of hook to succeed in the marketplace. In the case of *Memento*, it turned out to be the novelty of its structural innovations—the link between cognition and memory in relation to its philosophical inquiry into the nature of revenge and identity—that differentiates Nolan's thoroughly engaging film from the myriad formulaic thrillers routinely produced by Hollywood. Sophisticated audiences apparently enjoyed the challenge of attempting to solve *Memento*'s elaborate and intricate puzzle, even if all of the pieces didn't entirely add up to a complete or fully coherent picture. Rather than proving to be a serious flaw, the many paradoxes of *Memento* simply provided audiences with an excuse to see the film multiple times or to buy the special-edition DVD version once it was released, with an Easter egg that even allows viewers to watch the film in chronological sequence, if only to appreciate its innovative temporal structure more fully.

Part Four

Noncausal Structures

Chapter 10

Dream Logic and *Mulholland Dr.*

> A mystery is one of the most beautiful things in the world. It pulls you into the world, and the ideas have a way of putting in clues. They're not spoon-fed to you, but they're there. All you have to do is pay attention, and use your intuition.[1]
>
> --David Lynch

David Lynch's *Mulholland Dr.* (2001) builds on ideas previously explored in *Lost Highway* (1997), especially in terms of its bold experimentation with narrative structure. In *Lost Highway*, which Lynch cowrote with Barry Gifford, one story line transforms unexpectedly into another through abrupt character transformation—as jazz musician Fred Madison literally turns into Pete Drayton, a young garage mechanic, while he sits in a jail cell for the brutal murder of his wife—and then back again, as the first story eventually circles back on itself. Whereas *Lost Highway* ended up confusing critics and audiences, most of whom seemed to view its vexing character and plot shifts and suggestion of alternate realities as extreme weirdness for its own sake, the narrative complexity and dreamlike logic of *Mulholland Dr.* helped to turn Lynch's neo-noir mystery about the corrupting influence of Hollywood into a major critical hit. Originally written and then rejected as a two-hour pilot for ABC television, Lynch's film uses the inherent open-ended demands of an extended TV series to full advantage in reconfiguring the shelved pilot into a feature film. *Mulholland Dr.* combines virtually all the elements of "thread structure" with the kind of narrative logic found only

201

in dreams, as characters shift identities abruptly, time becomes elastic, and objects and events resonate with multiple meanings.

Linda Seger discusses *Mulholland Dr.* as a "looping structure," which she defines as a film that has "a beginning, middle, and end, but it doesn't play them in that order." Seger writes, "A looping structure can be beginning-end-middle, as in *Pulp Fiction*, or it can be the structure of *Mulholland Drive*, which seems to start with the end and then loops back to the beginning and middle and back to the very end."[2] Seger's concept of a looping structure emphasizes a reshuffling of the chronology of the narrative, but her term ignores a fundamental aspect of films such as *Mulholland Dr.* and *Pulp Fiction*, namely, the ensemble nature of them. Evan Smith's term "thread structure" actually seems to be a more appropriate description of such films.[3] Thread structure challenges the tightly woven classical unity of the conventional three-act paradigm by replacing "a single driving story line, the hallmark of linear structure," with "multiple story threads."[4] Thread structure shares a number of characteristics with ensemble films, such as Miranda July's *Me and You and Everyone We Know*, in which several distinct but related stories intersect. The need to create several different story lines and protagonists often results in some of the stories becoming less fully developed, or even truncated. In both kinds of structures, there is often less time and opportunity to provide the same level of exposition and character development typically found in single-protagonist films. As a result, characters sometimes serve more than one function in the story. The key difference between thread structure and ensemble films, however, hinges on whether or not the story unfolds in a linear manner. Ensemble films tend to be decidedly linear, while thread structure involves a nonlinear approach that consists of "intersecting stories that invite shifts in time frame and character viewpoint."[5]

Tarantino's *Pulp Fiction* (1994) serves as Smith's prototype for thread structure. Indeed *Pulp Fiction* employs an achronological multiple-plot structure that interconnects three different stories. Two professional criminals, Jules Winnfield and Vincent Vega, are sent by their African-American crime boss, Marsellus Wallace, to retrieve a briefcase full of money from several young punks; Butch, a boxer, refuses to throw a fight for Marsellus; and Vincent has an arranged date with Marsellus's wife, Mia, who nearly overdoses during a night on the town. These three stories are framed by a holdup involving a young couple in a diner. Manual writer Lew Hunter criticizes *Pulp Fiction's* structure as being too "convoluted" for audiences. He also objects to the film on strictly Aristotelian grounds, seeing it as "just a series of episodes strung together," but lacking a beginning, middle, and end.[6]

Pulp Fiction's achronological structure, however, works better than a strictly linear progression of the events. By reshuffling the chronology of the three stories and framing them with the holdup in the coffee shop, Tarantino succeeds in interweaving the separate stories in such a way that he manages to maintain audience interest far more than the typical multiple-plot film. For one thing, Tarantino's alternative structure forces the more linear and straightforward stories of Vincent's date with Mia and Butch's double-cross of Marsellus into the middle section, and uses the frame of the diner holdup and the story of Jules and Vincent's mission to retrieve Marsellus's briefcase as bookend equivalents of what would normally be considered first and third acts. Structurally, this helps to maintain both Vincent and Jules as the central protagonists. The film ends with them intent on following different paths. The events have convinced Jules to exit the crime business, while Vincent continues to work for Marsellus, which we already know from the Butch section will result in his own death.

The key scene in *Pulp Fiction* in terms of its revamped structure is the one where Jules and Vincent return the briefcase to Marsellus, for it is here that the two stories intersect through the chance meeting of Vincent and Butch and their immediate and visceral dislike for each other. Spared from disaster in the Mia sequence, Vincent accepts it as a lucky break. But, shortly after this, he decides to use the bathroom at the wrong time, and gets blown away by Butch who is in the apartment because of his dream about his father's gold watch and because Fabienne has forgotten to take it with her. Tarantino's reliance on notions of coincidence and the vicissitudes of chance gets stretched to the limit by having Butch run into Marsellus at an intersection and then by having the two of them stumble into a pawnshop run by a sexual pervert. Later in the film, although earlier in time, bullets will happen to miss Vincent and Jules at point-blank range, and Vincent's gun will go off accidentally in the car. *Pulp Fiction* reiterates over and over the greater role chance plays in determining the fate and actions of characters, in contrast to the more classically oriented logic of simple cause and effect.

In many ways, *Mulholland Dr.* presents an even more radical structural challenge to conventional storytelling than *Pulp Fiction* or, for that matter, *Memento*. In the first act, Lynch sets up six different plot threads involving a host of different characters. In fact, so many potential characters and plotlines are established that it becomes extremely difficult for the viewer to figure out which one of the characters is supposed to be the main protagonist. As *Mulholland Dr.* progresses, some of the plot threads recede into the background or get dropped entirely, as two of them shift to the foreground. Betty, a newly arrived aspiring actress, plays Nancy Drew in the noir mystery that constitutes one plotline as she attempts to aid Rita, an amnesia victim, rediscover her identity. Meanwhile Adam, an independent-minded film director, struggles against the studio forces that attempt to control who will get the lead female role in his '60s rock-and-roll musical. It is not until more than halfway through *Mulholland Dr.* that the plotlines involving Betty and Adam finally intersect, when the plot thread involving Betty's career resurfaces and the two finally eye each other, not once but twice, at the audition where Adam capitulates to the studio demands. Just as entire plotlines end up being dead ends, this shared moment between Adam and Betty never develops into anything, instead becoming another of the film's many red herrings. As it turns out, some kind of personality shift takes place between Betty and Rita, and virtually all the female characters in the film take on new identities in the final act, as Betty becomes Diane Selwyn and Rita turns into Camilla Rhodes. This occurs after Betty and Rita discover a decaying corpse in an apartment bedroom, and a surprise romantic plotline develops between the two women. Mulholland Drive, the location of the fateful car accident that originally causes Rita's amnesia, becomes the setting for Adam's elegant party where he intends to announce his engagement to Camilla. It turns out to be Diane, however, who is driven up there in a limousine, in a scene that mimics the opening one of the accident, as the film comes full circle. Spurned by Camilla, and (at least in her own mind) denied a chance at stardom by the machinations of the same studio cabal, Diane seeks revenge, as her life takes a downward spiral.

If the reality of many of the events in *Mulholland Dr.* becomes nearly impossible to pinpoint throughout, Lynch's elaborate puzzle confounds us in the same manner as our own dreams, even suggesting the possibility that the entire story may simply be Diane's dream or an extended hallucinatory rationale for her failure to succeed in the Hollywood dream factory. Like *Memento*, *Mulholland Dr.* revels in the kind of ambiguity more typically found in art films to ensure that no rational analysis can ever fully explain away its mystery. This is why a manual writer such as Linda Seger, steeped as she is in the conventional paradigm, takes a critical view of this film. She contends, "No matter how one looks at this film, some scenes don't make sense and some episodes and characters don't fit."[7] Her major criticism, however, boils down to the fact that *Mulholland Dr.* is not easy for the average viewer to follow or understand.

Mulholland Dr. opens with a snappy sequence of jitterbug dancers against a magenta screen and superimposed images of a smiling young woman. The camera then tracks over the rumpled dark red sheets of a seemingly occupied bed and ends on the pillow, as we hear the sounds of heavy breathing. Lacking a context and denied essential narrative information, such as the identity of the person in the bed, we are not sure how to interpret this image, but it will turn out to have great significance later on. The first plot thread becomes established when a street sign for Mulholland Drive appears, illuminated by the headlights of a car, as a limousine winds up the canyon road at night and credits roll over the scene. Just as a well-dressed woman in the backseat is about to be shot, a car carrying drag-racing teenagers plows into the vehicle. The dark-haired woman escapes from the wreck and walks into the city below. After finding a pearl earring at the crash site, two detectives speculate that someone must be missing. This initiates a second plotline, the accident investigation, but it will remain a dangling cause because the detectives never reappear again. The next morning, the brunette sneaks into the courtyard apartment of an older actress who is leaving town. The film then establishes a third narrative thread involving Winkie's restaurant on Sunset Boulevard. A patron (identified as Dan in the script for the pilot) discusses a terrifying nightmare about the place with a friend. The two men then proceed to enact the particulars of the dream, going out back to check whether a monster is really there. As they approach the corner, the dark face of a street derelict, made to seem horrific, suddenly emerges, causing Dan to die of fright and the third plot thread to be abruptly cut short.

Who is Dan? Who is the person with him? What is Dan's connection to the brunette in the accident? Since none of this information is actually provided, this scene, along with the previous one of the detectives, represents an extreme example of several of the characteristics of both ensemble stories and thread structure: a truncated story and almost no exposition or character development. A crucial sequence follows, but its meaning becomes obscured by Lynch's use of synecdoche, when a paralyzed dwarf (later identified as "Mr. Roque") calls someone—we only see the back of the man's head—to announce, "The girl is still missing." The message is then relayed to a third person—we only see the man's arm and a filthy yellow phone lit by a circular neon light—who dials another number. The camera pans down the wall, past a red lamp shade to a ringing black phone and an ashtray containing lots of cigarette butts. The sequence serves to deliver and to withhold important narrative information from the viewer, who has no way of knowing the meaning or the impact of the message. Thus, Lynch's initial strategy in *Mulholland Dr.* is to draw us into the mystery through a series of incidents that are deliberately left as dangling causes.

It is nearly eighteen minutes into the film before the blond young woman Betty Elms (whose face we recognize from the opening jitterbug sequence) arrives at Los Angeles airport and walks arm-in-arm with a smiling elderly lady named Irene. As Betty is leaving, Irene tells the aspiring actress, "Now, remember I'll be watching for you on the big screen." This line of dialogue establishes Betty's career aspirations to make it as a Hollywood actress as the film's fourth plotline. As Betty says goodbye to Irene and her husband (both of whom appeared momentarily with Betty in the opening jitterbug sequence), her expression changes abruptly when she thinks her luggage has disappeared. Another premonition of what may lie ahead for Betty occurs when we see Irene and her husband guffawing in the backseat of a car, perhaps at the young woman's naïveté. There is something very distorted about their reactions, suggesting some type of paranoid subjective viewpoint, but there is no indication at this point that we are seeing them from Betty's perspective. Betty arrives at her destination and meets Coco, the colorful landlady. As Betty explores her Aunt Ruth's apartment, she is shocked to find a naked woman in the shower. The woman turns out to be the dark-haired woman from the accident, who, adopting an identity from a movie poster for *Gilda*, tells Betty that her name is "Rita."

A fifth plotline becomes established in a meeting between Adam Kesher, a brash young film director, and various studio executives, including the Castigliane brothers, who insist that an actress named

Camilla Rhodes be cast as the female lead in Adam's new movie. The meeting is also monitored by Mr. Roque from another room. Adam refuses to acquiesce to their demands, and then batters the Castigliane brothers' limousine with a golf club before driving off in a sports car. After the studio executive consults with Mr. Roque, it becomes clear that a decision has been made to shut down Adam's production.

A sixth plot thread seems an unmistakable reference to *Pulp Fiction*. In an office building, two men laugh about a freak accident. The man in the black leather jacket (Joe) alludes to "Ed's famous black book," as the seated man responds, "Yeah, the history of the world in phone numbers." Joe then shoots him at point-blank range. As Joe wipes the gun clean with a handkerchief and attempts to place it in the man's hand, he inadvertently pulls the trigger, leading to a comedy of errors in which he shoots two other people before setting off the smoke alarm. Befuddled, Joe grabs the black book and disappears down the fire escape. Is the accident to which the men refer the same one involving Rita? Why does Joe kill the man? What is the importance of the black book? Although the scene seems unnecessarily cryptic, it succeeds in establishing Joe as some sort of professional hit man, the significance of which will be left as another dangling cause until much later in the film. It takes roughly forty minutes to introduce the six different plot threads.

Mr. Roque monitoring the meeting

Mulholland Dr. proceeds to cut back and forth between three of the narrative threads. After a conversation with Aunt Ruth, who suggests calling the police, Betty confronts Rita about her misunderstanding that Rita was a friend of her aunt, but Rita cries about the fact that she doesn't know her identity. After Betty suggests that the answer probably lies inside Rita's handbag, it turns out to contain stacks of $100 bills and an odd-shaped blue key. Just as Adam's resistance to the demands of the studio bosses serves as the first turning point in that story thread, Betty's decision to help Rita discover her identity functions as a first turning point in the mystery. This occurs approximately forty-four minutes into the film. Meanwhile, Joe and another man eat hot dogs as they walk with an unkempt young woman with blond hair. Joe asks her if any new girls have turned up on the streets, specifically, "A brunette? . . . maybe beat up?" This scene, in combination with the earlier reference to the accident, reinforces the fact that Joe must be connected somehow to Rita, but we are not sure how.

Much of the second act alternates between Rita's mystery and Adam's troubles. After hiding the purse containing the money and key in a hatbox, Betty proves to be an able sleuth, as she discovers two important clues. One of them turns out to be Mulholland Drive, the scene of a confirmed accident. The two women discover a second clue at Winkie's restaurant, when the waitress's name tag jogs Rita's memory to throw out the name "Diane Selwyn." Despite Rita's reluctance, the two locate an address and make plans to pay a visit. A strange psychic neighbor, however, appears at the door and announces that someone's in trouble. Coco shoos the woman away and delivers a script to Betty for an audition the following day. The arrival of the script reestablishes the plot thread involving Betty's whole purpose for coming to Los Angeles, which has, at least until now, been subsumed by the strange real-life noir mystery she has happened to stumble upon, in which she now plays the role of amateur detective. Meanwhile, Adam learns of the studio's hardball tactics from his assistant, Cynthia. At home, he discovers his wife having an affair with a pool man, who beats up Adam and throws him out of his own house. Adam then winds up at a seedy flophouse, where he discovers that he has developed credit problems. Cynthia confirms that Adam is now broke, and she suggests that he see a person called the Cowboy.

Shaken by this turn of events, Adam decides to meet with the Cowboy in Beachwood Canyon. As a bare lightbulb flashes, the Cowboy, wearing a large white Stetson and red bandanna, approaches out of the darkness. There is something surreal about his appearance—it's almost as if the production's costume person has managed to confuse genres—but the character turns out to be a pure Lynchian touch. In some of the most humorous dialogue in the film, the Cowboy suggests to Adam that "A man's attitude goes some ways toward how a man's life will be." He also chastises Adam for being a smart aleck, then switches to metaphor:

> COWBOY: There's sometimes a buggy. How many drivers does a buggy have?
> ADAM: One.
> COWBOY: So let's just say I'm drivin' this buggy and you fix your attitude and you can ride along with me.[8]

The Cowboy gives Adam explicit instructions to go back to work and recast the lead female part. He tells him that when he sees the girl whose photo he was shown earlier by the Castigliane brothers, he is to say, "This is the girl." The cowboy then threatens Adam, "Now, you will see me one more time if you do good. You will see me two more times if you do bad. Good night."

The next scene, which is set at Aunt Ruth's house, causes momentary confusion in our understanding of Betty's character, when she remarks, "You're still here?" When Rita indicates that she thought that was what Betty wanted, Betty snaps, "Nobody wants you here." The sting of Betty's response softens when we realize that Betty and Rita are merely rehearsing the lines for Betty's film audition. In the script, Betty plays a teenager having a sordid affair with a friend of her father's. The scene ends with a threat to kill him with a knife. As Betty mimes tears, she says, "Cry, cry, cry, and then I say with big emotion, 'I hate you . . . I hate us both.'" The two women ridicule the soap-opera nature of the material, but Rita insists that Betty is a really fine actress. Coco comes by and discovers Rita sitting in a bathrobe on the couch. When Betty pretends that Rita is an old friend, Coco does not hide the fact that she thinks Betty is lying by calling her story "a load of horse-pucky." Alluding to the psychic neighbor, Coco warns Betty that she needs to get rid of the "trouble."

As Betty approaches the studio for her audition, Lynch's pilot script suggests that she's "staring at a dream."[9] Once inside, the elderly and affable Wally Brown greets her warmly and introduces her to Bob

Booker, the director, Woody Katz, an actor who has already been cast as the male lead, and a casting agent, Linney James, who happens to be sitting in. As the lecherous older actor tries to take advantage of the intimacy of the scene, Betty surprises even herself by playing her part with a steamy eroticism. Although Bob Booker calls Betty's performance "forced maybe but still humanistic," everyone else seems to be genuinely bowled over by it, including Linney, who decides to take her over to a second audition.

Betty's second audition turns out to be even more significant because it becomes the point at which the two main plot threads finally intersect. It begins with a shot of a retro '60s recording studio where an actress lip-synchs to the song "Sixteen Reasons," by Connie Stevens, with four backup singers. The camera pulls back to reveal that we are viewing a movie set. As the bright-eyed Betty enters, Adam turns toward her and the two stare at each other with a look described in the pilot script as "they each seem to feel the thrill of the thunderbolt."[10] After Adam cuts the scene, the next actress is introduced as "Camilla Rhodes." As she mouths an uninspired rendition of Linda Scott's "I've Told Every Little Star," Adam calls a studio functionary and announces, "This is the girl." Betty, however, suddenly panics when she glances at her watch. As she again makes eye contact with Adam, a point that is emphasized by extreme close-ups of their eyes,

Adam Kesher at the casting session

Rita and Betty at the Sierra Bonita apartments

Betty excuses herself politely, and suddenly flees the recording studio. We then see her enter a cab with Rita.

Adam's capitulation to the Castigliane brothers, thus compromising the artistic integrity (a humorous conceit given the material) of his new film, followed by Betty's sudden abandonment of her career ambition to become a Hollywood actress, serve as the second major turning points for both plotlines, which intersect here at eighty-six minutes for the first time. Betty's "Cinderella-like" (this is even how the script describes it) flight from the audition also seems to arrest the potential development of a new romantic thread involving Adam. The most surprising aspect of Betty's behavior, however, is the fact that her priorities turn out to be much more bound up with Rita than we might, at least until this point, have suspected.

At the Sierra Bonita apartments, Betty and Rita find the name "Diane Selwyn" listed in the registry, but when they knock on the door of apartment twelve, a woman informs them she and Diane have switched apartments, but that Diane hasn't been around for a few days. After there's no answer at the other apartment, Betty climbs in through the window of the bungalow. Holding her nose, Betty then opens the door from the inside, and the two women proceed to discover (at ninety-six minutes) a decaying corpse lying in the bedroom. As Rita attempts to scream, Betty covers Rita's mouth with her hand, as the other tenant knocks on the door and then leaves. Rita screams—although we only hear the eerie music on the sound track—as she and Betty run out of the apartment and their images start to superimpose over themselves. The discovery of the rotting corpse serves as a second major turning point in the mystery plot thread to determine Rita's identity. This event will bring significant changes to the characters of the two women, who undergo a kind of *Persona*-like personality transference in the next scene.

In a close shot, Rita leans over a sink and attempts to cut off her hair, but Betty manages to restrain her. "I know what you have to do," Betty tells her, "but let me do it." When the two women then look in the mirror at the transformed Rita, she now has blond hair that is cut to look like Betty's, causing even Betty to remark, "You look like someone else." This is more or less where the pilot ended, but Lynch creates a surprising new plot thread when Betty invites Rita to share the bed. Rita takes off the blond wig, removes the towel that covers her naked body, and the two end up in a passionate embrace. "I'm in love with you," Betty confesses, with the same steamy desire we witnessed earlier in the audition with Woody Katz, suddenly bringing the repressed romantic plotline to the foreground. This admission provides us with a motivation for her behavior at the audition for Adam's film. Even though the introduction of this new romantic plotline comes as something of a surprise, there have actually been several clues, such as the remarks of the psychic neighbor, Coco's obvious disapproval of the developing relationship, and even the lyrics to the audition song "I've Told Every Little Star," which are about a secret undisclosed love.

The extended lovemaking scene cuts to the two of them asleep. Rita calls out the word "Silencio" several times during a nightmare, then gets Betty to accompany her to a tawdry Latino night spot called Club Silencio, where a magician performs what amounts to a deconstruction of cinematic illusionism in an old, nearly empty movie theater. A man playing the trumpet stops playing, but we still hear the sound. As the magician raises his arms, creating thunder and lightning, Betty quakes in her seat. A woman, who is introduced as Rebekah Del Rio, then comes out and sings an a cappella, Spanish-language version of Roy Orbison's "Crying," which brings both Betty and Rita to tears. The singer collapses, but the recording continues, as two men drag her off stage. Betty reaches into her handbag and takes out a blue box. The two women then return home and Rita takes down the hatbox containing her handbag. Betty disappears, but Rita removes the matching blue key, puts it in the lock, opens it, and the camera moves into the darkness inside, recalling Alice's fall down the rabbit hole in *Alice in Wonderland*. This occurs at 115 minutes, marking a third turning point. The film thus has four acts rather than three: a first act of forty-four minutes, a second act of forty-two minutes, a third act of twenty-nine minutes, and a fourth act of twenty-nine minutes.

Once we move inside the blue box and into the fourth and final act, the female characters, most notably Betty and Rita, experience a series of identity changes. Betty turns into Diane Selwyn and Rita becomes Camilla Rhodes. The transformation of Betty into Diane Selwyn recalls that of Fred Madison into Pete Drayton in *Lost Highway*, but there does seem to be a major difference. In *Lost Highway*, there is something literal about the transformation, a point that is made clear by the script:

INT. PRISON. FRED'S CELL. NIGHT

Fred's blank face begins to contort and take on the appearance, feature by feature, of Pete Drayton.

Fred Madison is becoming Pete Drayton.[11]

Not only do we witness it, but the prison guards do as well, as one of them comments, "Captain . . . this is some spooky shit we got here."[12] *Mulholland Dr.* likewise contains some very bizarre goings on, but the identity changes, which are indicated by shifts in camera angles, seem to be less rooted in uncanny occurrences than in obvious mental states. Is Diane dreaming? Is she suffering from a nervous breakdown? Has everything that has gone before—more than three-quarters of the film—been nothing more than an extended dream or hallucination? Indeed, the fourth act forces us to rethink virtually all our assumptions about what has gone before. The identity shift also causes a pronounced personality change in the two women. Betty/Diane, the ever-optimistic and assertive sleuth, has become reduced to a shadow of her former self, while Rita/Camilla, who had virtually no personality before, as a result of her memory loss, has now transformed into the classic Hollywood vamp. The power relations between the two women clearly reverse once they have become entangled romantically. Diane has been reduced to a pathetic mess, while Camilla has gained dominance over her.

One way to think about the structure of *Mulholland Dr.* is to see that the setup typically found in a first act has been deliberately withheld until the fourth act. The fourth act also ruptures the linear trajectory of the multiple story threads that comprise the first three acts. For the first three acts, *Mulholland Dr.* proceeds like a typical ensemble film, but once the lesbian romance becomes manifest, we begin to experience the time shifts and change in character viewpoints more clearly associated with thread structure, which serves to enhance the mystery. Delaying the main romantic plotline as well as the film's narrational frame until the fourth and final act prevents the viewer from realizing that the story has actually been unfolding through a series of flashbacks. The discovery of the rotting corpse turns out to be a prolepsis, that is, flash-forward, rather than a flashback, but this will only be revealed at the very end of the film.

After the blue box drops to the floor, Aunt Ruth enters her apartment, the camera tracks toward Diane Selwyn lying in bed, and the Cowboy opens the door, saying, "Hey pretty girl. Time to wake up." The scene fades to black as we hear the sound of more knocks on a door, then fades to a morning shot of Diane Selwyn, but as we get closer and the figure rises, we recognize that she's a more haggard-looking version of Betty. She puts on a robe and answers the door. The woman tenant from apartment twelve, addressing Betty as Diane, asks

The Cowboy appears for a second time

her where she's been, and demands that she return several possessions. As the woman retrieves an ashtray, the blue key sits on the edge of the coffee table. The woman mentions that a couple of detectives have been looking for Diane. After the woman leaves, Diane walks over to the kitchen sink. Seconds later, she turns and addresses Rita, whom she now calls Camilla. "You've come back," Diane says, her body shaking as if in a fever. The angle switches on Diane, who makes coffee. She pours herself a cup, then climbs over the couch. The angle changes slightly and she's no longer wearing a bathrobe, but dressed only in jean shorts. Diane straddles Camilla and fondles her naked breasts. Initially stimulated, the capricious Camilla tells Betty, "We shouldn't do this any more." Diane threatens Camilla, who pushes her away, leading Diane to speculate, "It's him, isn't it?"

Diane's dialogue hook is answered by the very next scene in which we watch Adam direct Camilla in a romantic scene on a movie set. Adam breaks one of the cardinal rules of directing by choosing to demonstrate how the part should be performed, as Diane watches jealously from nearby. Adam asks that the set be cleared, but Camilla requests that Diane be allowed to stay. Diane's eyes glisten with tears, as Adam nuzzles and kisses Camilla in the front seat of a convertible. Adam yells, "Kill the lights," as he kisses her passionately. The lights fade on the set and then on a close-up of Diane's face. The scene shifts back to the Sierra Bonita apartment. "Don't be mad," Camilla pleads, while Diane screams, "It's not easy for me," slamming the door in Camilla's face. We hear the sounds of Diane crying, as the camera tracks from the closed door to a shot of her masturbating on the couch, intermixed with subjective shifts in focus. The sound of a ringing phone nearby causes Diane to look over. The camera moves down the wall, past the red lamp shade, and settles on a shot of the table with the black phone and ashtray containing cigarette butts—it's the same shot that we were given earlier in the film without any sense of context. In a wider shot, Diane, wearing a black slip, walks into the room as the answering machine switches on, thus solving the earlier mystery. Once Diane picks up the phone, instead of receiving the message, "The girl is still missing," it turns out to be Camilla, who tells her that a car is waiting downstairs and gives her an address on Mulholland Drive.

Lynch's narrational strategy positions the viewer to play the role of a detective. As we have seen, he has planted several important clues early on. There is the tracking shot over the bed, along with the sound of heavy breathing, but we had no way of knowing that the person in the bed was Diane. If we did, then we might have understood it as a partial narrative frame for what transpires. The same is true of the ambiguous message, "The girl is still missing," which is relayed by someone—we will later determine the person's identity to be Joe—to a room that turns out to be Diane's bedroom. This news presumably pushes her over the edge, but we are only able to deduce that once we understand Diane's dire romantic predicament. The connection between that early phone call and Diane only becomes clarified when Diane gets Camilla's message regarding the surprise party on Mulholland Drive.

In this next scene, as happens in both *Lost Highway* and *Memento*, *Mulholland Dr.* doubles back on itself. We return to the opening limousine ride, including the same shots of car lights illuminating the street sign for Mulholland Drive, as the car again makes its way up the winding road, only this time it is actually Diane who is sitting in the backseat. When the vehicle stops, Diane quizzes the driver, asking, "What are you doing? We don't stop here . . ." Camilla comes out of the wooded growth and escorts Diane to a lavish party overlooking the city below. The grounds and pool look familiar. We recognize the location as Adam's house, once the director emerges and makes a toast "to love." Coco rushes over as well, and Adam introduces her as his mother, who repeats the same line she used when introducing herself to Betty the first time.

The next two scenes become crucial in untangling the mystery because they furnish us with a good deal of missing exposition. For instance, Diane tells about being from Deep River, Ontario, and about winning a jitterbug contest, which explains the opening image of her smiling face superimposed over the dancers. It is at the engagement party for Adam and Camilla that we see several of the people—Coco, the woman from the audition who kisses Camilla, the Cowboy, and one of the Castigliane brothers—who then get reconfigured in the dreams, memories, and hallucinations spinning wildly inside Diane's tortured mind. At the party we learn that Diane met Camilla when she auditioned for a film directed by Bob Booker. This information comes as something of a surprise because we might have assumed that they met at the audition for Adam's musical, in which we watched him say, "This is the girl." But the Camilla Rhodes at the audition is not really Camilla, but the woman who kisses her at the party.

Even the refrain "This is the girl," the mandate from the Castigliane brothers, turns out to be the phrase Diane uses when she hands the photo résumé to Joe in the next scene at Winkie's restaurant. Objects, such as the blue key and black book, have their origins here as well. The key gets connected to the blue box into which Rita falls, while the black book becomes the motive for Joe's earlier murder of the long-haired man. The waitress's name is not Diane, the clue that led Rita to throw out the name Diane Selwyn, but Betty, the identity Diane assumes in playing the role of detective in the mystery. The scene at Winkie's also provides the connection to the truncated story thread involving Dan's dream of the monster behind the restaurant. Dan is revealed to be simply another patron with whom Diane makes eye contact when she arranges with Joe to kill Camilla. The scene of Dan could easily be eliminated from the film, but it has an important thematic function, which is to demonstrate the power of the imagination to control reality. The scene with Dan appears to be a reference to Maya Deren's avant-garde classic *Meshes of the Afternoon* (1943), the psychosexual trance film she co-made with Alexander Hammid, which not only uses a dream structure—in which objects and events are transformed—but ends with Deren (playing herself) being killed by the powers of her own fertile imagination.

The scene at Winkie's dissolves into red-filtered subjective shots, as the camera tracks around the back of the diner toward the homeless derelict, with matted hair and soot covering his face, who frightened Dan to death earlier in the film. The homeless man examines the blue box, then places it in a paper bag on the ground. Irene and her husband (the folks who accompanied Betty/Diane on the plane to Los Angeles) appear as miniature cackling figures from inside the bag and disappear out of the frame. The camera then pans from the blue key on the edge of the table to the coffee cup to Diane, who, seemingly lost in thought, sits on the couch. She stares at the key and, at the sound of a knock, turns her head toward the door, under which the miniature laughing figures crawl into the apartment. We hear additional knocks as lights flicker over an extreme close-up shot of Diane's eye. Diane gets up from the couch and runs screaming. A lightning storm (similar to the one that the magician conjured up at Club Silencio) rages, as Irene and her husband taunt and chase her into her bedroom. Lying on the bed, Diane reaches into the night table drawer for a revolver, puts its to her mouth, and pulls the trigger, causing smoke to fill the room. This is followed by a dissolve to a close-up of the homeless "monster," superimposed over shots of Club Silencio, Los Angeles, images of a smiling Diane next to Camilla, the empty stage at Club Silencio, and the woman in the blue wig, who sits in the balcony. She says "Silencio," as the screen fades to black.

It is really only after *Mulholland Dr.* is over that the viewer can even begin to piece together the various strands of what has been deliberately constructed to be a mystery. The emergence of the lesbian love story—a plotline that has been suppressed for most of the film—certainly alters our understanding of the various events. The identity switch—a seemingly mind-boggling narrative twist—also causes the viewer to question which parts are dream and which parts are reality. Does the film shift into a nightmarish dream at this point? Or have we been watching a dream and now become grounded by reality?

The events of the final act cause a major revision of the story. In the amended version, Diane Selwyn, a naive young woman from Canada, arrives in Los Angeles after winning a jitterbug contest. Aspiring to become a Hollywood actress, she gets passed over for the lead role in *The Sylvia North Story* in favor of Camilla Rhodes. Diane falls in love with Camilla, her career never takes off, and she suffers a nervous breakdown after getting dumped by Camilla, who has taken up with the recently divorced film director Adam Kesher. After attending the surprise engagement party for Adam and Camilla at Adam's mansion on Mulholland Drive, Diane seeks revenge by arranging with a hit man at Winkie's diner to kill Camilla, who ends up being saved by a freak accident. The message that Camilla is missing (is this a euphemism?) causes Diane to have a complete nervous breakdown. Diane's intricate dream or fantasy, in which she plays detective by helping Camilla discover her identity, mirrors her own loss of self in falling madly in love with a Hollywood star. As the strung-out Diane huddles inside her Sierra Bonita bungalow, terrifying hallucinations cause her to put an end to her life.

Even though *Mulholland Dr.* turns out to be Diane's story in the end, Adam's plot thread provides an important parallel, providing another example of how the Hollywood dream factory has the power to destroy not only those with talent and ambition, but also those who attempt to assert their own individual creative ideas. Adam, who fancies himself an auteur, believes he can buck the system, but the combined forces of Mr. Roque, the Castigliane brothers, and the Cowboy soon manage to relegate him to the status of all the other hacks we witness in the scene where Betty/Diane auditions for Wally Brown's production. Just as the over-the-hill actor Woody Katz uses the audition scene to exploit Betty/Diane sexually, we later watch Adam do the same as he directs the romantic scene with Camilla in the convertible. Not surprisingly, Lynch's portrait of Hollywood turns out to be nothing short of a brutal satire. The studios are shown to be controlled by dwarfs such as Mr. Roque isolated in glass rooms. The executives cower before powerful financiers like the Castigliane brothers, who seem more concerned about the quality of the espresso than the films they are producing. They behave and act like mafiosi, a connection made literal by the telephone call linking Mr. Roque to Joe, the sleazy hit man, and by the large thug who shows up at Adam's house and punches out the pool man. And the Cowboy, a displaced refugee from another Hollywood genre entirely, seems an appropriately strange messenger of these controlling and repressive forces.

Adam's story thread becomes crucial in providing the necessary exposition for the viewer to understand the reasons for Diane's rapid descent. It delineates the world in which Diane hopes to succeed by suggesting that, no matter how great her talent or optimism, she faces a closed and arbitrary system that will reduce her to the shattered wreck of a person she eventually becomes. In Lynch's vision, the Hollywood dream turns out to be a horrific nightmare, where the division between dream and reality is hopelessly blurred.

Through an imaginative use of thread structure, *Mulholland Dr.* unfolds through Diane's own fractured subjectivity, causing the meaning of objects and events to reverberate in the endless hall of mirrors of her own mind. Along with pop songs Lynch so carefully incorporates into the narrative, Hollywood movies are the main purveyors of the kind of romantic fantasies to which the innocent Betty/Diane succumbs. As Phillip Lopate rightly points out, "*Mulholland Dr.* is a movie about movies, in more ways than one."[13] Lynch marshals other imaginative films—*Persona, Pulp Fiction,* and *Meshes of the Afternoon,* as well as dream logic itself—as part of his extensive arsenal to deconstruct the enormous power of the Hollywood dream factory, by depicting, as utterly befits the genre he is working in, its dark underside.

Chapter 11

Free Association and *Gummo*

A tabloid look at the decay of a small Midwestern town and the dark underside of adolescence, Harmony Korine's *Gummo* (1997) might be the most controversial American independent film of the 1990s. Not only does the film boldly ignore the conventions of mainstream plot, but it also aims to provoke its audience by presenting subject matter—animal abuse, racist venom, prostitution, child molestation, and murder—in a manner intended to be shocking and grotesque. *Gummo* pushes at the boundaries of acceptable good taste by raising issues about the presentation of the physically and mentally challenged, and by blurring the boundaries between documentary reality and scripted fiction. American independent films that have difficult content—*Bad Lieutenant* (1992), *The Living End* (1992), *In the Company of Men* (1997), and *Boys Don't Cry* (1999)—often couch such material within a more conventional form in order to make it more palatable. To its credit, *Gummo* resists this temptation by employing a far more experimental collage technique in which scenes are linked together not by cause and effect but by the more elusive logic of free association.

Most filmmakers who have attempted to work in this type of form have depended on editing to shape the material into a coherent finished film. *Gummo* exploits the editing process, as well as the spontaneous, improvised, and serendipitous events that can occur during actual filming, but the film nevertheless relies very heavily on Korine's engaging screenplay. Unlike so-called execution-dependent films, such as Jim Jarmusch's *Stranger Than Paradise* and *Down By Law,* or even

Gus Van Sant's *Elephant* (which didn't have a traditional script), *Gummo* succeeds on the page as well as the screen, which no doubt helped to convince Fine Line to finance such an unlikely feature film. On another level, given the demographics of its audience, Fine Line's interest in Korine and *Gummo* seems fairly transparent. At the time *Gummo* was produced, Korine was considered a certified youth-culture insider. He had already achieved notoriety and success, at age nineteen, as the screenwriter for Larry Clark's *Kids* (1995), an independent film that walked a fine line between authentic youth-culture expression and exploitation. Its graphic depiction of teen sexuality and drug consumption caused *Kids* to get an NC-17 rating, and Miramax to distribute it under a different label, but the film grossed $7 million in domestic release.

The more provocative and disturbing aspects of *Gummo*—those elements that appear to have riled movie critics and reviewers—are a bit less apparent in the screenplay.[1] Korine, for example, describes the early scene of someone drowning a cat in seven precise sentences, yet the effect on the page is not quite the same as its visceral impact on the screen.[2] Korine's screenplay nevertheless contains a remarkable level of specificity about its adolescent characters. It's apparent from reading the script that Korine has an exact sense of how each scene should look and sound. Here is how he describes Solomon and Tummler as they ride their bikes:

> *The two of them are riding their bikes down an empty street.*
>
> *Rows of small houses surround both sides of the street.*
>
> *Both boys have BB guns strapped to their backs.*
>
> *Solomon is wearing tight army pants with big pockets and an orange YMCA T-shirt. He has on a pair of generic high-top sneakers. His bike is red and simple, one wheel is a mag and the other is spoked.*
>
> *Tummler is wearing a pair of blue jeans with patches on them. There are little holes in his pants. He is wearing a blue flannel shirt with grease stains. He has a green backpack on. His sneakers are old running shoes with soles worn down. His bike is more glamorous; it is painted silver and has stickers on it. There is a racing plate on the front of the handlebars with the number 17 on it. He is sitting on a long padded banana seat. There is a skull and crossbones flag attached to the back of the bike. It flaps noisily in the wind.*[3]

Not only does the above description help to reveal character—the difference between the two characters (clothes, shoes, accessories, the type of bikes they're riding), but "authenticity" is also inscribed in the details. (As the industry well knows, kids—for whom style is everything—have the uncanny ability to spot a fake.) Korine also provides other levels of specificity in terms of the behavior of his characters, such as the scene where Solomon and Tummler break into Jarrod Wigely's house and Solomon exchanges the dirty pair of socks he's wearing for a fresh pair of Jarrod's. Solomon's gesture suggests his poverty, but, on a symbolic level, it represents an unconscious attempt by the young burglar to take possession of someone else's home.

Korine's grasp of youth culture extends to his dialogue. Whereas Korine's dialogue in *Kids* attempted to replicate realism by being long, rambling, and highly verbose, the dialogue in *Gummo* turns out to be much closer to a kind of poetic realism. In capturing the innocent banter of teenagers—the types of stupid things kids actually talk about—Korine includes bits of nonsense, or what could easily be snippets of overheard real-life conversation:

TUMMLER: Does your mom ever make you food?
SOLOMON: She makes me toast.
TUMMLER: Is that it?
SOLOMON: She cooks me lamb chops.
TUMMLER: You ever eaten crêpe suzette?

My characterization of the above passage as "nonsense" stems from the fact that what Solomon says doesn't prove true. Solomon's mother actually serves him spaghetti—not toast or lamb chops—when she shampoos his hair toward the end of the film. After Tummler recites what amounts to an oral suicide note, which is followed by a video clip of the band Slayer, Solomon says in voiceover, "Life is beautiful. Really it is. Full of beauty and illusions. Life is great. Without it, you'd be dead." Solomon's statement seems ironic, if not odd, given what has just transpired. While this could be interpreted as another contrast in character between the world views of Tummler and Solomon, Korine confirmed in an interview that Solomon's statement is actually an old vaudeville joke.[4] The inclusion of such materials represents Korine's enthusiasm for creating a collage of different bits of information, thus establishing weird juxtapositions while completely disguising his sources. That proves to be part of the poetry and mystery of Korine's screenplay for *Gummo*, which confirmed Korine's substantial talents as a writer attuned to the subtle nuances of youth culture.

Fine Line's marketing campaign for *Gummo*, which emphasized the twenty-three-year-old writer/director's youth-culture pedigree, took a distinctly auteurist slant. The press materials included a brief foreword by Gus Van Sant (who was the executive producer of *Kids*), as well as an enthusiastic interview with Korine conducted by none other than the German director Werner Herzog. Van Sant wrote, "Harmony Korine has come up with a completely original creation, as far as I can tell. To categorize it would be hard because it is so new, there would have to be a new category."[5] The film's coproducer, Robin O'Hara, who, like Van Sant, acknowledged specific influences, also insisted on Korine's originality: "The thing that's stunning about Harmony is he is an original, in every sense of the word."[6] Fine Line's publicity campaign and Korine's own interviews about *Gummo* sought to situate the film within a tradition of European art cinema by citing the films of Herzog, Fellini, and Godard. (Korine would later align himself with the Danish Dogme 95 manifesto with his next film, *julien donkey-boy* (1999), with Herzog cast in one of the lead roles.) The improvisational aspects of *Gummo*—the tension between spontaneity and scripted action—were likened to the films of John Cassavetes.

Whereas *Gummo's* nonlinear story, lack of plot, and mixture of documentary and fiction might seem new and original in the context of commercial cinema, it is not without precedent within the noncommercial tradition of American cinema. Ten years after Deren and Hammid's dream-inspired psychodrama *Meshes of the Afternoon*, Christopher Maclaine, the San Francisco-based Beat poet, took an amphetamine-inspired, nonlinear approach to narrative syntax in films such as *The End* (1953) and *The Man Who Invented Gold* (1957), which were largely underappreciated at the time.[7] In the 1960s, Jonas Mekas championed the idea of a plotless cinema as an antidote to what he perceived to be the stagnation of classical Hollywood, even going so far as to suggest that the only way to insure a rebirth of American cinema would be to shoot all screenwriters.[8] Ron Rice's underground classic *The Flower Thief* (1960) and David Brooks's lesser-known *The Wind Is Driving Him Toward the Open Sea* (1968) represent two important manifestations of this plotless impulse.

Not surprisingly, Korine attempted to distance himself from American avant-garde tradition as well as American independent cinema: "I'm a hundred per cent commercial filmmaker. I have nothing to do with independent directors, alternative cinema, I make Harmony movies. It's a cinema of obsession and passion. But at the same time, I can't differentiate between notions of underground. Underground film, underground music, alternative culture, to me it doesn't exist."[9] Korine's denial of the existence of alternative cinema no doubt allowed him to promote his own originality and to claim that *Gummo* represented a "new aesthetic."[10] There's a bit of an irony here. Although Korine found himself financed by a subsidiary of a major studio and insists that he's a totally commercial filmmaker, his work has, at least thus far, proven too avant-garde to attract a wide mainstream audience. Indeed, Benjamin Halligan argues that Korine's *Gummo* represents an attempt at self-annihilation in order to resist "being assimilated in the Neo-Underground"—a negation in the face of the cooption of independent films in the 1990s.[11]

Just as it is necessary to understand Korine's achievement within a larger cinematic tradition, it is equally important to point out that he did not create *Gummo* in a cultural vacuum. Korine's denial of the existence of an alternative culture is even more problematic given the fact that his artistic practice—he's written a novel, produced fanzines, and done installations in major art galleries—has undeniable roots in urban street culture. Korine has been associated with the artistic subculture centered around Aaron Rose's infamous Alleged Gallery on the Lower East Side of New York City. His work, which exhibits a do-it-yourself rawness, shares aesthetic concerns with that of other self-taught artists who also base their art primarily on their own life experiences. These include neo-graffiti and skateboard painters such as Barry McGee, Margaret Kilgallen, and Chris Johanson, designers such as Ryan McGinness, musicians such as Tommy Guerrero, and artists who also work in multiple disciplines, such as Mark Gonzales (who even appears in *Gummo* as the guy who wrestles the chair). All these artists, including Korine, were featured as part of a recent major museum exhibition entitled "Beautiful Losers: Contemporary Art and Street Culture."[12] Korine's contribution to "Beautiful Losers" included a video on the street magician David Blaine. Entitled *Above the Below* (2000), it documents the performance artist's feat of being suspended above the Thames River for forty-four days without food, and includes scenes involving self-mutilation. When asked in Korine's video what motivates him to attempt such risky feats of endurance, Blaine replies, "I love death. I hate life."

Art critic Jerry Saltz has coined the term "Modern Gothic" to describe the recent trend toward creepy, angst-ridden, and death-obsessed work by younger artists. Saltz cites several characteristics, notably, the "ironic edge" and transgressive nature of such work. He writes, "In the Gothic, the hero and the villain resemble one another; the wicked can be redeemed. Thus, fluid definitions of sexuality, self, and subject matter are typical. This keeps the Gothic elusive, deluded, and chic."[13] *Gummo*, with its fixation on death and the grotesque, and its references to the demonic, via the band Slayer, clearly anticipates the Modern Gothic sensibility that seems to have become more prominent since 9/11.[14]

Korine's screenplay for *Kids*, of course, was about skateboard subculture. It employed the very loose plot device of a young woman, Jenny, discovering that she has been infected with AIDS from a first-time sexual encounter with a skateboarder named Telly, who is obsessed with deflowering young virgins. Jenny searches to find Telly throughout much of the film, only to end up being raped by his friend Casper at a drunken orgy. *Kids* sidesteps the real dramatic implications of this plotline, merely using it as a narrative pretext to explore the sex lives and drug habits of disaffected teenagers in New York City. (As a result, the film provides neither a sense of closure, nor of lessons learned.)

Korine professes to be much more interested in individual scenes—slices of life—than in plot. According to Korine:

> With *Gummo* I wanted to create a new viewing experience with images coming from all directions. To free myself up to do that, I had to create some kind of scenario that would allow me to just show scenes, which is all I care about. I can't stand plots because I don't feel life has plots. There is no beginning, middle, or end, and it upsets me when things are tied up so perfectly.[15]

Rather than employing a conventional plot, *Gummo* uses a collage technique that mixes together still photographs, stock footage, documentary-like shots and interviews shot in other formats (such as Super 8 and digital video) with scripted scenes. All of this material further upsets our sense of the film's continuity by being shot in a variety of styles—from home movies to staged, television-like interviews.

Korine's technique of layering images and sound has been compared by at least one critic to "the looping and sampling process of drum-'n'-bass."[16] The soundtrack includes many examples drawn from children's folklore: foul-mouthed street lyrics, game songs, cheerleading songs, alphabet songs, religious songs, and animal-inspired song. The film likewise incorporates different types of music—from death metal and Buddy Holly to Madonna and Roy Orbison. In voiceovers and dialogue, we hear a variety of oral forms. Korine peppers the film with suicide notes, what sounds like a grade-school essay, celebrity gossip and rumor, neighborhood gossip, standup comedy, overheard conversations, stupid jokes, sexual puns, and a personal confession about sexual abuse by a parent. The film also abounds in references and allusions to American popular culture.

If *Gummo* lacks a traditional plot, is it merely a succession of disconnected individual scenes, as Korine claims, or does the film contain some type of narrative logic capable of holding its various parts together? Korine creates a number of scenes involving characters who never reappear again. Other characters, such as Cassidey (the prostitute with Down syndrome), Eddie (the tennis player with attention deficit disorder), the skinhead brothers who lift weights and get into a slugfest afterward, Ellen (the mentally challenged woman who actually appears in several scenes), and the man who battles the chair, connect to one of the various story lines or through voiceovers by either Solomon or Tummler. Yet none of these scenes turns out to have quite the impact as the ones that involve the six major characters and four different story lines, which connect only indirectly through a black cat.

Solomon and Tummler serve as the two protagonists in the film, thereby providing one story thread, as the two boys ride around town on mountain bikes looking for cats to kill with their BB guns. When we first meet Tummler, he sits in a junked car. As he feels up a teenage girl, he tells her, "You have a lump in your titty." In a conventional narrative, this would create a potential plotline, but we actually don't see this person again until much later in the film, when she discusses how her impending breast removal will affect her relationship with boys. Instead, Dot and Helen, the attractive white-haired sisters, develop into the potential romance characters, as we watch them apply strips of duct tape to their breasts and nipples in order to make them larger, before bouncing up and down on their attic bed to a Buddy Holly song. Dot has a crush on Eddie, but this story thread doesn't lead anywhere either. Jarrod Wigely becomes the antagonist to Tummler and Solomon when the two learn that he's competing with them for cat carcasses, which can be exchanged for money at the local supermarket. Jarrod, however, doesn't provide much in the way of dramatic conflict. When Tummler and Solomon track down Jarrod, they interrogate him about his methods and his sick grandmother. The two boys later break into Jarrod's house and discover photographs of him dressed in women's clothes. Tummler disconnects the grandmother's respirator as an act of revenge, but Jarrod doesn't reappear again, and no complications ever arise from Tummler's actions. Meanwhile Helen and Dot's black cat, Foot Foot, disappears. A final character, Bunny Boy, who functions as a free-floating element disconnected to the other story lines for most of the film, ends up kissing Dot and Helen, and retrieves the carcass of Foot Foot.

Solomon, age fourteen, idolizes his sidekick, Tummler, a suicidal and depressed older teen, whose face clearly reflects his inner turmoil. As Solomon describes him, "Tummler sees everything. Some say he's downright evil. He's got what it takes to be a legend. He's got a marvelous persona." Even their names suggest the unlikely juxtaposition between the Bible (Solomon) and the Yiddish word for an entertainer who encourages audience participation (Tummler).[17] A study in contrast also in terms of their size, Tummler and Solomon suggest a teenage version of Mutt and Jeff. Solomon, in particular, has cartoon-like features—an oversized, misshapen head on a scrawny, pint-sized body, and large ears, which make him look like a young Mr. Potato Head. Even before we meet either one, we hear Solomon's faint, slightly raspy voice over documentary-like images of a tornado and its aftermath:

SOLOMON (*V. O.*): Xenia, Ohio. Xenia, Ohio. A few years ago a tornado hit this place. It killed people left and right. Dogs died. Cats died. Houses were split open and you could see necklaces hanging from branches of trees. People's legs and neck bones were stickin' out. Oliver found a leg on his roof. A lot of people's fathers died and were killed by the great tornado. I saw a girl fly through the sky and I looked up her skirt. The school was smashed and some kids died. My neighbor was killed in half. He used to ride dirt bikes and his three-wheelers. They never found his head. I always thought that was funny. People

died in Xenia. Before dad died he had a bad case of the diabetes.[18]

Solomon's narration establishes natural disaster as the cause for much
of what we will witness in Xenia, an impoverished white-trash enclave
full of broken families, alienated teenagers, racist hate mongers, die-
hard homophobes, and physically and mentally challenged individuals.
Solomon's voiceover suggests that many fathers have died in the tornado, including possibly his own. Physical deformity is also linked to
the tornado—the leg found in the tree as well as the head of a neighbor
that was never found. Although Solomon's narration is decidedly
solemn and poetic, it's revealing of his character that he nevertheless
finds this gruesome detail to be humorous. The death of animals is also
highlighted. Not only do we see an image of a decaying dog impaled on
a TV antenna, but torturing and killing cats—a childhood trait usually
associated with later deviant pathology—will become a major sport
and diversion throughout *Gummo*, while at the same time providing
the kids with money to buy strawberry milk shakes, airplane glue, and
sex. Solomon reports seeing a girl fly through the air, but he includes
the telling detail that he looked up her skirt. Not surprisingly, sexuality
will become another prominent theme in the film.

The introduction of Bunny Boy—a skinny, androgynous skateboarder who wears a pink hat with large rabbit ears, dirty Bermuda
shorts, and sneakers—adds a surreal element to the story. In a series of
shots, Bunny Boy shivers in the cold on a barbed-wire-guarded over-
pass overlooking a highway. He stares at the camera and then off to the
side. Seemingly bored, he kicks at a puddle of water, then pees onto the
oncoming traffic below. As Bunny Boy sits and smokes a cigarette, we
see that he has the word "MAC" tattooed on three of his fingers and a
star on a fourth. Arms extended to form a Christ-like pose, Bunny Boy
stares directly at us. He shivers again, spits, kicks the fence, hangs from
the top of the enclosure, then rubs his rear end against the fence sug-
gestively, before he spits some more. Over all of this, we hear Almeda
Riddle's traditional children's song "My Little Rooster."

The film cuts from Bunny Boy to a struggling cat being carried by
the scruff of its neck and then drowned in a barrel of water. After the
scene with Tummler and the young woman with the cancer lump, and
an extended montage of Tummler and Solomon riding their dirt bikes
to the sound of death metal music, Tummler almost shoots a black cat,

but Solomon intervenes because it has a collar. A young girl named
Darby scoops up Foot Foot (whose name derives from a song by the
naive-retro group the Shaggs) and takes the cat inside, where her two
sisters, Dot and Helen, examine the animal to determine whether it's
pregnant. Meanwhile Solomon and Tummler learn about Jarrod
Wigely when they bring their bounty to the supermarket. In a subsequent scene where Tummler and Solomon get high from sniffing airplane glue, Tummler's dialogue exhibits a certain dreamy free
association. He begins to talk about a house for sale, relates it to his
brother shooting the mailbox, then connects this to the singer Roy
Orbison, who—like his brother—also shot things and wore dark sunglasses. The ensuing dialogue also reflects adolescents' love of sexual
puns.

> TUMMLER: I saw a house yesterday . . . near my house. I think it
>   was this lady's. I saw a sign, "for sale." It had a bullet
>   hole in the mailbox.
> SOLOMON: A hole?
> TUMMLER: A big old hole. I think my brother shot it down when
>   he was younger. I think it was him. He always used
>   to say Roy Orbison liked to shoot at things. Roy
>   always wore these dark sunglasses. My brother
>   always wore the same kind of sunglasses. He sang
>   that song, "Crying." You know that song.
> SOLOMON: What?
> TUMMLER: That song, "Crying."

Tummler sings the chorus of the song and tells Solomon his brother
used to sing "Crying." He confides to Solomon that his brother is gay,
and describes him as a transvestite. When Solomon asks whether his
brother was pretty, Tummler responds that he's "pretty enough to have
a boyfriend."

Because he eschews a traditional causal structure in favor of an
episodic one, Korine depends on the viewer to make connections
between and among a number of thematic motifs. For instance, an
association between Tummler's queer brother and Bunny Boy
becomes manifest in the next scene. As two kids with cowboy hats play
in a junkyard by smashing the windows of cars, Bunny Boy strolls into
the scene carrying his skateboard under his arm. The two kids shoot
Bunny Boy with their cap pistols, and he collapses on the ground. The

Tummler and Solomon sniffing glue

older boy yells, "He looks like a queer rabbit! All queer!" The younger
one chimes in, "That fag! He can kiss my ass! Rabbits are queers." The
older boy comes over again, saying, "Ah, those queer-ass rabbits." The
older one hurls Bunny Boy's yellow skateboard into the distance. The
younger one grabs one of Bunny Boy's long pink ears, "Hey, look at
those little fag bunny ears." The two boys continue to spew foul language with incredible intensity—almost as if they're junior Marines in
boot camp—as they hover over Bunny Boy. They continue to shoot at
him from up close. They poke at him, check his pockets for money,
toss one of his sneakers, and eventually take off, leaving the crumpled
body of Bunny Boy next to an old tire. Bunny Boy will later appear sitting in a public bathroom stall while playing a toy accordion—first
listlessly, then frantically.

The film seems to trade on the conventional association between
femininity (in men) and gay identity. After the junkyard scene between
Bunny Boy and the two redneck cowboys, when Dot comments on
Eddie's new layered haircut, "He looks pretty," which recalls Solomon's
earlier question to Tummler about his gay brother. The issue of queerness resurfaces again in a series of interrupted takes between the self-
pitying teen (played by Korine himself) and a gay African-American
dwarf. Swigging a beer and pouring much of it over his head, the
teenager laments his abusive upbringing and tries to persuade the

dwarf to kiss him, but he only manages to extract a hug. Additional connections between queerness and transvestitism arise in the character of sad-eyed Jarrod Wigely, who cares for his elderly grandmother, but also kills cats. In the scene where Tummler and Solomon extract revenge by breaking into Jarrod's house, Solomon finds photos of Jarrod in drag. The still photographs transform into a home movie of him dressed as a woman in various poses. Solomon also finds pornographic magazines, including "a gay one."

Sexuality as a thematic motif in *Gummo* also extends to scenes involving adults. A reference to lesbianism occurs in the scene where a mentally challenged individual (whose features are fogged out to hide his identity) talks about a woman's marriage breaking up as a result of a lesbian affair. After a brief image of two men, identical twins, taking a bath together—a title indicates that this footage is from Xenia in 1983—Tummler discusses a cocaine addict named Clifford Dumkin, who lives down the street. We see a series of pornographic Polaroids, with the eyes of the people blacked out. Tummler claims that Clifford engages in wife-swapping and sex parties, where he likes to have sex with women in front of the neighborhood kids. After Foot Foot later ends up missing, a man approaches Helen, Dot, and Darby in the bowling alley with a copy of their flyer and announces that he's seen

Bunny Boy playing the accordion in the bathroom

their cat. The three girls then take a drive with him. The man purports to be Freddie Prinze's brother, but the three sisters turn out to be unfamiliar with the TV show *Chico and the Man*.[19] After the driver, who claims to be a gossip writer for a newspaper, pulls into a parking lot, he tries to rub his hand on Helen's crotch. Helen slaps him. Dot screams, "Why'd you try an' touch her coochie?" The three sisters beat on the man before fleeing his car. As they continue to curse at him, the molester yells, "It's nothing new for trash like you."

There are also two bizarre scenes involving Solomon's mother that have decidedly incestuous overtones. In the first one, Solomon tapes silverware together and heads to the basement. Solomon stands in front of the mirror and lifts his homemade weights to the song "Like a Prayer" by Madonna. When his mother comes downstairs, she complains that such exercise will stunt his growth. She tells him, "I can see your shoulder popping out. . . . Look . . . The way it raises and gets smaller." This references Solomon's earlier line—"People's leg bones and neck bones were stickin' out"—in the opening narration. Solomon's mom takes out a pair of his dad's old tap shoes. She explains that his father took up tapping in lieu of getting hair transplants. Her dialogue lapses into further nonsense as she discusses the prospect of Marlene Dietrich falling in love with her husband if only she could have seen see him tap dance. Solomon's mom then starts to tap dance while Solomon continues to lift weights. She tries to get him to smile, but he refuses. She comes behind him and wraps her arms around him, asking, "Do you miss your dad? I do." When she gets no response from Solomon, his mother reaches over and suddenly puts a gun to his head.

> SOLOMON'S MOTHER: OK, you son of a bitch, if you don't smile I'm gonna kill you. OK? I've killed before, and I will kill again. I will pick up your brains all over the floor. You came out of my womb and I'll stick you right back in my womb. If you don't smile, I'm going to kill you.

She pulls the trigger, but Solomon again has no reaction. The absurdist scene nevertheless establishes the effect that her husband's death has on Solomon's mother, which provides a context for the later scene where she babies Solomon while he takes a bath.

The second scene has an even stronger sexual subtext. It occurs after a photo montage of Solomon, which then cuts to shots of him

Solomon in the bathtub of filthy water

washing himself in a bathtub full of filthy water. His mother brings him a tray of milk and spaghetti. As he eats, she begins to wash his hair with shampoo. She twists his soapy hair into a point on top, so that he looks like a Kewpie doll.[20] There's a knock at the door. His mother disappears from the frame, and we watch as the phallic point of soapy hair begins to droop to the sound of draining water, as a bunch of Barbie dolls (including one without a head) can be seen against the dark blue tiles of the wall. When Solomon's mom answers the door, she's greeted by African-American twins, Terry and Phelipo, who ask whether she wants to buy a Crunch bar. She buys one for a dollar and brings it to Solomon for dessert.

The last several scenes, which are bracketed by Roy Orbison's "Crying," suggest the way various images and sounds, through Korine's collage technique, ricochet in various directions across the entire film. The song has, of course, been set up earlier, in the glue-sniffing scene between Tummler and Solomon, when he creates the association between his brother shooting the mailbox and Roy Orbison, and makes a specific reference to "Crying." Tummler's queer brother becomes connected with Bunny Boy and then with Jarrod Wigely. The sheer buoyancy of the scene of Bunny Boy kissing Helen and Dot in the rain ends up tempered by the lyrics of the song, and, shortly afterward, we watch Tummler and Solomon empty their BB guns into the carcass of a black cat. Bunny Boy's gallant effort to retrieve Dot and

Bunny Boy kissing Dot in the fountain as Helen looks on

Helen's missing cat is rendered as an offering to the camera, thus allowing us to see the red heart-shaped tag and to confirm the identity of the cat as Foot Foot.[21] We never do get to witness Helen or Dot's reaction, but Foot Foot's death becomes associated with an aching sense of loss through Roy Orbison's song. Irony gets piled upon irony as Ellen sings "Jesus Loves Me. The Bible Tells Me So," which only provides a kind of mindless consolation. Yet, even though *Gummo* provides a rather bleak view of the human condition, strangely enough, the film does render some degree of hope and redemption through the character of Bunny Boy. In Bunny Boy—the lone and mute skateboarder—Korine has found a heroic and emblematic figure who embodies the fluidity of both identity and sexuality necessary for survival in a world that seems out of whack. In an earlier scene, the camera follows Bunny Boy, arms extended, as he skateboards down the hill to the sound of clapping and toy accordion music. The figure of scorn has become transformed into a figure of triumph, and, not surprisingly, it turns out to be Bunny Boy (the transvestite animal boy), rather than either Solomon or Tummler, who gets to kiss the pretty girls.

In *Gummo*, Korine calls attention to the body through his inclusion of the physically challenged—the albino woman without toes, the gay African-American dwarf, and Cassidey—as well as through the olfactory sense. For instance, the bigoted response of the young red-neck cowboys (in terms of American mythology, it's certainly not a coincidence that they're dressed as cowboys) to Bunny Boy's "difference" has everything to do with the sense of smell, especially as it relates to the body through repeated references to private parts and bodily fluids. When the cowboys first spot Bunny Boy, the older cowboy yells out, "Damn you, rabbit! You smell like fuckin' piss." Later, after they've shot him with their cap guns, the two cowboys continue to shout loudly at Bunny Boy, who lies motionless on the ground:

OLDER COWBOY: This shitty-ass rabbit stinks!
YOUNGER COWBOY: I know.
OLDER COWBOY: He smells like pussy! He smells like an asshole!
YOUNGER COWBOY: Motherfucker!
OLDER COWBOY: Smells like wetback dick!
YOUNGER COWBOY: It smells like a pile of bullshit!

Interestingly, Foot Foot stinks when we first encounter her. When Darby scoops up Foot Foot after Tummler nearly shoots her, she kisses the cat and remarks, "You smell like a dookie, girl." After she brings the cat upstairs, Dot greets her by saying, "Foot Foot, you stink a bitch." We later observe a scene where the three sisters wash Foot Foot, who doesn't seem to mind getting a bath. Jarrod's elderly grandmother is also distinguished by her foul smell, which we can only assume has to do with her bodily fluids. In the scene where Tummler and Solomon enter her bedroom, Solomon twice tells Tummler, "She stinks," but he also associates her with food (considered "unclean" by some religions and cultures), by remarking, "She smells like a baked ham." When Solomon enters Cassidey's bedroom to have sex, she demands to know whether he's clean and has washed with soap:

CASSIDEY: Let me smell your wrist.

Solomon sticks his wrist out and Cassidey sniffs it.

CASSIDEY: It smells good.
SOLOMON: How does it smell like?
CASSIDEY: Like fruit. Like cherries.
SOLOMON: My mom gives me cherry shampoo.
CASSIDEY: I like cherries. I put cherries on my ice cream. I like the name of Cherry. Cherries.

This scene takes on new meaning when Solomon's mother later shampoos his hair while he takes a bath and eats his dinner.

Korine's inclusion of mentally challenged individuals serves an important function in the film as well. After Ellen does a cheerleading routine with a pair of pom-poms, she speaks directly to the camera, as if she's being interviewed. Ellen talks about her inanimate doll as if it's a real live baby, then suddenly begins to discuss the fact that her mother makes her do chores and the need to keep everything clean. Her monologue shifts to her getting in trouble for breaking a jar of spaghetti sauce, which then somehow segues into the need for prayer. Just as Korine fractures linear story, he often does the same to the voiceovers and dialogue of various characters. Eddie, the tennis player whom Dot has a crush on, introduces the fact that he has ADD as a complete non sequitur into a conversation about the velocity of his serve. The dialogue of other characters in *Gummo* veers off on similar tangents, almost as if ADD has spread through the film like a contagious disease. Solomon's mother, for instance, provides an incoherent monologue about her husband in the tap dancing scene. The scene with Tummler's father provides another example. As Tummler and his father drive in a car, Tummler asks his dad about his deceased mother. In response, Tummler's dad launches into a long, rambling, and convoluted non sequitur about being a kid and watching his boss's good-looking wife walk around in her underwear. One additional example occurs in the scene where Tummler and Solomon interview Jarrod about killing cats and his elderly grandmother. After Jarrod indicates that his grandmother is catatonic, the boy next to him asks, "She used to throw darts, right?" Jarrod responds, "Yeah, she used to have a dartboard." Korine clearly delights in creating such illogical and absurd moments. It's all done with a straight face, because Jarrod, Solomon, and Tummler don't show any type of reaction to the boy's comment.

Korine seems to relish life's endless stream of absurdities—its contradictions, unpredictability, and strangeness. He's fascinated by the anomaly rather than the norm. He wants the meaning of images to remain open and fluid, rather than fixed, which is why he favors collage over traditional plot. Images in *Gummo* contain odd juxtapositions, such as Solomon wearing a red fireman's hat and whipping the carcass of a dead cat, a skateboarder in a partial rabbit costume, and a gay black dwarf who beats a huge pot-bellied redneck at arm wrestling. In such images and scenes, Korine seems intrigued by the imaginative sleight of hand in which the meaning of various images and events somehow gets confounded. It's a trait that springs from his love of American vaudeville, where such juxtapositions were common.

It's hard to know exactly where Korine is coming from at times. Often it's deliberately from left field, which no doubt partially accounts for some of the hostile responses to *Gummo*. Korine has certainly been castigated by mainstream critics who've found *Gummo* to be an offensive freak show that parades and exploits those less fortunate. Yet such criticism, as I've tried to show, fails to account for the way the film explores the various forms of "difference" as its theme. In depicting lower-class poverty—the endless clutter, filth, and bugs—Korine clearly shows that this, rather than Solomon's more literary conceit of blaming the tornado, has spawned the intolerance, hatred, racism, criminality, suicidal despair, animal cruelty, and the kind of inbreeding that no doubt accounts for much of the physical disfigurement and mental problems we witness throughout the film. *Gummo* (the film takes its name from the Marx brother who left show business) presents a rather grim portrait, not only of these two teenagers, but of Xenia as a whole.[22] The film manages to capture the poetry that resides in the gutter by focusing on the truly mind-boggling incongruities of such a milieu. *Gummo*'s real achievement, however, rests on its unusual narrative syntax—the way Korine is able to weave together its disparate scenes and events to create a viscerally assaulting, Modern Gothic portrait of "difference" in its various manifestations.

Chapter 12

The Character-Based
Structure of *Slacker*

The avant-garde pioneer Maya Deren championed the film poem, or what she later termed "vertical" (poetic) development over "horizontal" (dramatic) development.[1] Thus, a disavowal of dramatic narrative has been a central part of the avant-garde tradition, which sees itself as more connected to the larger framework of modern art. In a roundtable discussion on "Independence in the Cinema" conducted by the art magazine *October*, James Schamus discusses two original sins being committed in this regard. The theoretical mistake, he argues, "is the embedding of the understanding of cinema in primarily a visual arts context, and the lack of interest in the power of narrative."[2] The second mistake, he claims, had to do with the introduction of narrative into avant-garde film practice through films such as Cassavetes' *Shadows* and the New American Cinema Group in New York:

> You're in a new context in which, whatever the other outcomes of the cinematic games being played, films are approximately ninety-minute pieces of celluloid that tell stories and that can get distributed through the means and mechanisms that were set up by, more or less, the Hollywood studio system. So, suddenly, you're on a new path; you're marking out a new terrain, and that new path is leading you, at least in retrospect, to new modes of distribution, but also of representation and of signification, modes other than

those associated with the avant-garde cinema prior to this not-so-original sin of the introduction of the narrative form.[3]

As Schamus suggests, the new path of American independent cinema exists somewhere between commercial Hollywood and the avant-garde tradition, and that has proved a delicate balancing act for independent films that eschew the causality of classical narrative, such as *Mulholland Dr.*, *Gummo*, or my final example, *Slacker* (1991).

After spending several years trying to raise funds for a more conventionally scripted film without success, Richard Linklater decided to embark on a more alternative type of film project for his second feature, *Slacker*. Strongly influenced by his own background in acting, Linklater decided to shift the emphasis to what he called "structured improvisation"—loosely improvised situations involving nontraditional performers who essentially would be playing themselves.[4] Just as Harmony Korine's interest in scenes rather than in traditional plot pushed him toward the technique of collage, Linklater's preoccupation with both improvisation and snapshot character studies led him to devise the unconventional structure of *Slacker*, in which scenes are

Should Have Stayed at Bus Station in the cab

linked not by the mechanics of a tightly woven, causal plot, but by a conceptual framework, the loose interaction of its various characters, the narrow limits of the geography of a neighborhood, and the limited time span of a twenty-four-hour period.

The structure of *Slacker* is alluded to early in the film by the person in the cab, Should Have Stayed at Bus Station (played by Linklater himself), who talks about dreams and the notion of simultaneous or alternate realities:

> SHOULD HAVE STAYED AT BUS STATION: It's like every choice or decision you make . . . the thing you choose not to do, fractions off and becomes its own reality, you know, and just goes on from there, forever. I mean, it's like . . . you know in *The Wizard of Oz* where Dorothy meets the Scarecrow and they do that little dance at that crossroads and they think about going in all those directions and they end up going in that one direction? All those other directions, just because they thought about them, became separate realities. I mean, they just went on from there and lived the rest of their life . . . you know, entirely differ-ent movies, but we'll never see it because we're trapped in this one reality restriction type of thing.[5]

Linklater attempts to provide us with all those different realities or movies rather than restricting his film to a single protagonist or story. A scene begins with one character who interacts with another who then becomes the subject of the next scene, so that individual scenes branch off in unexpected directions. Although the interactions between characters appear to be seemingly chance occurrences—one character who happens to run into another—Linklater insists that the decision about which character to follow is not arbitrary: "I didn't want it to seem like the filmmakers or the camera were deciding things. It's whoever organically comes into the frame and interacts with someone else."[6] Each of the roughly ninety characters in the film gets his or her time in front of the camera only to have the film move on to the next one, so that no character ever reappears at a later point in the film. Some of these are major characters who speak long mono-logues, while others play more limited roles. In some cases, they merely provide a bridge from one scene into the next, such as the woman whom the camera follows into the coffee shop early in the film or the four kids who peep in Recluse's window.

Such a structure bears a resemblance to an ensemble film, such as *Me and You and Everyone We Know*. They are both character studies that create a composite portrait of a neighborhood, but there's a significant difference. July's film finds a way to connect the characters in the various plotlines, as do all ensemble films or multiple-plot films discussed in the preceding chapters, including *Gummo*. *Slacker* differs from an ensemble film like *Me and You and Everyone We Know* by having the plotlines multiply with each successive scene, but never letting the characters interact again. In this sense, *Slacker* turns out to be the exact opposite of a web-of-life plot or network narrative. This type of structure emphasizes relationship and connectedness and often employs what David Bordwell refers to as a "converging fates" device as a means of making that possible, whereas, both structurally and thematically, *Slacker* turns out to be about its characters' disconnectedness from each other.[7]

Like *Gummo*, *Slacker* doesn't have a three-act structure. Because the characters in *Slacker* never reconnect, there are no major turning points along the way to provide complications in a larger plot or to divide the film into separate acts. Linklater's use of a loose, episodic structure rather a conventional dramatic one matches the film's content. As Linklater explains:

> Well, you can only do what feels natural with whatever subject matter you're dealing with. But I have always wanted to experiment with the boundaries of narrative. I mean I like stories, I just tell them in a different way. I like creating multiple narratives in a story, or multifaceted characters, having a lot of mouths saying a lot of things, having a lot of different attitudes.[8]

By making each scene into its own mini-narrative, Linklater succeeds in creating a regional portrait of the college town of Austin, Texas, with its eclectic mix of young musicians, media freaks, petty criminals, conspiracy buffs, and aging anarchists. Even more important in terms of the film's eventual commercial success, *Slacker* was able to capture the spirit of a particular subculture that came to embody an entire generation of disaffected young people adrift in a sea of popular culture, namely, the Gen Xers, who also came to be known by the moniker of the film's title. By turning his camera on the mostly young and eccentric denizens of Austin, Linklater became a chronicler of the prevailing ethos of the time.

As John Pierson makes clear in *Spike, Mike, Slackers & Dykes*, the unconventional *Slacker* was hardly an easy sell in the marketplace.[9] Linklater had shown a truncated rough cut of the film at the Independent Feature Film Market in 1989, where *Slacker* attracted the attention of the German Television company WDR, which bought the territorial rights to the finished film. This deal allowed Linklater to borrow funds to complete the project. Responses to the completed version of *Slacker*, however, were decidedly mixed. At the American Independent section of the Berlin Film Festival Market in February of 1990, the film generated virtually no interest, with extremely small audiences and several walkouts. The film's commercial prospects became considerably more upbeat when *Slacker* had an enthusiastic screening at the Seattle Film Festival and received a positive review by Robert Horton in *Film Comment*.[10]

The film's momentum was again derailed when *Slacker* was turned down by the prestigious and market-influencing Toronto, New York, and Sundance film festivals. Linklater's smartest move, however, turned out to be his decision to four-wall the film at the Dobie Theater in Austin, where *Slacker* became a cult hit and played to sold out crowds for several months. The *Austin Chronicle* wrote an extended piece on the film, which showed a perceptive understanding of the film's subcultural relevance:

> Evidence that 20th-century radicalism has long been at the end of its tether pervades the movie; the people who inhabit it are overwhelmed by a sense of waiting for the fullness of time to bring word of something—anything—new. Most of them are too young to remember a time before official culture devoured or colonized everything that once held out a promise of vitality; they've claimed inertia as their birthright. The all-but-total decay of public life has atomized others into subcultures of which they are the only member, free radicals randomly seeking an absent center as the clock beats out its senseless song.[11]

The buzz of its successful theatrical local run brought *Slacker* back to the attention of John Pierson, who was able to have the film reconsidered for Sundance and to sell it to Orion Pictures before that company unexpectedly folded. From there, *Slacker* became a hard-won independent film success story.

The influences on Linklater, a self-professed cinephile who founded the Austin Film Society in 1987, range from European art films such as Max Ophuls's *La Ronde* (1950) and Luis Buñuel's *The Phantom of Liberty* (1974) to the actor-based, improvisational work of John Cassavetes. In an interview that accompanied the published screenplay for *Slacker*, Linklater described his approach:

> We would cast the right person, and then I'd write what I considered sample dialogue sometime before the first rehearsal. Then we would sit around a table and talk about the scene.... Certain characters did one hundred percent the text as I gave it to them, if it seemed to work. Most would add to it, and we'd work through things they didn't feel comfortable with. I think being a director is choosing.[12]

The people Linklater chose were nonactor friends of his and the crew's. By placing nonactors in fictional situations, Linklater, like Cassavetes or Van Sant in *Elephant*, was able to take advantage of the distinctive personalities of the people he cast. As a whole, they manage to imbue the film with a certain raw energy and vitality that contribute to the film's overall sense of realism.

Linklater did not begin the film with a conventional written script. Instead he had a roughly fifteen-page treatment that contained fifty-five scenes. He writes, "It's believed you need a script to organize a production around (what characters? what locations? what happens?) and I felt this would be enough to fit that purpose. It was known all along that within this structure, all was wide open."[13] Not all the scenes in the treatment wound up in the final film, as could be expected from such a method of working. Nearly a third of the scenes in the treatment were replaced and several others were altered during actual filming. Linklater did publish the script for the film, but it's simply a transcription of what actually ended up on the screen. In other words, the script was created after the fact.

Slacker begins with Should Have Stayed at Bus Station sleeping on a bus as the landscape moves by. Once the bus gets into town, he gives his lengthy philosophical monologue to an unresponsive cab driver, which keys the viewer to what follows. As Should Have Stayed at Bus Station walks down the street, we hear the sound of a loud crash and the screech of tires. The camera tracks in that direction, picking up a white Chevy station wagon as it swerves around the corner and out of the frame. We see groceries strewn about and a woman lying in the street. As Should Have Stayed at Bus Station recedes into the background to call for help on a pay phone, the camera tracks back. The white car pulls into the frame (as if it has circled the block), and a man hustles into the building. Once inside, he receives a phone call informing him about the hit-and-run accident. Despite indicating he's the son of the injured woman, the man seems incapable of feigning even the slightest emotional reaction. Besides his religious shrine and the high school yearbook photos he cuts out and burns, the only other motivational clue we have is the home-movie footage he projects: a looped image of his mother jump-starting his toy kiddie car with her foot—an ambiguous image, which, in this context, takes on a sinister spin. When the police take the guy away in handcuffs, a passing street musician asks a bystander what happened. We then follow the street musician as he sings a song about a "disturbed young man with a tan," a seeming reference to Hit-and-Run Son.

A young woman drops a quarter into the street musician's guitar case and heads to a café. As she goes to the counter, we watch an

Hit-and-Run Son projecting a childhood movie

espresso being made and hear the off-screen voice of Dostoyevsky Wannabe. We follow another guy, Giant Cappuccino, over to a table, where Dostoyevsky Wannabe recites a passage from *The Gambler*, which poses the question of whether true freedom can be found in passivity. A character named Looking for Missing Friend asks Giant Cappuccino about a friend named Gary, but neither he nor Dostoyevsky Wannabe have seen him. After Looking for Missing Friend leaves the café, a paranoid guy, Been on Moon, follows him and launches into a lengthy monologue about various government conspiracies involving UFOs, the colonization of space, the greenhouse effect, mass abductions, and secret mind-control experiments. Been on Moon tells Looking for Missing Friend:

> BEEN ON MOON: So they must like children, too, because the statistics from the FBI since nineteen-eighty say that three-hundred fifty thousand children are just missing . . . they disappeared. There're not that many perverts around. You know, the worst thing about this, pal, is that you're in close proximity to all this. I mean, Houston's just right down the road, you know, the main headquarters: NASA. Sure, and the main headquarters around the world: Geneva, New York, and Moscow.[14]

As they approach a house, Looking for Missing Friend excuses himself and goes inside, while Been on Moon attempts to engage a passing couple who enter the living room of their co-op house. Inside, two guys play a reflex-testing game, while another rants about George Bush and compares his election to what happened in Nazi Germany. One of the game players tells the couple that Paul has moved out, leaving only a series of postcards behind. They go upstairs to Paul's room where they read what's written on the postcards, one of which is of Uncle Fester from *The Addams Family*. The postcards tell a story about a character named Juan Apagato, but the story appears to have strong autobiographical overtones. One of the cards describes the monotony of Juan's daily routines. The last one contains an ominous threat: "Watch for the next episode: Juan joins up with an emerging European terrorist organization and soon returns to the U. S. with a supply of homemade nuclear weapons."

In a narrative sense, each vignette raises a number of questions. First and foremost, we wonder: What is the connection between Should Have Stayed at Bus Station, Hit-and-Run Son, Looking for Missing

Friend, Gary (the missing person), and the various conspiracy theories of Been on Moon, or the story Paul relates on the postcards? In a classic Hollywood film, the viewer would have figured out the central protagonist by this point (roughly twenty-four minutes), as well as the premise and direction of the story. *Slacker*, however, lacks a central protagonist who might provide a greater sense of unity. Instead, each scene introduces a new character, only to have that character be replaced by still another one. For the most part, no further reference is made to the character who has been replaced. The fact, however, that two missing individuals, Gary and Paul, have becomes the focal point of the last two scenes creates the strong suggestion that the rest of the film will involve solving the mystery of their disappearance. This idea is reinforced by the missing-person poster that is clearly visible on the telephone pole in the foreground of the shot as the camera tracks along with Been on Moon and Looking for Missing Friend.

Should Have Stayed at Bus Station hints that a dreamlike logic might serve to connect the various scenes, but *Slacker* differs from a film that actually incorporates dream structure, such as *Mulholland Dr.*, in a number of important ways. For one thing, the basic structure of *Slacker* follows its own conceptual logic. As *Slacker* shifts from character to character, the viewer might be baffled by the relationship between scenes, but the overall structure of the film remains clear and rational. In *Mulholland Dr.*, on the other hand, David Lynch attempts to replicate the illogical experience of a dream. Part of the mystery of *Mulholland Dr.* results from its cleverly disguised point of view. Whereas *Mulholland Dr.* turns out to reflect the psyche of its tormented main character, Betty/Diane, there are certainly no indications that *Slacker* represents that of Should Have Stayed at Bus Station, despite his opening monologue.

Rather than pursuing the mysterious disappearances of Gary and Paul, as we might expect, *Slacker* shifts direction once a band member from a group called Ultimate Losers turns up at the apartment. When Ultimate Loser learns that Paul has moved out, he simply asks whether he can have Paul's vacated room, and then heads back outside. He runs into a young woman named Stephanie, who indicates she has just returned from Dallas, where her parents have had her committed to a mental hospital. Their stilted conversation is interrupted by a hyperactive young woman called Pap Smear Pusher, who rants about someone who opened fire on the freeway before turning the gun on himself. She then tries to sell them Madonna's pap smear by boasting, "I mean, it's a little bit getting closer to the rock God herself than just a poster." Before they part, Ultimate Loser puts Stephanie on the guest list for his next concert, but the possible romantic implications of this, as well as the reasons for her hospitalization, simply get left as dangling causes.

The dangling causes in *Slacker* serve an important function. Just as David Lynch's withholding of information in *Mulholland Dr.* helps to keep viewers engaged in that story, Linklater creates enough semblance of narrative—murder, missing persons, possible romance, and psychic predictions of imminent death—to maintain audience interest in *Slacker*. Like certain structural films of the late 1960s and '70s, such as Hollis Frampton's *Zorns Lemma* (1970), the structure of *Slacker* also functions like a game. Part of the pleasure for the viewer of *Slacker* involves trying to anticipate how a particular scene might evolve or how the various scenes eventually might connect. Whereas

Pap Smear Pusher

Jim Jarmusch created a guessing game about the direction of *Stranger Than Paradise* by having an ambivalent protagonist, Linklater achieves a similar effect through an emphasis on *Slacker's* unfolding structure.

After Ultimate Loser leaves Stephanie, the camera follows two other people who've been listening to a political rant. The woman would like to leave the country, but her male friend responds:

> ANTI-TRAVELER: I don't know . . . I've traveled, and all it is is bad water, bad food, you get sick, you got to deal with strange people, and when you get back you can't tell whether it really happened to you or if you just saw it on TV . . .[15]

They continue past two women, one of whom informs her companion, "The next person who passes us will be dead within a fortnight." Things immediately begin to go wrong for Happy-Go-Lucky Guy, including nearly getting run over by a car.

Our concerns about the fate of Happy-Go-Lucky Guy recede, as Recluse joins his girlfriend, who watches a TV program about a gruesome serial killer. She pesters Recluse to go outside, but, like Anti-Traveler, he simply vents:

> RECLUSE: I hate shit like that . . . all that nature, and the sunlight's so oppressive now. And you don't just go to the lake. You have to prepare for it—you have to get suntan lotion and insecticide . . . it's like premeditated fun. It's too hot outside anyway.[16]

He proposes sex instead, but their snuggling is interrupted by neighborhood kids peeking in the window. The kids kick a Coke machine to get free cans of soda, which they try to sell to three guys, who later enact a misogynistic ritual on a bridge. We then follow one of them as he meets up with his girlfriend, but the two get into an argument after she gives a street person a quarter and the can of soda he has given her. The boyfriend has philosophical objections to helping the indigent. When she calls him an asshole, he responds: "You know, I don't think anyone who's ever done anything hasn't been considered an asshole by the general populace," citing Freud and Bob Dylan as examples.

The girlfriend goes into a bookstore where she runs into a former classmate who turns out to be a JFK assassin buff. He gives her a long-winded primer on various conspiracy books. Of course, he happens to be writing one himself. He later tries to engage a guy working on his car about assassination trivia, but a friend comes by and the two of them head off to steal car parts. They pick up a hitchhiker, who bad-mouths his stepfather, whose funeral he's just attended. After they let him out, Hitchhiker gets interviewed by two people with a video camera at an outdoor café. In response to a question about what he does for a living, Hitchhiker denounces work. "All that does," he tells the interviewers, "is fill the bellies of the pigs who exploit us." He adds, "To all you workers out there: Every single commodity you produce is a piece of your own death."

At a convenience store, we learn from the security guard that Hitchhiker has been in prison. The security guard asks Hitchhiker to take over for him while he chases after a shoplifter who has left the store. Old Anarchist passes by with his daughter, Delia, who recognizes the shoplifter from her ethics class. When they arrive home, they discover a burglar with a gun. The potential drama of the situation, however, deflates once Old Anarchist invites the burglar to take anything he wants. He relieves Burglar of his gun and assures him that he wouldn't consider calling the police. Old Anarchist offers Burglar a cup of coffee, shakes hands, and asks him his name. Burglar answers, "Paul . . . Yazimsky."

Burglar's revelation catches us by surprise. Is Burglar the same Paul who had moved out of his room at the co-op house, leaving behind a series of cryptic postcards? Although Paul's fate was left as a dangling cause, this potential plotline appears to have been dropped as the film moved on to other characters. There's no way for us to know for sure whether Burglar is indeed the same person, but this demonstrates how *Slacker* presents enough bits of plot to tease the viewer into expecting greater narrative coherence than the film delivers. Coming where it does in the film's structure, the possible discovery of Paul at roughly sixty minutes could represent a second turning point. Yet there are several arguments against this. For one thing, it's completely speculative to assume that this Paul is actually the same person. In addition, the revelation would seem too weakly inflected to serve as a turning point. Even if it were, the issue hasn't been raised in the middle act. Nor does the film dwell on the connection, as Old Anarchist digresses from Paul Yazimsky's ethnic background to such topics as McKinley's assassin, the Spanish Civil War, his desire to blow up the Texas Legislature, and (as they walk in the direction of the infamous tower at the University

Paul and Old Anarchist in front of the Texas tower

of Texas) the crazed sniper Charles Whitman, whom Old Anarchist obviously admires. He concludes:

> OLD ANARCHIST: It's taken my entire life, but I can now say that I've practically given up on not only my own people but for mankind in its entirety. I can only address myself to singular human beings now.[17]

After Old Anarchist leaves to take a phone call, Burglar comments that he's "never met anyone that fought in the Spanish Civil War." Delia sets him straight, but acknowledges that she loves her father. As Burglar leaves, Delia tosses him his gun, and Old Anarchist tells him, "Remember, the passion for destruction is also a creative passion."

Burglar rejoins his two friends in a stolen Cadillac. He has taken a rare book about the Marquis de Sade instead of a TV. Disgusted by this, Cadillac Crook makes Burglar drive him to the house of a friend, Video Backpacker, who sits in a room full of TV monitors. Video Backpacker has forsaken the outside world for the pleasures of the video image—over which he has greater control. He brings out a tape made by a graduate student studying history who took his thesis committee hostage before "a SWAT team came in and off'ed him."

Afterward, Cadillac Crook heads across the street, where a woman (Having a Breakthrough Day) offers him his choice of cards from a deck. He reads, "Withdrawing in disgust is not the same thing as apathy." Cadillac Crook takes a second card, which reads, "It's not building a wall but making a brick." Having a Breakthrough Day remarks that this is a perfect description of her day:

> HAVING A BREAKTHROUGH DAY: Okay, well, I mean, it's like I've had a total recalibration of my mind. It's like I've been banging my head against this nineteenth-century-type thought mode/constructs . . . human constructs. Well, the wall doesn't exist, it's not there. They tell you to look for the light at the end of the tunnel . . . well, there is no tunnel. There is no structure. The underlying order is chaos. Man, I mean everything is in one big ball of fluctuating matter . . . a constant state of change. I mean, it's like across that great quantum divide is this new consciousness and I don't know what it's going to be like but I know that we're all a part of it. I mean, it's new physics—you can't look at something without changing it . . . anything. I mean, that's almost beyond my imagination. It's like that butterfly flapping its wings in Galveston and somewhere down the road a pace it'll . . . (*to approaching friend*) Well hey . . . (*completing thought*) . . . create a monsoon in China.[18]

It's hard not to read either the card or Having a Breakthrough Day's response as anything but a reflexive commentary on the film by invoking new physics, chaos theory, and a change in consciousness as an intellectual rationale for *Slacker*'s unorthodox approach to narrative. Interestingly, Bordwell cites both chaos theory and the butterfly effect in his discussion of network narrative or degrees-of-separation plots, but he reaches an opposite conclusion: "Whatever new shapes degrees-of-separation plots take, most remain coherent and comprehensible, thanks to the principles of causality, temporal sequence and duration, character wants and needs, and motivic harmony that have characterized mainstream storytelling (not just in cinema) for at least a century."[19] *Slacker* is coherent and comprehensible, but it ruptures the causal connections between the various character strands by leaving the dangling causes dangling, as a reflection of life's seeming chaos.

Several scenes later, Going to Catch Show picks up a woman who has flirted with him at the bar of a music club. Linklater once again undermines viewer expectations by eliding the scene of Going to Catch Show's one-night stand, or what would be considered the crucial part in a classical narrative. Instead of this, we only see the woman get dressed and leave his apartment early the next morning. She passes an old man, who walks along and records his reflections about life into a cassette recorder. A car passes by, its loudspeaker blaring about a free weapons give-away program. A convertible with five early-morning beer drinkers pulls up next to Ranting Driver. Two of them point Super 8 cameras. The point of view switches to that of the Super 8 camera, as the revelers head out of town and up an embankment overlooking the river. The images become more staccato and abstract. One of the guys suddenly hurls the camera off the cliff, creating a swirling effect, which ends the movie.

Slacker tends to meander as it moves from character to character. Despite the fact that there's no overarching plot, individual scenes nevertheless have progression. Should Have Stayed at Bus Station takes a cab ride from the bus station, despite his fantasies. Hit-and-Run Son does run over his mother with his car as she returns from the grocery store, which causes him to be led away in handcuffs. This event provides material for the street musician's song. Looking for Missing Friend never finds his friend, Gary, but he continues to look for him, rejecting Been on Moon's paranoid explanations. Paul has turned his abrupt move out of the co-op house into a revolutionary parable, but he may, in fact, have become a burglar. The two car buffs steal parts from the junkyard. Other characters are unmasked, such as the Hitchhiker, who turns out to have been in jail, or Old Anarchist, who is revealed to be delusional. Burglar steals a rare edition of the Marquis de Sade rather than a TV for Video Backpacker. Finally, Going to Catch Show (rather than Steve) does actually succeed in picking up a woman. The overall movement turns out to be predominantly one of stasis rather than development, yet another day passes for these characters.

Scenes in *Slacker* also have thematic links. As a result of living in a media-saturated culture, a number of characters seem to get confused between images and reality, or between their own fantasies and what exists outside their heads. Individuality often involves taking a contrarian view, whether it's about traveling, nature, helping those less fortunate, crime, government conspiracies, snipers and assassins, or even figures from popular culture, such as Scooby Doo and the Smurfs. For quite a few of the characters, paranoia and their own mental problems, or even their refusal to leave their houses, attest to their heightened sensitivity and personal rebellion against the conformism of consumer culture—at least in their own minds. Recluse's girlfriend is one of the only characters to take issue with the whole notion of apathy, when she complains, "You're just what they want."

Linklater does a masterful job of creating a wry, humorous portrait of regional oases of alternative lifestyles that often grow up around college towns throughout America, such as Austin; Berkeley, California; Ann Arbor, Michigan; Athens, Georgia; or Madison, Wisconsin. The characters in *Slacker* have given up hope of a radical change in society, even while they mouth its empty rhetoric. Part of the fascination of *Slacker* comes from seeing through the verbal posturing that substitutes for meaningful action for these people, all the time understanding that it's not their fault. Part of their burden—the slacker syndrome itself—stems from being born at the wrong historical time.

In creating such characters, Linklater experiments with the conventions of dialogue. Although dialogue implies an exchange between two or more people, the characters in *Slacker* use speech as their own individual protest against the world, as a sign of their own aliveness. For the most part, the characters in *Slacker* talk *at* each other rather than *to* each other. This is evident in the very beginning of the movie when the Linklater character, Should Have Stayed at Bus Station, uses the backseat of a taxicab to spew forth his dreams and personal philosophical theories about multiple or alternative realities to a driver who never acknowledges his presence. As Linklater commented in an interview, "With *Slacker* it was like I woke up and said, What if everybody started talking, expressing who they thought they were and what they believed? What if anyone could approach anyone else and just start rambling?"[20] There is an obvious connection between Linklater's notion of uninhibited personal expression and what might be considered madness. A number of other characters in *Slacker*, such as Been on Moon, Pap Smear Pusher, T-Shirt Terrorist, Traumatized, JFK Buff, Old Anarchist, Video Backpacker, and Having a Breakthrough Day launch into decidedly one-sided tirades.

Such long-winded monologues by *Slacker*'s characters would be decried by the manuals, which emphasize brevity and conciseness. Robert McKee writes:

> First, screen dialogue requires compression and economy. Screen dialogue must say the maximum in the fewest possible words. Second, it must have direction. Each exchange of dialogue must turn the beats of the scene in one direction or another across the changing behaviors, without repetition. Third, it should have purpose. Each line or exchange of dialogue executes a step in design that builds and arcs the scene around its Turning Point. All this precision, yet it must sound like talk, using an informal and natural vocabulary, complete with contractions, slang, even, if necessary, profanity.[21]

The manuals also emphasize the difference between everyday speech and movie dialogue. Dialogue should not mirror everyday speech, which tends to be a rambling and unfocused attempt to fill up the awkward silences between people. According to Walter, "The way people really talk is to pass time. But in movies the way people talk must be pointed, purposeful."[22] Walter advises against long speeches: "In real life people do not make long, unwieldy speeches to each other. Neither should they in films."[23]

The dialogue in *Slacker*, with its verbal excesses, may not conform to either Walter or McKee's guidelines, but it mimics similar long-winded outbursts by Mr. Pink in *Reservoir Dogs* or Carl Showalter in *Fargo*. Linklater is not afraid to use the clichés of young people's speech to give his characters' lines a certain authentic ring. Pap Smear Pusher begins her harangue, "Yo, hey dude. . . . Man, I am freaking out so severely." A character's thoughts may also vector off in several directions, almost as if she or he is unable to decide what's important or relevant. For example, right before Pap Smear Pusher enters, Stephanie (the woman whose parents have had her hospitalized in Dallas) asks Ultimate Loser what he's been up to. He responds:

> ULTIMATE LOSER: Same old same old . . . just lollygagging around. Still unemployed. I'm in this band . . . well, the one I was in before but we've changed our name. We're the Ultimate Losers now. And, ah, the singer's still a jerk. We're playing this Friday . . . if you want to come I can put you on the list. I'm sleeping a lot . . .[24]

Ultimate Loser struggles to answer Stephanie's question. He's unemployed, playing in a band with a different name, and sleeping a lot, but he also throws in the gratuitous fact that the lead singer's still a jerk, as if this detail might be a significant key to any or all of the above. The lines about the lead singer and sleeping a lot, while non sequiturs on one level also help to make Ultimate Loser's dialogue seem more realistic, since the inclusion of such lines more closely mimics the odd turns of normal human conversation. As Roger Ebert wrote in his review at the time of the film's release:

> The point is not really what is said, but the tone of voice, the word choices, the conversational strategies, the sense of life going on all the time, everywhere, all over town. In a conventional Hollywood movie, as the brain-dead characters repeat the few robotic phrases permitted them by the formulas of the screenplay, they walk down streets and sometimes I yearn to just peel away from them, cut across a lawn, walk through the wall of a house, and enter the spontaneous lives of the people living there. *Slacker* is a movie that grants itself that freedom.[25]

So convincingly does *Slacker*'s dialogue succeed in capturing the realistic sound of actual talk that many viewers mistakenly assume that it's been improvised on the spot rather than scripted.

Linklater's dialogue shares an affinity with the type of dialogue found in Cassavetes' films, which should not be at all surprising given the similarities of their approaches. In writing about Cassavetes' dialogue, Todd Berliner discusses the paradox that "realistic" Hollywood dialogue is unlike actual real speech because it masks its own contrivance. He argues in favor of Cassavetes' particular brand of realism, "a realism created not by concealing one's art, but by revealing the similarity between the act of creating art and the art of living." He goes on to elaborate:

> Though I have only indirect statements to support the contention (such as the quotation that opens this essay), I suspect that Cassavetes saw real life as a kind of performance, that in his films he sought to represent people in the act of representing themselves, and that he intended us to blend actorial behavior with the behavior of the characters his actors impersonate. But whether or not he intended the effect, the feeling of actorial improvisation, when

coupled with characters who seem to make up their statements as they go along, serves to combine actor and role (and hence art and reality) far more thoroughly than with more conventional, tightly constructed dialogue.[26]

In *Slacker*, we get the same sort of tension between real life and performance that we get in Cassavetes' films. The characters in *Slacker* seem to be deliberately playing to both the camera and each other, fully aware of the artifice involved, which is not so different from the way they behave in their actual lives.

The comparison with Cassavetes has to do with Linklater's improvisational approach to character and dialogue, but Cassavetes' films are much more firmly rooted in narrative. There's a conceptual logic to *Slacker*, a concern for an overall system, that pushes it closer to the more avant-garde tradition of structural film, just as Lynch mimics the dream structure of Deren's early pyschodrama, or Korine engages in a similar free-associative image play found in the plotless cinema of Ron Rice. *Slacker*, like Korine's *Gummo* and Lynch's *Mulholland Dr.*, undermines the causality of classical narrative, which provides the very grounding for the hybrid narrational strategy employed by independent cinema. When *Slacker* played at Sundance, Linklater later recalled feeling a bit intimidated to have made this "weird movie," which was being screened with "all these other films that are seemingly real movies." He continued, "And then those came out the next year and didn't do anything because they were just real and normal. Where this weird thing actually did much better."[27] Novelty can help to differentiate indie films in the marketplace, but, as Schamus reminds us, they still have to succeed in an economic system largely set up and controlled by the major studios.

Conclusion

Classical Hollywood narration is not intrinsically superior to either art-cinema narration or the combination represented by American independent cinema. Robert McKee mounts a number of arguments in favor of classical narration, but his ultimate argument rests on the fact that the archplot is simply more commercial than either the antiplot or miniplot. Although both art cinema and American independent cinema constitute niche markets, box office alone hardly seems to be an appropriate gauge of the merits of a particular film or screenplay. Unlike international art cinema, which involves different financing and tends to succeed on the festival circuit, American independent cinema, almost by necessity, has to incorporate certain classical elements as part of its narration in order to compete against studio product in the marketplace. American independent films also need to have some type of hook to succeed at the box office, which is why novelty can often play such an important role, especially for those independent films that share the greatest affinity with art cinema.

An alternative screenwriting model broad enough to encompass American independent cinema would have a circular shape rather than McKee's triangular one. A circular shape implies that the spectrum of screenwriting possibilities represents a non-hierarchical continuum. The active, goal-driven protagonist represents only one of several possible options. A protagonist can be obsessively active, passive, or ambivalent, as should be obvious from the preceding analyses of *Me and You and Everyone We Know*, *Safe*, and *Stranger than Paradise*. Taking a cue from *Pyscho*'s screenwriter, Joseph Stefano, the Coen brothers demonstrate in *Fargo* that it's even possible to shift protagonists during the course of a film. The degree of agency attributed to a protagonist will have an obvious bearing on the story, especially in terms of flattening character and dramatic arcs, but various choices can be equally appropriate depending on the material.

Although the manuals insist that the protagonist in a film provides narrative agency, a film like *Gas Food Lodging* reminds us that the actions of a more secondary character, such as Trudi, can be equally effective in creating the turning points in a story. Another character, including a romance character or antagonist, can also serve that function, especially when a protagonist is either passive or ambivalent. In classical narration, a protagonist usually has a single goal or two intertwined goals that move the story forward, but a film like *Gas Food Lodging* involves a protagonist whose goals shift continually. Shade starts out with clearly defined goals, fails to achieve any of them, but still manages to find some semblance of hope in the catastrophe of her sister's pregnancy and her baby niece's adoption when she discovers the reason for Dank's failure to return.

While classical narration favors a single protagonist, more than one main character has become quite common in recent contemporary independent films. The introduction of more than one protagonist often results in multiple story lines, which have a decided impact on the structure of the films. *Trust* involves two separate stories, *Gas Food Lodging* focuses on three, while an ensemble film, such as *Me and You and Everyone We Know*, has a great many major characters and story lines. In multiple-plot structures, the various plotlines can be ascribed equal weight or one of the story lines can take precedent over the others. How those various plot threads interweave with each other (or don't), as well as the timing of those interconnections, become important factors in the overall structure. The two initially separate plotlines of *Trust* converge at the first turning point, when Maria and Matthew become involved. The other story lines, which really function more as subplots than independent plotlines, involve Rachel's kidnapping of the baby and Jean's connivance to get Matthew to marry Peg. Oddly enough, neither subplot has a major effect on what happens in the central romantic story line, but they nevertheless create an important thematic link.

Ensemble films, such as *Me and You and Everyone We Know*, often have slow setups in order to establish the multiple characters and story lines. As a result, ensemble films create snapshot portraits of their characters and do not allow time for the same type of motivated character development as most classical or art films. Miranda July uses several personal epiphanies to propel her ensemble narrative. Ensemble films often tend to be character-driven rather than plot-driven. While they often have major turning points connected to a main plotline, ensemble films frequently switch between events in the parallel plotlines as a way of keeping an audience engaged. The lives of characters in ensemble films also intersect at various points, which provides narrative coherence to the story. Ensemble films differ from a thread structure, such as *Mulholland Dr.*, in being linear rather than nonlinear.

With the rare exception of certain noncausal films, such as Richard Linklater's *Slacker* and Harmony Korine's *Gummo*, which emphasize individual scenes and thematic association rather than traditional dramatic plot, most American independent films employ the type of three-act structures found in classical narration. Many devise interesting alternative storytelling strategies other than strict linear progression, and the novelty of some of them provide hooks for movie audiences looking for more intellectual challenges. That seems particularly true of films such as *Reservoir Dogs*, *Elephant*, *Mulholland Dr.*, and *Memento*. The allure of such films has to do with their temporality, how they play with the element of time in telling their stories. By showing us the prelude to the diamond heist and then cutting directly to its aftermath, *Reservoir Dogs* cleverly delays providing important exposition usually contained in the first-act setup in order to heighten the suspense of the film's inciting incident, namely, that one of the gang members has to be a police infiltrator. *Reservoir Dogs* simply wouldn't work as effectively if its story were told linearly, and the flashbacks serve to parcel out the exposition at various intervals when needed, rather than incorporating it into the first act. *Elephant* sets up an elaborate temporal pattern of duration and simultaneity and then violates it in order to keep its overall structure from becoming predictable when it unexpectedly flashes back to Alex arriving home from school on the previous day.

Both *Memento* and *Mulholland Dr.* use flashback structures to filter their stories through the exaggerated subjectivity of their protagonists. Time goes forward and backward in *Memento*, which depends on a paranoid protagonist, who also suffers from anterior-grade (short-term) memory loss, to narrate the story. In Lenny's version of the events, he functions as a kind of vengeful hero, but it is only in the final act (or, to be more accurate, once the film is over) that we come to understand that he's a delusional murderer. Our perception of Diane Selwyn also changes radically in the final act of *Mulholland Dr.*, when we realize that what we've been watching actually occurs in her tortured psyche. In developing his neo-noir mystery, *Mulholland Dr.*, David Lynch introduces so many different plotlines and characters that it takes a long time for a viewer to figure out the protagonist of the story. Entire plot threads get dropped or turn into dead ends, as more typically happens in art-cinema narration. Lynch shows that it is possible to delay the intersection of the story lines involving Betty and Adam until more than halfway through the film when the two eye each other at the musical audition. This potential plotline becomes a red herring, but another involving Betty/Diane and Rita/Camilla surfaces unexpectedly later on. We come to realize eventually that the film's traditional setup has been delayed until the final act, where Lynch ruptures the causality of classical narration as various characters mutate into entirely different personalities through the type of weird associational logic we experience only in dreams. As also happens with *Memento*, it is only after *Mulholland Dr.* is over that it becomes even possible to piece together the parts of what seems to be a narrative puzzle. Despite Linda Seger's claims to the contrary, both films manage to cohere upon reflection and further analysis, despite their penchant for ambiguity.

Art cinema has always attempted to avoid the maximum clarity and comprehensibility demanded by classical Hollywood cinema by substituting ambiguity in its place. We also see this in a number of American independent films, most notably *Stranger Than Paradise*, *Safe*, and *Elephant*. *Memento* takes the notion of ambiguity to sophisticated heights by managing to create a puzzle structure that turns the experience of film viewing into a confounding game. Lynch does this as well in *Mulholland Dr.* by deliberately withholding important exposition through the repression of certain plotlines and the use of synecdoche, thereby positioning the viewer to play the role of detective in his mystery. He fools us into believing one thing, even while providing vague clues for what turns out to be an incredibly mind-boggling narrative twist. Instead of the game structure of *Memento*, Lynch uses dream structure as his subversive weapon to parody the notion of the Hollywood dream factory as a place that stifles true creativity and imagination. Like many American independent films, both films utilize a recognizable genre, in this case, film noir, to provide a grounding for the viewer. Despite its confounding structure, exaggerated subjective point of view, and downright baffling elements, *Memento* balances all of these by depending on viewers to be familiar with recognizable figures of the genre: the wronged tragic hero, the crooked cop, and the femme fatale. *Mulholland Dr.* uses and confuses genre by having one of its film noir characters turn out to be a cowboy.

Whereas screenwriters have a broad range of options in deciding on the agency of the protagonist, the type of characterization employed in American independent cinema runs from clearly recognizable genre types to the more inscrutable characters found in *Stranger Than Paradise*. If character traits and motives seem less clearly defined in art cinema, there's a similar tendency in American independent film. David Bordwell's contention that "art cinema presents psychological effects in search of their causes" has relevance to the types of characters we find in American independent cinema.[1] It certainly describes Carol White, whose body revolts against her desire to keep things superficial, and it also applies to Willie in *Stranger Than Paradise*, Christine in *Me and You and Everyone We Know*, Mr. White in *Reservoir Dogs*, Alex and Eric in *Elephant*, Solomon and Tummler in *Gummo*, or any of the myriad characters who populate *Slacker*. We understand the behavior of these characters from our observation of them and their interactions with the other characters, but we do not fully understand the motives for their actions, which often remain either buried or contradictory. Solomon, for instance, refuses to shoot Foot Foot early in *Gummo* because she has a collar, but this doesn't prevent Tummler and him from killing the cat later on.

Many characters in American independent films often seem less reflective and introspective than their counterparts in art cinema. Willie certainly hasn't a clue about his own actions, Carol White turns out to be incapable of talking about herself either in therapy or in a group session, and neither can Jerry nor Marge see beyond their narrow small-town world views. It never occurs to Jerry that something could go wrong with his kidnapping scheme, even though his young son can figure this out. Marge seems equally bewildered by Grimsrud's violent behavior and her old classmate's lies about his wife dying of leukemia. Maria in *Trust* starts out unreflective, but her quest for learning and self-discovery represents an unusual journey of spiritual discovery for an American independent film, even though it's one more commonly found in art cinema. In this respect, Shade's character stands in marked contrast to that of her sister and mother. Her birth order and the Spanish melodramas she watches at the local movie theater allow her to gain more insight into her own life and those around her. Trudi has one moment of insight after she makes love to Dank in the incandescent cave, but she resorts to further mindless and self-destructive behavior once he doesn't return. Trudi's one attempt to offer big-sisterly advice results in Shade suffering humiliation when she makes a miscalculated play for her gay friend.

Character arcs are usually found in classical narration, but not necessarily in art-cinema narration, so American independent films have the option of either using them or not. Dramatic structures, which have active, goal-driven protagonists and strong antagonists, are more apt to employ character arcs. Episodic structures—those with passive or ambivalent protagonists and no external antagonist—simply don't rely on them. The notion of character arcs does not seem relevant in the case of such films as *Stranger Than Paradise, Safe, Elephant, Gummo*, or *Slacker*. Independent films also tend to flatten the dramatic arcs of classical narration through a variety of strategies, including the use of coincidence, such as when Eva obtains money by mistake at the end of *Stranger Than Paradise*, Maria locates Rachel's husband in *Trust*, Shade twice runs into her estranged father in *Gas Food Lodging*, or Robby's Internet chat-room partner turns out to be the museum curator in *Me and You and Everyone We Know*. An ambivalent or passive protagonist can flatten drama; multiple characters and plotlines can diffuse drama; temporal duration or the lack of a strong protagonist can minimize drama. Certain independent films, such as *Mulholland Dr., Slacker* and *Gummo*, employ unorthodox noncausal structures that create problems for the narrative because their characters don't have an opportunity to interact with each other in any sort of conventional dramatic plot, even though we have that expectation and the films play with those expectations while merely creating more thematic, structural, and associational links. Because narrative is so central to commercial features, films that employ noncausal structures usually prove to be more challenging for a mass audience.

American independent cinema entered the mainstream in the 1990s as a result of the innovations in story structure and as a number of more character-driven films drew stars who were willing to defer or reduce their high salaries for the opportunity to play more challenging roles. Once this led to Oscar nominations and awards, independent films gained an additional element of prestige. The studios attempted to capitalize on the indie phenomenon by creating their own specialty units. They sought to bring independent talent under their wing or they gave their own "maverick" directors—Paul Thomas Anderson, Wes Anderson, David O. Russell, Spike Jonze, and David Fincher— enough creative autonomy to provide a studio-backed alternative to independently produced films.[2] As might be expected, the lines or divisions between the two began to blur and pseudo-independent films clouded the picture even more. Given such a context, even bona fide practitioners like Jarmusch have become wary of the term "independent." Jarmusch told an interviewer, "I'm so sick of that word. I reach for my revolver when I hear the word 'quirky.' Or 'edgy.' Those words are now becoming labels that are slapped on products to sell them."[3] It is hardly surprising that American independent cinema should be experiencing a crisis of identity.

The escalating costs of marketing and theatrical exhibition have made it increasingly expensive and difficult for independent films to compete against studio or studio-subsidized products, especially when many independent distributors have either been swallowed up by the major studios or gone out of business. Anyone interested in understanding the harsh economic aspects of producing and distributing independent films need only to read James Schamus's enlightening article on the subject in order to grasp how a $10 million box office draw usually results in a net loss.[4] It's no wonder then that independent film's greatest threat continues to be cooption by the major studios, which in the meantime have transformed into giant media conglomerates.

When Richard Linklater has directed a remake of *Bad News Bears* (2005) and Christopher Nolan has directed *Batman Begins* (2005), it's understandable why some commentators have begun once again to claim independent cinema's demise. Yet not all independent filmmakers have succumbed to working for either the major studios or their subsidiaries on a consistent basis. Jarmusch has had an exemplary independent career for the past twenty years, before making *Broken Flowers* (2005) for Focus Features, the same company (run by Schamus) which also produced Todd Haynes's *Far from Heaven* (2002). It is also interesting to note that Gus Van Sant appears to be moving in the opposite direction. After working as a director-for-hire and achieving notable commercial success with *Good Will Hunting* (1997) and *Finding Forrester* (2000), he has returned to his independent roots by making a trilogy of films—*Gerry, Elephant,* and *Last Days* (2005), his biopic on the rock musician Kurt Cobain—which have been influenced by the formal simplicity of Eastern European art cinema. Like Van Sant, Lynch has given up "film" for the flexibility of digital video, and chosen to work on a scaled-down basis, which allows him to have even greater artistic control. Despite a productive career, Hal Hartley still remains very much outside the system. His latest film, *The Girl from Monday,* played at Sundance, the Museum of Modern Art, and was distributed on DVD through an unusual arrangement between his new releasing company, Possible Films, and Netflix.[5]

There is no doubt that emerging technologies will impact the future direction of independent film in ways we are only beginning to understand. Digital technology already allows independent features to be made more cheaply than ever before. Museums and art galleries are providing alternate exhibition channels, even commissioning large-scale media works, as in the case of Matthew Barney. Spurred by audience demand, there is industry-wide discussion of the possibility of simultaneously releasing films in theaters and on DVD. The DVD phenomenon has given independent films a second life, especially as online DVD rental companies, such as Netflix and GreenCine, have created a market for smaller independent films previously relegated to the festival circuit.[6] Netflix even has begun to make exclusive deals with independent filmmakers, as in the case of Hartley's new film. Video-on-demand (VOD) will allow home viewers to have access to virtually unlimited choices in media, with personalization software customizing preferred content to individual users. All of these developments could benefit independent films in the long run.

In the meantime, films like Gregg Araki's *Mysterious Skin* (2005), Van Sant's *Last Days* (2005), Noah Baumbach's *The Squid and the Whale* (2005), and July's *Me and You and Everyone We Know* (2005), demonstrate the continued vitality of independent films, despite efforts to gloss over differences between independent cinema and mainstream Hollywood. As an example of the attempt to conflate the two, *MovieMaker's* first-annual edition *Beginner's Guide to Making Movies 2004* featured eleven filmmakers on the cover, including Quentin Tarantino, Allison Anders, Linklater, and Jarmusch.[7] The citation of these filmmakers, most of whom began their careers by being associated with American independent cinema, suggests that their breakthrough films ought to serve as models for beginners interested in making movies. The advice offered in the various short articles on screenwriting, however, runs contrary to the achievements of the early films of the writer/directors featured on the magazine's cover. Instead of providing an analysis of how these independent filmmakers have managed to skirt the rules and conventions of traditional screenwriting, the articles simply rehash the basic advice contained in the manuals.

Many of the films cited on the cover of *MovieMaker*, most notably *Slacker, Gas Food Lodging, Stranger Than Paradise*, and *Reservoir Dogs*, achieved their success precisely by deviating from the conventions of classical Hollywood films, which manages to get recycled here as tips for the beginning screenwriter. Jarmusch's *Stranger Than Paradise*, with its ambivalent protagonist, internal conflict, and meandering episodic plot, would hardly seem to be an appropriate model for classical dramatic structure, and Anders, who has been openly critical of the goal-oriented three-act structure as overtly masculine, seems an equally odd poster child for the conventional paradigm. Linklater's *Slacker*, to cite a final example, does not have a three-act structure, a goal-driven protagonist, or even a strong antagonist. Many independent films don't conform to the guidelines that appear on the checklists.

The comments of independent filmmakers such as Linklater, Jarmusch, Haynes, Anders, Korine, Van Sant, and July suggest that they have developed their own methods of writing screenplays that clearly seem at odds with those of the manuals. In an interview in *Filmmaker*, Steve Buscemi, the actor/screenwriter/director talks about his experiences taking John Truby's screenwriting workshop:

> I learned about what should go into a commercial screenplay. But when I tried to apply [his instruction] to what I wanted to write, I got stuck. I think good scripts incorporate all these things intuitively. What helped me—there was a retrospective of Cassavetes at MoMA, so I saw all his films in one shot. It totally freed me up. His movies inspired me to just write and not worry about structure. One of the things Truby said was you have to know your beginning, middle and end before you start, or else you're going to get into trouble. I think it's o.k. to get in trouble, it's o.k. to lose yourself in these characters and find out where they're going. And if you have to start all over again, fine.[8]

As Buscemi suggests, the manual approach can be inhibiting as well as constricting through an overemphasis on plot structure at the expense of character. In addition, it only guarantees that your screenplay will end up being conventional.

All truly independent films manage to provide some element of novelty—whether in terms of form or subject matter—that can't be reduced to a set of rules. As Jarmusch puts it, "There are no rules. There are as many ways to make a film as there are potential filmmakers. It's an open form."[9] This is not to suggest that screenwriting is better mastered by a fly-by-the-seat-of-your-pants approach. Screenwriters need to have a broad understanding of the entire spectrum of narrative procedures available to them. Real innovation in screenwriting, as the various American independent films in this study boldly attest, comes not from an ignorance of narrative film conventions, but from being able to see beyond their limitations.

Notes

Introduction

1. Harvey Weinstein quoted in Benjamin Svetkey, "The Distributors," *Entertainment Weekly*, Special Issue: "The New Hollywood: Inside the World of Independent Films" (November/December 1997): 35.

2. Christine Vachon with David Edelstein, *Shooting to Kill: How an Independent Producer Blasts through the Barriers to Make Movies that Matter* (New York: Avon Books, 1998), 16–17.

3. Jonathan Bing, "Will U's Focus Prove Blurry?" *Variety* (1–14 July 2002): 1.

4. Jon Jost, "End of the Indies: Death of the Sayles Men," *Film Comment*, 25, 1 (January/February 1989): 44.

5. *Ibid.*, 43.

6. Ted Hope, "Indie Film Is Dead," *Filmmaker*, 4, 1 (Fall 1995): 18.

7. James Schamus, "Don't Worry, Be Happy: Producer James Schamus Responds to 'Indie Film Is Dead,'" *Filmmaker*, 4, 1 (Fall 1995): 60.

8. Jim Jarmusch quoted in Lynn Hirschberg, "The Last of the Indies," *New York Times Magazine* (31 July 2005): 20.

9. Owen Gleiberman, "The Worst," *Entertainment Weekly* (20/27 December 2002): 108.

10. Julie Dash quoted in Patricia Thomson, "The Screenplay's the Thing," *The Independent* (December 1988): 27.

11. Syd Field, *Screenplay: The Foundations of Screenwriting* (New York: Dell Publishing, 1979, 1982), 12.

12. *Ibid.*, 9.

13. Syd Field, *The Screenwriter's Workbook* (New York: Dell Publishing, 1984), 155.

14. Richard Walter, *Screenwriting: The Art, Craft and Business of Film and Television Writing* (New York: New American Library, 1988), 37.

15. *Ibid.*, 44.

16. *Ibid.*

17. *Ibid.*, 46.

18. *Ibid.*, 52.

19. *Ibid.*, 53.

20. *Ibid.*, 61.

21. Richard Walter, *The Whole Picture: Strategies for Screenwriting Success in the New Hollywood* (New York: Plume, 1997), 3.

22. *Ibid.*, 19.

23. Linda Seger, *Making a Good Script Great*, 2d ed. (Hollywood: Samuel French, 1987, 1994), 20.

24. *Ibid.*, 21.

25. *Ibid.*, 25.

26. *Ibid.*, 35.

27. *Ibid.*

28. *Ibid.*, 32.

29. *Ibid.*, 99.

30. *Ibid.*

31. Linda Seger, *Advanced Screenwriting: Raising Your Script to the Academy Award Level* (Los Angeles: Silman-James Press, 2003), xv.

32. Charlie Kaufman and Donald Kaufman, *Adaptation: The Shooting Script* (New York: Newmarket Press, 2002), 11.

33. Robert McKee, *Story: Substance, Structure, Style, and the Principles of Screenwriting* (New York: Regan Books, 1997), 3.

34. *Ibid.*, 41.

35. *Ibid.*, 45.

36. *Ibid.*, 46.

37. *Ibid.*, 62.

38. *Ibid.*, 218.

39. *Ibid.*, 220–221.

40. Jim Jarmusch and Joel Coen, for example, received their MFA degrees from NYU, Allison Anders from UCLA, and David Lynch from the American Film Institute. Hal Hartley came out of a strong production program at SUNY-Purchase and Todd Haynes graduated from the semiotics program at Brown.

41. David Bordwell, "The Art Cinema as a Mode of Film Practice," *Film Criticism*, 4, 1 (1979): 57. For a detailed discussion of art cinema narration, see pp. 56–64.

42. David Bordwell, *Narration in the Fiction Film* (Madison: University of Wisconsin Press, 1985), 207.

43. See Ken Dancyger and Jeff Rush, *Alternative Screenwriting: Writing Beyond the Rules*, 2d ed. (Boston: Focal Press, 1995), 39–49.

44. Kristin Thompson, *Storytelling in the New Hollywood: Understanding Classical Narrative Technique* (Cambridge, Mass., and London: Harvard University Press, 1999), 37.

45. See Evan Smith, "Thread Structure: Rewriting the Hollywood Formula," *Journal of Film and Video*, 51, 3–4 (Fall–Winter 1999–2000): 88–96.

46. Richard Linklater, *Slacker* (New York: St. Martin's Press, 1992), 10.

47. Bob Verini, "Independent People: Crafting Characters for the Low-Budget Movie," *scr(i)pt*, 5, 6 (November/December 1999): 45.

48. *Ibid.*, 46.

49. McKee, 138.

50. *Ibid.*, 104.

51. Seger, *Making a Good Script Great*, 186.

52. Walter, *Screenwriting: The Art, Craft and Business of Film and Television Writing*, 69.

53. Syd Field, *Screenplay: The Foundations of Screenwriting*, 53.

54. Thompson, 14.

55. Sarah Kozloff, *Overhearing Film Dialogue* (Berkeley and Los Angeles: University of California Press, 2000), 28.

56. *Ibid.*, 74. Kozloff cites Bernard M. Dupriez, *A Dictionary of Literary Devices, Gradus, A–Z*, trans. and adapted by Albert W. Halsall (Toronto: University of Toronto Press, 1991), 132.

57. Thompson, 12.

58. Field, *Screenplay. The Foundations of Screenwriting*, 58.

59. *Ibid.*, 63.

Chapter 1

1. Jarmusch quoted in Lawrence Van Gelder, "'Stranger Than Paradise': Its Story Could Be a Movie," *The New York Times* (21 October 1984, Section 2): 33.

2. Jarmusch quoted in Harlan Jacobson, "Jim Jarmusch," *Film Comment* 21, 1 (January/February 1985). Reprinted in Ludvig Hertzberg, ed., *Jim Jarmusch Interviews* (Jackson: University of Mississippi Press, 2001), 13.

3. See Linda Seger, *Creating Unforgettable Characters* (New York: Henry Holt and Company, 1990), 29. Seger begins her discussion of the core of the character by stating, "Characters need to be consistent."

4. Jarmusch quoted in Richard Linnett, "As American as You Are: Jim Jarmusch and 'Stranger Than Paradise,'" *Cineaste*, XIV, 1 (1985): 27.

5. See Syd Field, *The Screenwriter's Workbook* (New York: Dell Publishing, 1984), 71–73.

6. Flo Leibowitz, "Neither Hollywood nor Godard: The Strange Case of *Stranger Than Paradise*," *Persistence of Vision* 6 (Summer 1988): 20–21.

7. Ray Carney, *Shadows* (London: BFI Publishing, 2001), 48.

8. Jarmusch quoted in Peter Keough, "Home and Away," *Sight and Sound*, 2, 4 (August 1992): 9. Reprinted in Hertzberg, 110.

9. See Jim Jarmusch, *A Film Proposal: Stranger Than Paradise* (unpublished screenplay, 1982). When Jarmusch showed the fifty-nine-page script for his next feature, *Down By Law*, to distribution companies and potential backers, their reaction was that it wasn't a full-length feature. See Jane Shapiro, "Stranger Than Paradise," *Village Voice* (16 September 1986). Reprinted in Hertzberg, 61.

10. Christine Vachon quoted in Oren Moverman, Interview: "And All Is Well in Our World—Making *Safe*: Todd Haynes, Julianne Moore and Christine Vachon" in *Projections 5: Filmmakers on Filmmaking*, eds. John Boorman and Walter Donohue (London and Boston: Faber and Faber, 1996), 225.

11. See Peter Belisto, "Jim Jarmusch," in Peter Belisto, ed., *Notes from the Pop Underground* (The Last Gasp of San Francisco, 1985), 56–71. Reprinted in Hertzberg, 35.

12. Jarmusch quoted in Jacobson, 18.

13. John Piccarella, "Guess Who's Coming to Dinner," *High Fidelity* (November 1985): 75.

14. Jarmusch quoted in Van Gelder, 23.

15. Jarmusch quoted in Linnett, 27.

16. See John Pierson, *Spike, Mike, Slackers & Dykes: A Guided Tour Across a Decade of American Independent Cinema* (New York: Hyperion Miramax Books, 1995), 25.

Chapter 2

1. See Michael Hauge, *Writing Screenplays That Sell* (New York: McGraw-Hill, 1988), 21.

2. Todd McCarthy, Review: *Safe*, *Variety* (27 January 1995).

3. See "The 50 Most Important Independent Films," *Filmmaker*, 5, 1 (Fall 1996): 40–45, 51–60.

4. See "Rules of the Game: First Annual *Village Voice* Film Critics Poll," *Village Voice*, XLIV, 52 (4 January 2000): 41.

5. Christine Vachon with David Edelstein, *Shooting to Kill: How an Independent Producer Blasts through the Barriers to Make Movies That Matter* (New York: Avon Books, 1998), 8.

6. For a discussion of reception issues surrounding the film, see Justin Wyatt, *Poison* (Wiltshire, England: Flick Books, 1998).

7. Christine Vachon quoted in Oren Moverman, Interview: "And All Is Well in Our World—Making *Safe*: Todd Haynes, Julianne Moore and Christine Vachon," in *Projections 5: Filmmakers on Filmmaking*, eds. John Boorman and Walter Donohue (London and Boston: Faber and Faber, 1996), 226.

8. Roger Ebert, Review: *Safe*, *Chicago Sun-Times* (28 July 1995).

9. Todd Haynes, Far from Heaven, Safe, *and* Superstar: the Karen Carpenter Story: *Three Screenplays* (New York: Grove Press, 2003), 179.

10. *Ibid.*, "Three Screenplays: An Introduction," x.

11. *Ibid.*, 108.

12. Haynes quoted in Moverman, 203.

13. Haynes, 137–138.

14. *Ibid.*, 104.

15. Haynes quoted in Moverman, 201–202.

16. Haynes, 103.

17. *Ibid.*, 105.

18. *Ibid.,* 126. In the script, this image comes from a later scene of Carol outside her house at night when the patrol car drives by.

19. *Ibid.,* 115.

20. Haynes quoted in Alison Maclean, "Todd Haynes," *Bomb* (Summer 1995): 50.

21. Haynes, 143.

Chapter 3

1. Linda Aronson, *Screenwriting Updated: New (and Conventional) Ways of Writing for the Screen* (Los Angeles: Silman-James, 2001), 61.

2. See Eddie Robson, *Coen Brothers* (London: Virgin Books, 2003), 160.

3. Ethan Cohen quoted in Robson, 163.

4. Ethan and Joel Coen, *Fargo* (London and Boston: Faber and Faber, 1996), 75.

5. Richard Walter, *Screenwriting: The Art, Craft, and Business of Film and Television Writing* (New York: Plume, 1986), 48.

6. Syd Field, *The Screenwriter's Workbook* (New York: Dell Publishing, 1984), 141.

7. John Egan, "The '90's New Wave," *scr(i)pt*, 3, 6 (November/ December 1997): 18.

8. *Ibid.*

9. *Ibid.,* 19, 61.

10. See Robert McKee, *Story: Substance, Structure, Style, and the Principles of Screenwriting* (New York: Regan Books, 1997), 226–232.

11. *Ibid.,* 137.

12. Amanda Sheahan Wells, *Psycho* (London: York Press, 2001), 34.

13. Alfred Hitchcock quoted in François Truffaut, *Hitchcock*, rev. ed. (New York: Simon and Schuster, 1984), 269.

14. Ethan Coen, "Introduction," in Ethan and Joel Coen, x.

15. Thomas Goetz, "Tongue Twisting," *Village Voice* (12 March 1996): 46.

16. Ethan and Joel Coen, 6–7.

17. *Ibid.,* 10–11.

18. *Ibid.,* 20.

19. My analysis of the structure of *Fargo* also differs significantly from Linda Seger's. She writes: "At the first turning point, Marge gets a phone call about a murder. She begins the case. At the second turning point the police hear that something strange is going on at the lake. This leads Marge to the lake, where she finds one of the bad guys and the body parts of another." See Seger's *Advanced Screenwriting: Raising Your Script to the Academy Award Level* (Los Angeles: Silman-James, 2003), 83.

20. Thomas Pope, *Good Scripts, Bad Scripts* (New York: Three Rivers Press, 1998), 103.

21. *Ibid.,* 104.

22. *Ibid.*

23. *Ibid.,* 105.

24. *Ibid.,* 106.

Chapter 4

1. Linda Seger, *Making a Good Script Great,* 2d ed. (Hollywood: Samuel French, 1987, 1994), 39.

2. *Ibid.,* 41

3. Hal Hartley, Simple Men *and* Trust (Winchester, Mass., and London: Faber and Faber, 1992), 109.

4. *Ibid.,* 110.

5. *Ibid.,* 123.

6. *Ibid.,* 139.

7. *Ibid.,* 140–141.

8. Hartley quoted in Graham Fuller, "Hal Hartley: Finding the Essential," in Hartley, xiv-xv.

9. *Ibid.,* xxi.

10. Hartley, 178.

11. Hartley quoted in Fuller, xiii.

12. Hartley, 163–165.

13. David Mamet, *On Directing Film* (New York: Viking Penguin, 1991), 4. Although flattered by the comparison, Hartley claims to know very little about Mamet. See Fuller, xxxi.

14. Mamet, 2.

15. Hartley, 156.

Chapter 5

1. Syd Field, *Screenplay: The Foundations of Screenwriting* (New York: Dell Publishing, 1979, 1982), 111.

2. Linda Seger, *Making a Good Script Great,* 2d ed. (Hollywood: Samuel French, 1987, 1994), 29, 31.

3. Michael Hauge, *Writing Screenplays That Sell* (New York: McGraw-Hill, 1988), 83.

4. Kristin Thompson, *Storytelling in the New Hollywood: Understanding Classical Narrative Technique* (Cambridge, Mass.: Harvard University Press, 1999), 29.

5. Anders quoted in Celeste Adams, "Working Class Heroes: The Film World of Allison Anders," *Filmmaker,* 1 (Fall 1992): 18.

6. Anders quoted in Anthony C. Ferrante, "Allison Anders Telling Her Own Story," *scr(i)pt* 2, 5 (September/October 1996): 32.

7. *Ibid.,* 33.

8. Anders quoted in Stephen Lowenstein, ed., *My First Movie: Twenty Celebrated Directors Talk About Their First Film* (New York: Pantheon Books, 2000), 61.

9. Allison Anders, *Gas-Food-Lodging* (unpublished screenplay, 2nd draft, 26 November 1990), 62.

10. Anders quoted in Lowenstein, 58.

11. *Ibid.*

12. Georgia Brown, "Rest Stop Ahead," Review: *Gas Food Lodging, Village Voice* (4 August 1992): 56.

13. Todd Haynes, "Three Screenplays: An Introduction," in Far From Heaven, Safe, *and* Superstar: The Karen Carpenter Story: *Three Screenplays* (New York: Grove Press, 2003), xi.

Chapter 6

1. There are exceptions to this. See, for instance, Linda J. Cowgill, *Secrets of Screenplay Structure: How to Recognize and Emulate the Structural Frameworks of Great Films* (Los Angeles: Lone Eagle Publishing, 1999); and Linda Aronson, *Screenwriting Updated: New (and Conventional) Ways of Writing for the Screen* (Los Angeles: Silman-James Press, 2001).

2. Todd Solondz quoted in Scott Macauley, Interview: "That Lovin' Feeling," *Filmmaker*, 7, 1 (Fall 1998): 37.

3. Miranda July quoted in Rebecca Murray, "Miranda July Talks About *Me and You and Everyone We Know*," http://movies.about.com/od/meandyouandevery one/a/meandyou061505.htm.

4. Ron Meyer quoted in Lynn Hirschberg, "Crabgrass Gothic," *The New York Times Magazine* (27 September 1998): 38.

5. Christine Vachon quoted in Dan Cox, "October Axes 'Happiness'; Good Steps In," *Variety* (13–19 July 1998): 18.

6. James Schamus, "The Pursuit of *Happiness*: Making an Art of Marketing an Explosive Film," *The Nation* (5–12 April 1999): 35.

7. Cox, 18.

8. July quoted in Murray.

9. Both *Nest of Tens* and *Getting Stronger Everyday* are available from the Video Data Bank in Chicago.

10. For a discussion of network narratives, see David Bordwell, *The Way Hollywood Tells It: Story and Style in Modern Movies* (Berkeley, Los Angeles, London: University of California Press, 2006), 99–103.

11. Kristin Thompson, *Storytelling in the New Hollywood: Understanding Hollywood Technique* (Cambridge, Mass.: Harvard University Press, 1999), 12.

12. Cowgill, 131.

13. Thompson, 20.

Chapter 7

1. Tarantino quoted in Jeff Dawson, *Quentin Tarantino: The Cinema of Cool* (New York: Applause Books, 1995), 69–70.

2. Syd Field, *Screenplay: The Foundations of Screenwriting* (New York: Dell Publishing, 1979, 1982), 132.

3. Richard Walter, *Screenwriting: The Art, Craft, and Business of Film and Television Writing* (New York: New American Library, 1988), 141.

4. Linda Seger, *Making a Good Script Great*, 2d ed. (Hollywood: Samuel French, 1987, 1994), 154.

5. *Ibid.*

6. Robert McKee, *Story: Substance, Structure, Style, and the Principles of Screenwriting* (New York: Regan Books, 1997), 342.

7. Tarantino quoted in Graham Fuller, "Answers First, Questions Later: Quentin Tarantino interviewed by Graham Fuller," in John Boorman and Walter Donahue, eds., *Projections 3: Filmmakers on Filmmaking* (London: Faber and Faber, 1994), 184.

8. Tarantino quoted in Gavin Smith, "Interview with Quentin Tarantino: When You Know You're in Good Hands," *Film Comment* (July-August 1994). Reprinted in Gerald Peary, ed., *Quentin Tarantino Interviews* (Jackson: University of Mississippi Press, 1998), 110.

9. Mary M. Dalton and Steve Jarrett, "Review Essay: *Reservoir Dogs*," *Creative Screenwriting*, 1, 4 (Winter 1994): 10.

10. See Sarah Kosloff, *Overhearing Film Dialogue* (Berkeley and Los Angeles: University of California Press, 2000), 201–234.

11. Field, 67–68.

12. Walter, 101.

13. Quentin Tarantino, *Reservoir Dogs and True Romance: Screenplays by Quentin Tarantino* (New York: Grove Press, 1994), 19.

14. Tarantino quoted in Dawson, 84.

15. Tarantino, 50–51. The dialogue has been adapted to what appears in the film.

16. For a similar breakdown of the act structure of *Reservoir Dogs,* see Linda J. Cowgill, *Secrets of Screenplay Structure: How to Recognize and Emulate the Structural Frameworks of Great Films* (Los Angeles: Lone Eagle, 1999), 164–165.

17. Charles Deemer, "The Screenplays of Quentin Tarantino," *Creative Screenwriting*, 1, 4 (Winter 1994): 61.

18. Tarantino, 91–92. The dialogue has been adapted to what actually appears in the film.

19. Tarantino, in fact, borrowed so much from Ringo Lam's *City of Fire* that it led to charges of plagiarism. See Dawson, 90–91. (Dawson mistakenly identifies Lam as Lan, and the date of *City of Fire* as 1989 instead of 1987.)

20. The screenplay contained an additional line of motivation, which was excised from the film: "But he seemed like a good kid, and I was impatient and greedy and all the things that fuck you up." See Tarantino, 106.

21. Harvey Weinstein quoted in Jami Bernard, *Quentin Tarantino: The Man and His Movies* (New York: Harper Perennial, 1995), 160.

22. Tarantino quoted in Gerald Peary, "A Talk with Quentin Tarantino," in Peary, 29.

23. Tarantino, 61–63.

24. Todd McCarthy, "Review: *Reservoir Dogs*," *Variety* (27 January 1992). Reprinted in Paul A. Woods, ed., *Quentin Tarantino: The Film Geek Files* (London: Plexus, 2000), 16.

25. Ella Taylor, "Quentin Tarantino's *Reservoir Dogs* and the Thrill of Excess," *LA Weekly* (16 October 1992). Reprinted in Peary, 47–48.

Chapter 8

1. Jonas Mekas, "Shoot the Screenwriters," *Village Voice* (25 November 1959). Reprinted in *Movie Journal: The Rise of a New American Cinema, 1959–1971* (New York: Collier Books, 1972), 6–7. The full quote appears as an epigraph to the Introduction.

2. Jonathan Rosenbaum, "*The Savage Eye/Shadows*," in *The American New Wave 1958–1967* (Minneapolis: Walker Art Center, 1982), 32.

3. Cassavetes quoted in Stephanie Watson, "Spontaneous Cinema? In the Shadows with John Cassavetes," in *Naked Lens: Beat Cinema*, ed. Jack Sargeant (London: Creation Books, 1997), 61–62. Watson cites Colin Young and Gideon Brachmann [*sic*] in "New Wave—Or Gesture," *Film Quarterly*, 14, 3 (Spring 1961): 7.

4. *Ibid.*, 62.

5. Ray Carney, "No Exit: John Cassavetes' *Shadows*," in *Beat Culture and the New America 1950–1965*, ed. Lisa Phillips (New York and Paris: Whitney Museum of American Art in Association with Flammarion, 1995), 236.

6. Jonas Mekas, "Two Versions of *Shadows*," *Village Voice* (27 January 1960). Reprinted in *Movie Journal: The Rise of a New American Cinema, 1959–1971*, 10. Although the missing first version has finally been located, the only version available remains the second version. For a discussion of the continuing controversy surrounding *Shadows*, see Tom Charity, "Open Ear Open Eye," *Sight & Sound*, 14, 3 (March 2004): 26–28. According to Charity, Mekas has softened his position on the second version.

7. "The First Independent Film Award" in Appendix, *Film Culture Reader*, ed. P. Adams Sitney (New York and Washington: Praeger Publishers, 1970), 423.

8. Mekas, "Two Versions of *Shadows*," 10.

9. Van Sant quoted in Jeffrey M. Somogyi, "Flying Blind," *Screenwriter Magazine*, XII, 4: 28.

10. *Ibid.*

11. *Ibid.*

12. In October of 2005, JT LeRoy was revealed to be a literary hoax. Rather than a gay teenage literary sensation, LeRoy turns out to be a pseudonym for an older woman named Laura Alpert. See Stephen Beachy, "Who Is the Real JT LeRoy?" *New York* 38, 36 (17 October 2005): 30.

13. See "Conception," *Elephant* Publicity Materials, http://www.elephant movie.com/production/2conception.html.

14. Van Sant quoted in Scott Macaulay, "Tracking Shots," *Filmmaker*, 12, 1 (Fall 2003): 44.

15. *Ibid.*

16. Van Sant quoted in Somogyi, 28.

17. Van Sant quoted in Patricia Thomson, "Walking the Halls of Fate," *American Cinematographer*, 84, 10 (October 2003): 64.

18. See Dave Cullen, "The Depressive and the Psychopath," *Slate* (20 April 2004), http://www.slate.com/id/2099203/.

19. Van Sant quoted in Amy Taubin, "Part of the Problem: Stepping into the Arena of High School, Gus Van Sant's *Elephant* Confronts the Specter of Columbine," *Film Comment*, 39, 5 (September/October 2003): 26.

20. *Ibid.*, 26–29.

21. Kent Jones, "Corridors of Powerlessness," *Film Comment*, 39, 5 (September/October 2003): 28.

22. Van Sant quoted in S. F. Said, "Shock Corridors," *Sight & Sound*, 14, 2 (February 2004): 18.

23. Van Sant quoted in Taubin, 33.

24. *Ibid.*

Chapter 9

1. Linda Seger, *Advanced Screenwriting: Raising Your Script to the Academy Award Level* (Los Angeles: Silman-James Press, 2003), 19.

2. Christopher Nolan quoted in Annie Nocenti, "Christopher Nolan's Revenge Redux," *The Independent* 24, 2 (March 2001): 33.

3. James Mottram, *The Making of* Memento (London: Faber and Faber, 2002), 34.

4. Nolan quoted in Nocenti, 35.

5. *Ibid.*, 33.

6. Seger, 19.

7. Christopher Nolan, Memento *and* Following (London: Faber and Faber, 2001), 221–222. The dialogue has been adapted to what appears in the film.

8. For a discussion of neo-noir, see Sharon Y. Cobb, "Writing the New Noir Film," *Creative Screenwriting*, 7, 5 (September/October 2000): 35–37. This article was first published in *Film Noir Reader 2*, eds. Alain Silver and James Ursini (New York: Limelight, 1999).

9. Nolan, 222. The dialogue has been adapted to what appears in the film.

10. Nolan quoted in Daniel Fierman, "Memory Games," *Entertainment Weekly* (22 June 2001): 24.

11. Christopher McQuarrie quoted in David Konow, "The Way of the Screenwriter: Christopher McQuarrie," *Creative Screenwriting*, 7, 5 (September/October 2000): 40.

12. Richard Kelly quoted in Bob Longino, "Cult Hit Refuses Easy Answers for Artistic Truth, Filmmaker Says: Interview with Richard Kelly, Director of *Donnie Darko*," *The Atlanta Constitution* (27 June 2003).

13. Seger, 20.

Chapter 10

1. David Lynch quoted in Scott Macaulay, "The Dream Factory," *Filmmaker*, 10, 1 (Fall 2001): 66.

2. Linda Seger, *Advanced Screenwriting: Raising Your Script to the Academy Award Level* (Los Angeles: Sillman-James Press, 2003), 24–25.

3. See Evan Smith, "Thread Structure: Rewriting the Hollywood Formula," *Journal of Film and Video*, 51, 3–4 (Fall–Winter 1999–2000): 88–96.

4. *Ibid.*, 88.

5. *Ibid.*, 93.

6. Lew Hunter quoted in Richard Whiteside, "Structure Wars: Part One," *scr(i)pt*, 5, 2 (March/April 1999): 44–45.

7. Seger, 28.

8. David Lynch, Mulholland Drive *Pilot —The Screenplay* (1/5/1999), http://www.lynchnet.com/mdrive/mdscript.html.

9. *Ibid.*

10. *Ibid.*

11. David Lynch and Barry Gifford, *Lost Highway* (London and Boston: Faber and Faber, 1997), 49.

12. *Ibid.*, 51.

13. Philip Lopate, "Welcome to L.A.," *Film Comment*, 37, 5 (September/October 2001): 47.

Chapter 11

1. Although *Gummo* won major prizes at the Venice and Rotterdam film festivals, not only did Janet Maslin deem it the "worst movie of the year" in her scathing *New York Times* review, but J. Hoberman, one of the most sympathetic critics of alternative cinema was equally hostile in his response, calling the film "genuinely disgusting" and later dismissing Korine as "the glue-sniffer's Jean-Luc Godard." See Janet Maslin, "Cats, Grandma and Other Disposables," Review: *Gummo*, *New York Times* (17 October 1997): E12. See also J. Hoberman, "Parting Shots: The 37th New York Film Festival," *Village Voice* (22–28 September 1999): 124; and J. Hoberman, "Young Blood," *Village Voice* (6–12 October 1999): 139.

2. Harmony Korine, *Collected Screenplays 1:* Jokes, Gummo, julien donkey-boy (London: Faber and Faber, 2002), 77.

3. *Ibid.*, 80.

4. See Jefferson Hack, "Harmony Korine," in *Star Culture: The Collected Interviews from Dazed & Confused Magazine*, eds. Mark Sanders and Jefferson Hack (London: Phaidon Press, 2000), 194.

5. Gus Van Sant, "Forward," in "*Gummo*: About the Film," Fine Line publicity materials, http://www.finelinefeatures.com/gummo/topabout.html.

6. Robin O'Hara quoted in "*Gummo*: About the Production," Fine Line publicity materials, http://www.finelinefeatures.com/gummo/topabout.html.

7. For a discussion of the films of Chistopher Maclaine, see J. J. Murphy, "Christopher Maclaine—Approaching 'The End,'" in *Film Culture*, 70–71 (1983): 88–100. Maclaine is cited as one of the forgotten visionaries by a character in *Slacker*. For a discussion of David Brooks, see also J. J. Murphy, "The Films of David Brooks," in the same issue of *Film Culture*, 206–212.

8. See Jonas Mekas, *Movie Journal: The Rise of a New American Cinema, 1959–1971* (New York: Collier Books, 1972), 6–7, 23–24.

9. Korine quoted in Hack, "Harmony Korine," 195.

10. See Werner Herzog, "*Gummo*'s Whammo," *Interview*, 27, 11 (November 1997), 88. See also http://www.finelinefeatures.com/gummo/topabout.html.

11. See Benjamin Halligan, "What Is the Neo-Underground and What Isn't: A First Consideration of Harmony Korine," in *Underground U.S.A.: Filmmaking Beyond the Hollywood Canon*, eds. Xavier Mendik and Steven Jay Schneider (London: Wallflower Press, 2002), 160.

12. Coproduced by the Contemporary Arts Center in Cincinnati and Yerba Buena Center for the Arts, San Francisco, "Beautiful Losers: Contemporary Art and Street Culture" was an exhibition of work by more than fifty artists inspired by skateboarding culture. See *Beautiful Losers: Contemporary Art and Street Culture*, eds. Aaron Rose and Christian Strike (New York: Iconoclast and D. A. P., 2004). For additional information on contemporary artists and skateboard culture, including Harmony Korine, see also the special issue "The Disobedients," *Tokion* 29 (May/June 2002).

13. Jerry Saltz, "Modern Gothic," *Village Voice* (4–10 February 2004): C85. For another view of the same phenomenon, see Michael Cohen, "The New Gothic: Scary Monsters and Super Creeps," *Flash Art*, 36, 231 (July–September 2003): 108–110.

14. For an interesting discussion of the grotesque, see Marie de Brugerolle, "Disparities and Deformations: Our Grotesque," *Flash Art* 37, 236 (May–June 2004): 75.

15. Korine quoted in Werner Herzog, "*Gummo*'s Whammo."

16. Hack, "Harmony Korine," 193.

17. The Yiddish word "tumler" derives from "tumlen," or "to make a racket."

18. Korine, 73–74.

19. *Chico and the Man*, which featured Freddie Prinze, was a popular situation comedy that aired on the NBC network from 1974–1978.

20. Tad Tuleja, *The New York Public Library Book of Popular Americana* (New York: Stonesong Press, 1994), 207. The entry for Kewpie reads, "A child's doll manufactured since 1913 and modeled on figures created by Rose O'Neill (1874–1944). She accompanied a 1909 poem in *Ladies' Home Journal* with a drawing of a 'Cupidlike' creature, explaining 'Kewpie means a small Cupid, just as a puppy means a small dog.' Inexpensive Kewpies appear as carnival prizes." The carnival reference seems particularly relevant to *Gummo*.

21. While it's ambiguous in the film whether Tummler and Solomon have killed Foot Foot, the screenplay clearly indicates that they have done so, despite Solomon's earlier refusal to kill a house cat (as indicated by its collar). This is another example of Korine undercutting causal connections in the film. More logically, we might assume that Foot Foot wound up being one of Jarrod's victims, since we've watched him mix glass with tuna fish at the dumpster. In the screenplay, however, Korine writes, "Tummler and Solomon are shooting Foot Foot to death with their BB guns." See Korine, 164.

22. In an interview with David Letterman on *The Late Show* (17 October 1997), Korine claims that Gummo quit because he liked to "wear women's clothes" and "sell cardboard boxes." See http://www.harmonykorine.com/interview010.html. Korine's comment is interesting in terms of the theme of difference, and references to transvestism in the film, but I cannot confirm the veracity of Korine's statement, other than that Gummo worked in the garment industry.

Chapter 12

1. See "Poetry and Film: A Symposium with Maya Deren, Arthur Miller, Dylan Thomas, Parker Tyler. Chairman, Willard Maas. Organized by Amos Vogel," *Film Culture* 29 (Summer 1963). Reprinted in P. Adams Sitney, *Film Culture Reader* (New York and Washington, D.C.: Praeger Publishers, 1970), 175.

2. James Schamus quoted in Stuart Klawans, Annette Michelson, Richard Peña, James Schamus, and Malcolm Turvey, "Roundtable: Independence in the Cinema," *October* 91 (Winter 2000): 4.

3. *Ibid.*, 5.

4. Richard Linklater, *Slacker* (New York: St. Martin's Press, 1992), 118.

5. *Ibid.*, 40.

6. *Ibid.*, 126.

7. See David Bordwell, *The Way Hollywood Tells It: Story and Style in Modern Movies* (Berkeley, Los Angeles, London: University of California Press, 2006), 97.

8. Linklater quoted in Lane Relyea, "What, Me Work?: Lane Relyea Talks with Richard Linklater," *Artforum* (April 1993): 76–77.

9. See John Pierson, *Spike, Mike, Slackers & Dykes: A Guided Tour Across a Decade of American Independent Cinema* (New York: Hyperion Miramax Books, 1995), 185–197.

10. See Robert Horton, "Stranger Than Texas," *Film Comment*, 26, 4 (July/August 1990): 77–78.

11. Chris Walters, "Freedom's Just Another Word for Nothing to Do," *The Austin Chronicle* (27 July 1990). Reprinted in Linklater, 118.

12. Linklater, 119.

13. *Ibid.*, 23.

14. *Ibid.*, 47.

15. *Ibid.*, 57.

16. *Ibid.*, 62.

17. *Ibid.*, 85.

18. *Ibid.*, 94.

19. Bordwell, 100.

20. Linklater quoted in Relyea, 75.

21. Robert McKee, *Story: Substance, Structure, Style, and the Principles of Screenwriting* (New York: Regan Books, 1997), 389.

22. Richard Walter, *Screenwriting: The Art, Craft, and Business of Film and Television Writing* (New York: Plume, 1988), 88.

23. *Ibid.,* 101.

24. Linklater, 54.

25. Roger Ebert, Review: *Slacker, Chicago Sun Times* (23 August 1991).

26. Todd Berliner, "Hollywood Movie Dialogue and the 'Real Realism' of John Cassavetes," *Film Quarterly,* 52, 3 (Spring 1999): 9.

27. Richard Linklater quoted in Eugene Hernandez and Andy Kaufman, "FUTURE 5: Richard Linklater, 'Slacker' for the New Millennium," *indieWIRE,* http://www.indiewire.com/people/int_Linklater_Rich_010112.html.

Conclusion

1. David Bordwell, *Narration in the Fiction Film* (Madison: University of Wisconsin Press, 1985), 208.

2. For a discussion of the enormous difficulties and restraints of making films under the aegis of Hollywood, please see Sharon Waxman, *Rebels on the Backlot: Six Maverick Directors and How They Conquered the Hollywood System* (New York: Harper-Collins, 2005).

3. Jim Jarmusch quoted in Lynn Hirschberg, "The Last of the Indies," *New York Times Magazine* (31 July 2005): 20.

4. See James Schamus, "To the Rear of the Back End: The Economics of Independent Cinema," in *Contemporary Hollywood Cinema,* eds. Steve Neale and Murray Smith (London and New York: Routledge, 1998), 91–105.

5. See Scott Macaulay, "Micro-Caps," *Filmmaker,* 13, 2 (Winter 2005): 76–77.

6. See Elizabeth Angell, "Netflix and the Afterlife of Indies," *The Independent,* 28, 7 (September 2005): 44–47.

7. See *MovieMaker,* Vol. 10, Special Issue: "Beginner's Guide to Making Movies 2004." The complete list of filmmakers includes: Quentin Tarantino, John Cassavetes, Robert Rodriguez, Allison Anders, Richard Linklater, Jim Jarmusch, Orson Welles, Spike Lee, John Sayles, Sophia Coppola, and Steven Soderbergh.

8. Steve Buscemi quoted in "Shooters: A Conversation between Steve Buscemi and Eric Bogosian," *Filmmaker,* 5, 1 (Fall 1996): 48.

9. Jim Jarmusch, "My Golden Rules," *MovieMaker,* 11, 53 (Winter 2004): 122.

Selected Bibliography

Andrew, Geoff. *Stranger Than Paradise: Maverick Film-Makers in Recent American Cinema.* New York: Limelight, 1999.

Aronson, Linda. *Screenwriting Updated: New (and Conventional) Ways of Writing for the Screen.* Los Angeles: Silman-James, 2001.

Bernard, Jami. *Quentin Tarantino: The Man and his Movies.* New York: Harper Perennial, 1995.

Boorman, John, and Walter Donahue, eds. *Projections 3: Filmmakers on Filmmaking.* London: Faber and Faber, 1994.

———, eds. *Projections 5: Filmmakers on Filmmaking.* London and Boston: Faber and Faber, 1996.

Bordwell, David. *Narration in the Fiction Film.* Madison: University of Wisconsin Press, 1985.

———. *The Way Hollywood Tells It: Story and Style in Modern Movies.* Berkeley, Los Angeles, and London: University of California Press, 2006.

Carney, Ray. *Shadows.* London: BFI Publishing, 2001.

———, ed. *The Films of John Cassavetes: Pragmatism, Modernism, and the Movies.* Cambridge: Cambridge University Press, 1994.

———, ed. *Cassavetes on Cassavetes.* London and New York: Faber and Faber, 2001.

Charity, Tom. *John Cassavetes: Lifeworks.* London: Omnibus Press, 2001.

Coen, Ethan, and Joel Coen. *Fargo.* London and Boston: Faber and Faber, 1996.

Cowgill, Linda J. *Secrets of Screenplay Structure: How to Recognize and Emulate the Structural Frameworks of Great Films.* Los Angeles: Lone Eagle Publishing, 1999.

Dancyger, Ken, and Jeff Rush. *Alternative Screenwriting: Writing Beyond the Rules.* 2d ed. Boston: Focal Press, 1995.

Dawson, Jeff. *Quentin Tarantino: The Cinema of Cool.* New York: Applause Books, 1995.

Field, Syd. *Screenplay: The Foundations of Screenwriting.* New York: Dell Publishing, 1979, 1982.

———. *The Screenwriter's Workbook.* New York: Dell Publishing, 1984.

————. *The Screenwriter's Problem Solver: How to Recognize, Identify, and Define Screenwriting Problems.* New York: Dell Publishing, 1998.

Hartley, Hal. *Simple Men and Trust.* Winchester, MA, and London: Faber and Faber, 1992.

Hauge, Michael. *Writing Screenplays That Sell.* New York: McGraw-Hill, 1988.

Haynes, Todd. *Far From Heaven, Safe, and Superstar: the Karen Carpenter Story: Three Screenplays.* New York: Grove Press, 2003.

Hertzberg, Ludvig, ed. *Jim Jarmusch Interviews.* Jackson: University of Mississippi Press, 2001.

Hillier, Jim, ed. *American Independent Cinema: A Sight and Sound Reader.* London: British Film Institute, 2001.

Holmlund, Chris, and Justin Wyatt, eds. *Contemporary American Independent Film: From the Margins to the Mainstream.* London and New York: Routledge, 2005.

Horton, Andrew. *Writing the Character-Centered Screenplay.* Berkeley, Los Angeles, and London: University of California Press, 1994.

Jost, Jon. "End of the Indies: Death of the Sayles Men," *Film Comment,* 25, 1 (January/February 1989).

King, Geoff. *American Independent Cinema.* Bloomington and Indianapolis: Indiana University Press, 2005.

Klawans, Stuart, Annette Michelson, Richard Peña, James Schamus, and Malcolm Turvey. "Roundtable: Independence in the Cinema." *October* 91 (Winter 2000).

Korine, Harmony. *Collected Screenplays 1: Jokes, Gummo, julien donkey-boy.* London: Faber and Faber, 2002.

Kozloff, Sarah. *Overhearing Film Dialogue.* Berkeley and Los Angeles: University of California Press, 2000.

Larsen, Ernest. *The Usual Suspects.* London: BFI Publishing, 2002.

Levy, Emanuel. *Cinema of Outsiders: The Rise of American Independent Film.* New York and London: New York University Press, 1999.

Lewis, Jon, ed. *The New American Cinema.* Durham, NC, and London: Duke University Press, 1998.

————, ed. *The End of Cinema As We Know It: American Film in the Nineties.* New York: New York University Press, 2001.

Linklater, Richard. *Slacker.* New York: St. Martin's Press, 1992.

Lippy, Tod, ed. *Projections 11: New York Film-makers on New York Film-making.* London: Faber and Faber, 2000.

Lowenstein, Stephen, ed. *My First Movie: Twenty Celebrated Directors Talk About Their First Film.* New York: Pantheon Books, 2000.

Luhr, William G., ed. *The Coen Brothers' Fargo.* Cambridge: Cambridge University Press, 2004.

Lynch, David. *Mulholland Drive Pilot—The Screenplay.* January 5, 1999.

————, and Barry Gifford. *Lost Highway.* London and Boston: Faber and Faber, 1997.

Mamet, David. *On Directing Film.* New York: Viking Penguin, 1991.

McKee, Robert. *Story: Substance, Structure, Style, and the Principles of Screenwriting*. New York: Regan Books, 1997.

Mekas, Jonas. *Movie Journal: The Rise of a New American Cinema, 1959–1971*. New York: Collier Books, 1972.

Mendik, Xavier, and Steven Jay Schneider, eds. *Underground U.S.A.: Filmmaking Beyond the Hollywood Canon*. London: Wallflower Press, 2002.

Merritt, Greg. *Celluloid Mavericks: A History of American Independent Film*. New York: Thunder's Mouth Press, 2000.

Mottram, James. *The Making of* Memento. London: Faber and Faber, 2002.

Nolan, Christopher. Memento *and* Following. London: Faber and Faber, 2001.

Peary, Gerald, ed. *Quentin Tarantino Interviews*. Jackson, MS: University of Mississippi Press, 1998.

Phillips, Lisa, ed. *Beat Culture and the New America 1950–1965*. New York and Paris: Whitney Museum of American Art in Association with Flammarion, 1995.

Pierson, John. *Spike, Mike, Slackers & Dykes: A Guided Tour Across a Decade of American Independent Cinema*. New York: Hyperion Miramax Books, 1995.

Pope, Thomas. *Good Scripts, Bad Scripts*. New York: Three Rivers Press, 1998.

Robson, Eddie. *Coen Brothers*. London: Virgin Books, 2003.

Rose, Aaron, and Christian Strike, eds. *Beautiful Losers: Contemporary Art and Street Culture*. New York: Iconoclast and D. A. P., 2004.

Rosenbaum, Jonathan. "The Savage Eye/Shadows." In *The American New Wave 1958-1967*. Minneapolis: Walker Art Center, 1982.

Sanders, Mark, and Jefferson Hack, eds. *Star Culture: The Collected Interviews from Dazed & Confused Magazine*. London: Phaidon Press, 2000.

Sargeant, Jack, ed. *Naked Lens: Beat Cinema*. London: Creation Books, 1997.

Schamus, James. "To the Rear of the Back End: The Economics of Independent Cinema." In Steve Neale and Murray Smith, eds., *Contemporary Hollywood Cinema*. London and New York: Routledge, 1998.

Seger, Linda. *Making a Good Script Great*. 2d ed. Hollywood: Samuel French, 1987, 1994.

———. *Creating Unforgettable Characters*. New York: Henry Holt and Company, 1990.

———. *Advanced Screenwriting: Raising your Script to the Academy Award Level*. Los Angeles: Silman-James Press, 2003.

Sitney, P. Adams, ed. *Film Culture Reader*. New York and Washington: Praeger Publishers, 1970.

Smith, Evan. "Thread Structure: Rewriting the Hollywood Formula." *Journal of Film and Video* 51, 3–4 (Fall/Winter 1999–2000).

Tarantino, Quentin. Reservoir Dogs *and* True Romance: *Screenplays by Quentin Tarantino*. New York: Grove Press, 1994.

Thompson, Kristin. *Storytelling in the New Hollywood: Understanding Classical Narrative Technique*. Cambridge, MA, and London: Harvard University Press, 1999.

———. *Storytelling in Film and Television*. Cambridge, MA, and London: Harvard University Press, 2003.

Truffaut, Francois. *Hitchcock*. Rev. Ed. New York: Simon and Schuster, 1984.

Vachon, Christine, with David Edelstein. *Shooting to Kill: How an Independent Producer Blasts through the Barriers to Make Movies that Matter*. New York: Avon Books, 1998.

Walter, Richard. *Screenwriting: The Art, Craft, and Business of Film and Television Writing*. New York: New American Library, 1988.

———. *The Whole Picture: Strategies for Screenwriting Success in the New Hollywood*. New York: Plume, 1997.

Wells, Amanda Sheahan. *Psycho*. London: York Press, 2001.

Wyatt, Justin. *Poison*. Wiltshire, England: Flick Books, 1998.

Index